Sometimes There Is No Other Side

Sometimes There Is No Other Side

Chicanos and the Myth of Equality

RODOLFO F. ACUÑA

University of Notre Dame Press
Notre Dame and London

Library of Congress Cataloging-in-Publication Data

Acuña, Rodolfo.
  Sometimes there is no other side : Chicanos and the myth of
equality / Rodolfo F. Acuña.
    p. cm.
  Includes bibliographical references and index.
  ISBN 0-268-01762-X (cloth : alk. paper). — ISBN 0-268-01763-8
(pbk. : alk. paper)
    1. Hispanic Americans—Civil rights—History—20th century.
2. Hispanic Americans—Study and teaching.   3. Hispanic Americans—
Education (Higher)   4. Race discrimination—United States.
5. Conservatism—United States—History—20th century.   I. Title.
E184.S75A66   1998
305.868073—dc21   97-46840
                                                            CIP

∞ *The paper used in this publication meets the minimum requirements of the
American National Standard for Information Sciences—Permanence of Paper
for Printed Library Materials, ANSI Z39.48-1984.*

Contents

Preface   vii

1.   The Children of *Bakke*   1

2.   It's the Law   33

3.   Ideological Combat:
The War over Who Controls History   57

4.   The Culture of the Academy   83

5.   Chicana/o Studies and the American Paradigm   103

6.   A Case Study:
Acuña v. The Regents of the University of California   123

7.   Truth and Objectivity: Thomas Kuhn Applied   167

8.   The Trustees of the Truth   183

9.   El Rodeo: Truth and Consequences   203

Notes   229

Selected Bibliography   255

Index   281

Preface

The title of this book, *Sometimes There Is No Other Side: Chicanos and the Myth of Equality*, was inspired by the legendary journalist, Edward R. Murrow. When U.S. government officials cautioned Murrow that his stories about the Holocaust had not been proved, and that they were, after all, based solely on the side of the victims, Murrow responded, "Sometimes there is no other side." Murrow later recalled that even during World War II, news agencies ignored or diminished reports about the death camps, saying that the independent stories (those of the survivors) had not been confirmed or that the "statistics were imprecise, [and] one-sided."

This book follows Murrow's theme. It is about how truth and objectivity are determined, and what roles the courts and academe play in establishing an American paradigm which predetermines what is accepted as truth. The book comes at a time when minority scholars are under increased pressure to tone down their message, to accept the American paradigm, and to adopt fictions, such as the rhetoric that Mexicans are not victims. The acceptance of the present American paradigm mutes the voices of the exploited sectors of society. Hence my message, just as the title indicates, is that survivors of inhumanity are victims. Their side is often more valid than that of the perpetrator, and should be told in the plainest language possible.

This book is also inspired by a long and bitter lawsuit against the University of California at Santa Barbara, during which I listened to two dozen or so depositions of learned scholars on the weighty subjects of truth and objectivity. Instead of offering vigorous critiques, the deponents resorted to clichés about the scholar's role in society: one scholar after the other pompously testified that the mission of the university was the search for truth through scholarly objectivity. What amazed me was that these scholars, from disparate disciplines, sounded so much alike, almost universally agreeing on common definitions and interpreting society through what I call the American paradigm.

How could these intelligent, well-educated professors be so at odds with how I saw the world? How could their perceptions of the universe differ so much from the majority of scholars of color whom I knew? And how could they be so certain that they were right? My first reaction was to dismiss them as pompous sycophants who could not make it in the real world, comfortable with the adage, "Those who can't, teach, and those who can't teach, do research." However, it is wrongheaded to dismiss them so cavalierly. For as much as I may dislike what I heard, these professors collectively have the power to define truth and objectivity.

For a majority of U.S. scholars, truth is that carefully schooled notion that middle-class professionals define as *accepted* knowledge. The study of history and the other social sciences in the U.S. is determined by a small body of scholars who define what is the proper subject of inquiry and what qualifies as scholarship. In this way they establish a hegemonic view and, under the banner of scholarly objectivity and truth, dismiss the historical memory of scholars such as myself who do not accept their paradigm. The courts also adhere to the American paradigm. They define what is truth and create and maintain an aura of objectivity that gives moral authority and legitimacy to their version of the American paradigm. In this way, scholars and justices function like the shamans of old.

This book is about the American paradigm, which is formed by neoliberal (positivist) theory. Fundamental to the paradigm are loyalty to government and Western civilization, and a core of beliefs shared by the dominant class of Euro-Americans about the superiority of their civilization and culture. The academy and the courts base their moral authority on the myth that these institutions objectively (and thus, justly) interpret fact.

The narrative makes reference to a law suit that I filed in 1992 and successfully litigated against the University of California at Santa Barbara. The case study is used to illustrate my points. I would like to make clear that this is not my final analysis of the law suit, fought in both the state and federal courts. In the course of litigation, I accumulated a mountain of primary documents, which include depositions, more than three hundred personnel files (which are under a protective order), internal documents, motions, responses, a trial transcript, interviews, and so on, that I am slowly reflecting upon.

If the American paradigm is to be shifted, and if the history and study of the "other" in American society is to be taken into account, it is important to strike down the notion that institutions such as the academy and the jurisprudence system are fair and treat everyone equally. The notion that the United States is (or strives to be) a "color-blind" society must be demythicized. The message must change; it must show how the American paradigm mythicizes history and works as a form of social control, consequently creating the glass-ceiling that keeps the "other" in their places.

As in most of my books, working-class Chicanas/os and Latinas/os are my target audience. Unfortunately, these sectors of society often are "true believers." They are the people who believe they can win the lottery; who fight wars for others' interests; who accept lower wages; who don't cheat on their income taxes; and who still ultimately believe in God and flag, and incredulously believe that they are included in the American Dream. I rely heavily on the narrative as a method of discourse because I believe that it is the most forceful way to expose the paradigm constructed by academe and the courts.

I have chosen to apply the model of Thomas Kuhn throughout the narrative because, in its simplicity, it forces the reader to define the meaning of truth and objectivity. Much too often, theory and method are used to obscure rather than expose injustice. Alternative models are set up to avoid concepts such as truth and objectivity instead of seeking to attack the current definition and to create struggle at that level.

Fortunately, skepticism is at an all-time high in the United States. Latinos are beginning to question whether other Americans consider them equal or even Americans. A partial explanation for this skepticism is California's anti-immigrant Proposition

187, which took its toll, as did the so-called California Civil Rights Initiative—Proposition 209, the anti–affirmative action measure. The issues were clear in the case of 187, and four-fifths of voting Latinos statewide opposed the proposition, while their white counterparts overwhelmingly voted for it. Although these Latino voters were citizens, they recognized the racist motives of the proponents of 187 and the racist premise that "illegal" meant anyone who looked like them. This assumption was confirmed by the passage of the federal Welfare Reform Act of 1996, which even took away benefits from documented immigrants. As a consequence, during the 1996 elections, close to 80 percent of Latinos (depending on the exit poll) returned to the Democratic party, expressing hostility to California Governor Pete Wilson.

It doesn't take a genius to deduce that there is something fundamentally wrong in a society where an "'Airport Posse' Takes San Diego Border Control Into Its Own Hands" (as the *Washington Post* reported on May 23, 1996), and whose members cruise San Diego's busy Lindbergh airport, wearing T-shirts boldly declaring "U.S. Citizen Patrol" and eyeing passengers they suspect of being undocumented workers, which means anyone who looks brown or speaks Spanish. This citizen patrol isn't looking for Canadians. Its members may be patriotic citizens to many white Americans who cheer them on, but to most brown people they are vigilantes who should be arrested before they harm innocent people. The posse operated for several weeks in response to callers to a conservative radio talk show who claimed that suspicious-looking people were using the airport to evade Border Patrol highway checkpoints. Certainly these actions did not go unnoticed by Chicanas/os and other Latinos. The so-called posse was stopped only when counterdemonstrators confronted them. Fearing physical confrontations, the court issued an injunction against both parties because, according to the court, they had created "a climate potentially disruptive to airport operations." The Immigration and Naturalization Service took what it termed a "neutral position" in the controversy, saying that posse members "have as much free speech right as the fellow with the tambourine." One of the leaders of the "posse" likened border control to a "domestic Vietnam War," saying that the lack of political will has encouraged a flood of illegal immigrants:

In Vietnam, we had the manpower and firepower to win but not the will. In the war against illegal immigration, we have the manpower and firepower, but not the will. We're supplying the will.

On another front, a poll conducted by the Spanish-language *La Opinión* newspaper and Spanish-language KVEA-TV of documented and undocumented immigrants (14 percent of the five hundred Latinos polled identified themselves as undocumented immigrants) was released in May 1996. According to *La Opinión's* associate publisher, Monica Lozano,

> We were concerned that the growing anti-immigrant sentiment in Los Angeles was having a negative psychological effect on Latinos which could lead to very serious undesirable consequences. We felt it our responsibility to measure the effect and how it was changing the lives of Latinos in the area.

The poll reported that 80 percent felt they were treated with racism or contempt by whites; sixty-nine percent said anti-immigration sentiment had substantially increased since the 1994 passage of Proposition 187, which threatened to cut off welfare and education benefits for illegal immigrants; thirty-seven percent said they felt "worried or threatened"; sixteen percent answered "yes" to the question, "Have you or any member of your family been a victim of racism, discrimination, or contempt of any kind in recent months?" A large majority of Latinos (65 percent) said that incidents of police brutality against them are common. The findings suggest that Latinos feel a growing sense of uneasiness due to the continued political focus on "illegal immigrants," a term often considered synonymous in California with Mexicans. According to the principal investigator of the poll, "The environment that Latinos are living in is ugly . . . The way they feel they're being treated, the way they feel they're being dealt with, has changed." Still, most Latinos (57 percent) felt that the best way to respond to attacks against their community was through political empowerment and not through more radical measures.

Chapter 1 of this book, "The Children of *Bakke*," discusses Proposition 209, the so-called California Civil Rights Initiative, in the context of the infamous 1978 *Bakke* decision. This case marked a change in the rationality of the courts. It shifted the focus from racial equality to the issues explicit in California's Proposition 209, which will undoubtedly have a far-reaching impact on relations between whites and people of color in the United States. Regardless of whether 209 is overturned by the courts, the heated discourse will continue. The passage of this ballot initiative is not a fad but rather is very much part of the neoliberal American paradigm that was awakened by the U.S. Supreme Court decision in *Regents of the University of California v. Bakke,* which created a language, neutered race as a variable, and popularized the myth of the United States as a color-blind society.

Chapter 2, "It's the Law," discusses the dominant American paradigm in the context of Thomas Kuhn's concept of paradigms. The focus of the chapter is on positivist legal theory, although it includes a brief discussion of natural law theory and of critical legal studies. Thomas Kuhn's theory of paradigms and paradigm shifts explains the macro views of society and how they interact with micro interests of minorities. The courts and academe have a defined culture, and this culture is upheld and defended by mainstream judges and scholars. The approved theoretical rationality is rooted in positivism and neoliberalism, which supposedly use a scientific methodology to search for the truth in the law and society. This legal theory determines the dominant concepts of justice and thus the outcome of court cases.

Chapter 3, "Ideological Combat: The War over Who Controls History," deals with the war that has been launched by the New Right and its success in defining the language of that war. The importance of the concepts of truth and objectivity is analyzed, and the reaction of a coalition of conservative and liberal historians in defense of the American paradigm is critiqued. A militant "culture war" has been conducted by the New Right to control higher education. Soon after William Simon sounded the clarion for conservatives to form think tanks and political proactive organizations, entities such as the National Association of Scholars (NAS) appeared to combat the changes that were taking place in American society and to preserve Western civilization. The courts and academe became the battlegrounds.

Chapter 4, "The Culture of the Academy," narrates resistance to change within academe. It explains how the culture of the university works against the acceptance of ethnic studies programs. It discusses the reaction of the University of California faculty to the Pister Report, which recommended changing the reward system of the academy by giving more credit to teaching and applied research. It was viewed by many professors as an entitlement program which lowered the quality of the university. The history of American higher education is one of change and the incorporation of other knowledge systems. These paradigm shifts have taken place only after intense struggle and pressure on the institutions. Since the nineteenth century, higher education in the United States has added disciplines such as engineering, sociology, and history. In recent times, fields such as multicultural, women's, and ethnic studies have also pressed academe to be included, only to be rejected by the culture of higher education. Like other institutions, academe demands conformity and controls its scholars through the faculty governance and reward processes. The present attitude toward Chicana/o studies and ethnic studies in general is not an aberration.

Chapter 5, "Chicana/o Studies and the American Paradigm," focuses on the state and future of Chicana/o studies and its interaction with the American paradigm. This essay explores the definitions of truth and objectivity in relationship to Chicana/o studies. It stresses the importance for the Chicana/o scholar of maintaining credibility in the culture war that is raging in academe. The war is really not about scholarship but rather about the challenge to the American paradigm by Chicana/o studies and the "other." The tension is how to include what is essentially an alien field of study within the American paradigm. In other words, how do you study Chicanos through an acceptable neo-liberal model? The lack of conformity by Chicana/o studies and the inherent racism of the system puts it in the middle of the "culture war."

Chapter 6, "A Case Study: *Acuña v. The Regents of the University Of California*," summarizes my case against the University of California at Santa Barbara. It gives insight into the academic review process and the political climate in higher education. It indicates how academe and the courts, deriving their rationality from a common source, reinforce the prevailing positivist paradigm. The culture of confidentiality in academe makes it almost impossible to prove discrimination. Conformity is enforced in academe through the faculty governance process, which keeps intact the American paradigm. Throughout the five-year period that I spent in litigation, one of the most formidable barriers was the neoliberal mentality of academe and the courts. The case produced mountains of empirical data, proving my hypothesis that the culture of academe and the courts rejects ethnic studies because they are incompatible with the American paradigm. An appendix to the chapter reproduces the text of two crucial reports by university review committees as part of the evidence of the neoliberal bias of academe.

Chapter 7, "Truth and Objectivity: Thomas Kuhn Applied," presents and analyzes portions of the deposition of David Holtby by my attorney, Eliot Grossman. The deposition shows the legal difficulty in breaking through the accepted narrative. The presumption is that scholars are objective and tell the truth, and that the scientific method is at the essence of American scholarship. This view of scholarship has been revolutionized by Kuhn's theory of paradigms. The American paradigm encompasses the values, culture, and beliefs of a society, and approves the methodology through which society is interpreted. There are very few empirical models that illustrate the function of paradigms in the social sciences, but courtroom testimony and depositions provide an ideal laboratory. Under normal circumstances, oppositional paradigms do not have the opportunity to challenge the dominant paradigm. Attorney Grossman used Kunh's concept of paradigms to cross-examine David Holtby, editor of the University of New Mexico Press, in regard to scholarship and the concepts of truth and objectivity, and thereby to defend the oppositional paradigm.

Chapter 8, "The Trustees of the Truth," presents and analyzes portions of a second deposition, that of David Sprecher, the university provost at the time of my review. Sprecher had been touted as a careful scholar, one on whose judgment other scholars relied. What becomes evident in the course of the deposition is that, while the work of a candidate is expected to be meritorious, the review process is nonscholarly at best, based on capriciousness as well as bias. Research universities have enjoyed privileges that are not normal in a free society. Peer group reviews and the administration of the academies have until recently been above public scrutiny. This changed only in 1990, due to the *University of Pennsylvania v. EEOC*, which held that the documents in peer group reviews were necessary for victims of discrimination to prove their cases. The deposition of Sprecher in particular turns the light on the conduct of most scholarly reviews, demythicizing the governance process and debunking the fable that scholars are dedicated to the search for truth and objectivity.

The last chapter, "El Rodeo: Truth and Consequences," summarizes the theme of truth and objectivity in the context of 209 and my case. The passage of Proposition 209 represented a tremendous victory for the New Right, and it gave these forces tremendous energy in the so-called culture war. The victory of the 209 forces is based on their ability to exploit a language of opposition that has flourished since the 1978 *Bakke* decision. The war is framed by claims to objectivity and encased in a coherent narrative and discourse. This book exposes the link between the judicial system, higher education, and the American paradigm, and the New Right's reassertion of hegemony over these institutions. By looking at culture, language, and symbols used by the academic reviewers in my case, *Acuña v. The Regents of the University of California, et al.*, I provide an insight into a pattern of power agendas and their meanings in the overall struggle for inclusion of other knowledge. Proposition 209 has caused irreparable damage to race relations. It raises the question whether people of color should continue to support academe—whether minorities should pay taxes to support a privileged elite, which excludes knowledge that is needed to bring about solutions to pressing societal problems. The chapter discusses the importance of advocacy by Chicana/o scholars in setting the narrative straight, forcing a paradigm shift.

I would like to recognize the support of the Chicana/o and Latina/o communities during the lawsuit and the writing of the present book. My case against the University of California would not have been possible without their support and the support of my attorneys, who gave selflessly. Moisés Vázquez, the lead attorney, stuck with me to the last at great personal and economic sacrifice. I learned a lot from his quick and analytic mind. Moisés was the horse that brought me to the finish line. The National Coalition of Universities in the Public Interest, its director, Leonard Minsky, and his daughter, Beth, kept this case alive during the first two years. Their legal analysis and assistance were invaluable. I thank the Southern California Chapter of the American Civil Liberties Union, especially attorney Silvia Argueta and paralegal Virginia Alvárez, without whom we would not have gotten to trial. Thanks to Angelina Nelson, who at the time was a law student. Students are often quick to promise, but Angelina kept her promises. I thank Armando Durón, who first answered the call and recruited others. Special thanks to Jesús Cruz, who worked for peanuts and was often the sole thread between success and failure. Thanks to the trial attorneys: Robert Racine, our procedural expert; Miguel Calballero, one of the sincerest human beings I know; Millie Escobedo, who after Silvia Argueta was our youngest and gutsiest member; and Eliot Grossman, who always plays it on the edge, but whose intellectual brilliance kept me on my toes. Thanks to the California Immigrant Workers' Association, which made Calballero available. To all of the other friends and members of the legal team—Yvonne Flores, Silvia Cruz, Patricia Fukishima, Mark Poindexter, Andrés Bustamante, and Dan Jasso—who took depositions and gave of their time, I thank you. I thank the witnesses, Drs. Ramón Ruiz, Carlos Vélez-Ibañez, Ray Padilla, María Chairez, Mary Pardo, and Antonia Castañeda. I thank Mauricio Mazón and Deena González. Special thanks to Yolanda Broyles-González, without whom the victory would not have been possible. Thanks to Local 399 and organizers Rocio Saenz, Patricia Recino, and Jono Shaffer; to Local 11 and its president, María Elena Durazo; to Local 660 and its former general manager, Gil Cedillo, and to Kathy Ochoa, who were among the earliest supporters; and to the California Faculty Association, the California Teachers' Association, and the American Federation of Teachers. I especially thank Pat Nichelson, president of the CFA and a valued friend; el Congreso students at UCSB, especially Alma, Mike, Lupe, Alicía, and the gang; the Mechista at California State University at Northridge, especially Miguel Pérez, Gabriela Chavira, Ramón Muñiz, and Carlos alias "Herb"; and the

Mechistas throughout California. Thanks to Benny Torres, a hard-working and committed friend, who keeps telling me to read the first edition of *Occupied America*; to the Santa Barbara Chicana/o community, especially Armando Vallejo, Carlos Ornelas, and Rogelio Trujillo; to columnists Roberto Rodríguez and Patrisia González, whose articles always gave us a push and whose moral authority is increasing with every piece; and to the members of the jury in my federal case, who based their decision on fairness and the dying concept of justice. Most important, I thank the F.O.R. Acuña Committee, whose members kept us afloat with fundraisers, and without whom we could not have taken on the octopus: especially, Mary Pardo, Raquel Salinas, Cristina Shallcross, Diana Martínez, Marta López-Garza, Victor Carrillo, Jaime Corral, Vince Lorenzo, Rafael González, María de la Luz Blair, Rita Moreno, and all my friends. I'll always have you in my heart, and regret that time and space prevents me from singling out every one of you. Your links with the Chicana/o arts communities were invaluable. It is my sincere belief that the strongest part of our community is among the visual and performing artists, who are keeping the movement alive. Dozens of artists and musicians deserve to be singled out. For now, special thanks to Marcos Loya, Quetzal, and Malaquias Montoya. Thanks to Nancy Stein, whose early advice is appreciated, and to Rebecca DeBoer, the editor, who whipped this book into shape and whom I greatly admire.

I always thank my deceased parents for having made me a Mexican. I also thank the Casillas family of Oxnard, and my deceased compadre, Arnulfo Casillas. His family is always there. I thank my grown sons, Frank and Walter, and my grandchildren, whom I love. Everyone has to have people close to them—an immediate family which roots one. My support network above all includes my wife, Lupita Compean, with whom I have had the most productive years of my life, and my daughter Angela, who gives me a purpose in life. Lupita is my greatest critic, my greatest supporter, and my moral and intellectual superior. She is courageous. Angela is my future.

Rodolfo F. Acuña
California State University at Northridge

1

The Children of *Bakke*

Proposition 209, passed by California voters on November 5, 1996, is a watershed event for race relations in the United States. Like every other social disaster, it affects different groups in different ways, with the perceptions of the various groups also differing. In my conversations with Chicano and Latino activists, for example, they opposed Proposition 209 not so much because they believe that affirmative action is the ultimate salvation for working-class Latinos, but because they perceive 209 as the beginning of the end of Euro-America's commitment to social and economic equality for all. Symbolically, the old signs of "No Mexicans or Dogs Need Apply" have been pulled out of the attic. Their perception of affirmative action differs markedly from that of their Euro-American allies, who seem to romanticize affirmative action and who assume that affirmative action was working.

The reality to many Latinos is that affirmative action did not cure all of their problems. For instance, the income and education gap between Latinos and Euro-Americans has increased dramatically in the last two decades. At the same time, however, the Mexican American middle class has expanded significantly since 1965. Undoubtedly, affirmative action along with the Voting Rights Act of 1965 played a role in this expansion by creating the political space for activists to push for more people of color in politics, employment, and education. It created the language that justified the inclusion of Latinos and other minorities and women.

There were tangible results. For example, when I arrived at California State University at Northridge (CSUN) in the spring of 1969, there were about fifty students of Mexican extraction. This number has since grown to more than three thousand; a similar

1

phenomenon of growth occurred on campuses throughout the United States. As a result, today more Mexican Americans attend universities than at any time in our history, something that would not have happened without the environment created by affirmative action. Affirmative action gave us the justification for our being at the university, and the right to expect that administrators listen to our demands.

Even with these gains, success is limited in relation to the population of Latinos, which has dramatically increased in places like California since 1969. Despite the growth in the number of Mexican American students at CSUN, for instance, they still only comprise about 12 percent of the student body. In comparison, Latino students represent two-thirds of the public school students in Los Angeles.

Indeed, in postgraduate education, the sector that produces most of the future power brokers, Latinos are not doing well. In 1992, Latina females at the University of California (UC) system comprised only 3.7 percent of its Master of Arts students, 1.8 percent of its Ph.D. students, 4.9 percent of its law students, and 3.8 percent of its medical students. The percentage of Latino males was slightly higher in all categories except for M.A.'s, where Latinas outnumbered Latinos.[1] The UC is important because it enrolls more graduate Latino students than any other institution of higher learning in the country. Affirmative action has also failed to move institutions of higher learning to hire qualified Mexican American professors. At California State University at Northridge, less than 3 percent of the tenure-track professors are of Mexican extraction, a portrait that is repeated at most universities in California.

Myth has it that universities are populated by liberal and left-of-center professors. In reality, the academy is moderate to conservative. As a rule, college administrators and faculty have not been cooperative in hiring Latinos and other minorities. They have to be dragged into hiring one Latino at a time. Although many University of California faculty senates rushed to vote in favor of affirmative action following passage of Proposition 209, a Roper Center for Public Opinion Research poll, reported in the *Christian Science Monitor* on December 2, 1996, found that a majority of the nation's higher-education faculties opposed racial and gender preferences in student admissions and faculty employment. Nearly two-thirds of eight hundred faculty members interviewed would support a ban on preferences similar to the recently passed California Civil Rights Initiative (CCRI), Proposition 209. Organizations such as the American Council of Learned Societies and the American Association of University Professors came out against 209, yet in the privacy of a polling interview or secret ballot, faculty members across the political spectrum see affirmative action at best as problematic. It is also significant that a growing number of right-wing think tanks are housing themselves in prestigious universities.

It can be argued that the sheer growth in the Latino population has more to do with the dramatic increase of Chicanos in the universities and the public sector than the enforcement of affirmative action. This growth has led to the election of Latinos to public office, which in turn has led to the hiring of Latino public employees. The employment of Latinos in the public sector in Los Angeles, for example, lagged until the mid-1980s, when Latinos were elected to the LA City Council and to the Board of Supervisors. Local government then hired increasing numbers of Latinos in entry-level and middle-management jobs.[2] In higher education their increasing numbers also drove the rationale for their inclusion as students. Yet affirmative action was important because it justified the special outreach to Latinos (and others); it became a symbol as well as a genuine remedy. With the passage of Proposition 209, which marks the death of affirmative action, this remedy for discrimination is about to be taken away. The law is now on the other side.

The Message of 209

The potential impact of the so-called California Civil Rights Initiative goes beyond the Latino community. Anti–affirmative action organizations are poised in at least twenty states to emulate the California measure by banning programs that assist women and minorities in government employment, contracting, and public education. Anti–affirmative action zealots are also poised in the conservative Republican-controlled Congress to use the California law as a basis for rolling back affirmative action on the federal level.[3]

In this assault on affirmative action, these forces are defining the American paradigm, even laying claim to championing the legacy of Martin Luther King.[4] "Culture War" warriors such as John H. Bunzel, past president of San Jose State University, a former member of the U.S. Commission on Civil Rights, and a senior research fellow at Stanford's Hoover Institution, an ultra-conservative right-wing think tank, writes:

> When California voters passed Proposition 209 and outlawed government-sponsored affirmative-action programs, they were sending a simple message to politicians and bureaucrats: If affirmative action requires racial preferences, end it—because you can't mend it.[5]

Bunzel's involvement as a leader in the protracted war against affirmative action dates back two decades. He, more than most, has forged the message of the anti–affirmative action forces, contributing to the evolution of today's right-wing ideology. He has provided a "bright light" for the opponents of affirmative action:

> It is precisely this kind of moral simplicity, however, that makes Proposition 209 so troublesome. The proposition's backers asserted the superiority of pure principle. They asked, "Doesn't everyone agree that we want a color-blind and equal-opportunity society?"

Bunzel adds that

> The use of race to overcome past and present racism has resulted in "excesses" and has frequently violated the promise of equal protection to all citizens. It seems fair to say that Proposition 209 is as blunt an instrument in confronting these "excesses" as affirmative action has often been in using race to overcome racism.

While one can disagree strenuously with Bunzel's rhetoric, one must give him and his cabal credit: they have forged a powerful narrative and tapped into an American paradigm that has been molded by more than two hundred years of history. The supporters of 209 claim that they are attempting to create a "color-blind society," professing that if you want a color-blind society you need a color-blind policy. It sounds reasonable, if you ignore the public discourse and forget about motive. The discourse centers around questions such as merit versus equality, with race as the sole basis of analysis. Affirmative action becomes a metaphor for limiting preference to promising black or Latino students with lower-than-the-highest SAT scores and high school grade-point averages lower than those of meritorious whites. The debate almost always degenerates into a question of policies that admit minority students who, according to the "culture warriors," lack the academic qualifications to make it to graduation, and into sweeping generalizations about black and brown students.

The message of opponents of 209 was never as clear as that of the culture warriors. It lacked a defined political trajectory. What the opponents of 209 should have been saying was that most Americans were unified in the hope that the U.S. could achieve a "color-blind society" by integrating society through the most logical fashion possible, namely, by creating an equal society. Education has always been a vehicle for integration, and equal access to jobs and contracts is a way to achieve economic equality. The only way to integrate society is to erase class differences which, in the U.S., are often based on color. (The same logic applies to gender differences.) Instead of getting this message out to the public, opponents of 209 sent the weak message, the insipid message, that yes, affirmative action has its flaws, but let's not throw out the baby with the bath water, let's fix it!

Because opponents of 209 did not want to offend anyone, they missed a golden opportunity to discuss special privileges in the U.S. For example, following the logic that it takes a color-blind policy to produce a color-blind society, it seems reasonable to conclude that in order to bring about equality of opportunity, a policy that abolishes special economic privileges must also be initiated. The children of the ruling classes are regularly given special consideration in admission not only to private but also to public universities, for instance. It is reported that Harvard University admits about 20 percent of its entering class using the criterion that the student is the son or daughter of an alumnus/a or donor.[6]

Proposition 209 clearly reflects political rather than policy aims. In the case of 209, the underlying legal issue is right to equal protection as codified in the Fourteenth Amendment of the Constitution, enacted after the Civil War to protect the rights of newly freed slaves. The Supreme Court, based on that clause, has upheld certain policy efforts to redress discrimination, including forms of affirmative action. The American Civil Liberties Union (ACLU) challenged Proposition 209 as a violation of the Fourteenth Amendment, claiming that it freezes current discrimination in place and takes away remedies to correct that inequality. This position contradicts the argument that the Fourteenth Amendment rights of white Americans and Asians are being violated by race- and gender-based preferences. The opponents of 209 state the obvious: supporters of 209 basically don't want the federal government to enforce race and gender discrimination laws.

The debate over affirmative action has divided Americans. A national poll by CBS News and the *New York Times* in August 1996 found support for affirmative action running slightly ahead of abolition sentiment, 45 percent to 43 percent. Twelve percent of participants didn't know or didn't answer the poll questions. It can be assumed that a majority of the latter support the abolition of affirmative action, but they refuse to publicly state their preference because affirmative action is correctly perceived as a race issue.

Protest and the Voters

What has happened in the immediate aftermath of 209? Do minorities really care? During the anti-209 campaign there was surprisingly little popular protest. The press reported on hundreds of angry, chanting students protesting the end of affirmative action at the University of California at Berkeley.[7] At my own campus, 150 riot-dressed Los Angeles Police charged a handful of protestors who had vowed to stop the demise of affirmative action by any means necessary. However, these kinds of protests were rare. Even after the passage of 209, the *San Francisco Chronicle* of December 5, 1996, reported that the protests against the passage of Proposition 209 fizzled fast. Not even minority students could be found to march, "and even fewer ditched class," according to the *Chronicle*.

Why didn't the controversy over affirmative action reach the same level of intensity in the Latino community as it did over Proposition 187? Simply put, 209 is not the kind of issue that inspires mass support. In the 1960s, huge numbers of students took to the streets to protest what they saw as a clear-cut, life-and-death issue: the Vietnam War, which affected almost everyone. In the case of affirmative action, most Americans perceive it as a race issue that does not impact their lives. In the 1960s, middle-class Euro-Americans defied their parents to demonstrate for free speech and civil rights. Today, aside from the same few white liberals and radicals who always support human rights issues, the affirmative action fight is led by Latinos, Blacks, Native Americans, and some Asian Americans. It is a "minority thing." The sense of brotherhood and sisterhood which dominated the 1960s is, for the most part, gone. The bottom line is that it is difficult to be enthusiastic about someone else's interests.

Despite the lack of street protest, the polarization produced by the rhetoric surrounding 209 is evident, and California is increasingly being divided along color lines. Propositions 187 and 209 have had a dramatic impact on Chicanos and Latinos. However, it is an impact that cannot easily be measured. As mentioned, the campaign to defeat 187 was much more intense. Tens of thousands of students walked out of Los Angeles schools. Between 100,000 and 150,000 Chicanos and other Latinos marched in opposition to 187 in October 1994.[8] The public and Spanish-language media alike understood the issue, and the latter helped mobilize the former. In contrast, the implications of Proposition 209 were not entirely clear to Spanish-language reporters. Many of these middle-class Latin American reporters are not conversant with domestic issues such as affirmative action and consequently, did not sufficiently understand the importance of 209 and their duty to educate the public. Moreover, the Latino leadership did not play as visible a role as it did with Proposition 187. In order to overcome the public perception that it was a minority issue, Euro-Americans took the lead in the public campaign against 209. Most of these volunteers were Democrats with split loyalties. Indeed, the Democratic party played a negative role in stifling popular discontent. They muted the message, fearing that it might cost Clinton votes. They rationalized that the survival of the progressive agenda was contingent on his reelection. In the process, they sold out affirmative action.

Although many Euro-Americans worked hard to defeat 209, the Chicano and Latino communities felt the sting of defeat. The election results suggest that the community as a whole became more passive-aggressive. There is no doubt that its members were angered by the discourse surrounding 187 and 209 and began to vote in increasing numbers for Spanish-surname candidates. In 1990, Governor Pete Wilson got 38 percent of the Latino vote; in 1996, Dole got only 20 percent in California. At the same time, Latino voting in California increased by approximately 40 percent (since 1992). Some pundits suggest that the Latino backlash from Proposition 209 enabled Democrats to pick up three congressional seats in California. A Democratic Latina, Loretta Sánchez, beat the ultrareactionary Representative Bob Dornan in Orange County. Latinos, according to exit polls, voted 3-1 against Proposition 209 and 3-1 for Democratic candidates. At the same time, they increased their vote from 7 percent of the state voting population in 1992 to at least 10 percent in 1996 (some exit polls say as much as 13 percent). The state's Latino population in 1996 was between 27 and 30 percent of the total population and rising, with the registration of Latino voters increasing at each election.

Proposition 209 undoubtedly gave the edge to Orange County financial adviser Loretta Sánchez. "What [Governor] Pete Wilson and the Republican anti-immigrant drill did was to unify the Latino vote more than anything else that we had seen before," Sánchez said. Key to Sánchez's victory was that Dornan and the GOP apparently didn't take into account the growing constituency of Latinos, who make up about half the district's population.[9] Ironically, Sánchez, using her husband's Anglo surname, previously ran for the Santa Ana City Council and lost. Her victory was in great part attributed to the use of her Spanish-surname. Latinos have shown a greater tendency since 187 to vote for Spanish-surname candidates.[10]

African Americans voted against Proposition 209 by 74 percent, and Latinos by 76 percent. Asian Americans also voted against it, although only by 61 percent. White males voted for 209 by a 66 percent margin and white females by 58 percent; whites make up three-fourths of the voters. It would be ridiculous to suggest that only African Americans and Latinos care deeply about equality. However, the fact remains that while many Euro-Americans support the concept of equality, the glass ceiling that was retrofitted by Proposition 209 has a greater impact on African Americans and Latinos. These communities have higher proportions of low-income people. But even in the case of blacks and browns, the death of affirmative action hits the growing middle class hardest. It effectively slows down the upward movement of working-class Latinos and blacks into professions, the white collar sector, and middle-management jobs. Inside those communities it sends a message to the children of the poor that they need not apply. It also tells them that American society is no longer committed to the idea of equality.

Why a majority of white women supported Proposition 209 will have to be studied further. However, it would be fair to suggest that many voted for 209 because white women, although discriminated against, are part of that middle-class culture that has benefited from the dominant society and in no small measure has nurtured its racist sentiments.

Further examples of voter polarization surfaced in the spring 1997 elections. A March 1997 *Los Angeles Times* article suggested that as a result of 187 and 209, there had been "a fierce Latino backlash in November. . . ."[11] With the election of three new Latino Democrats to the state Assembly, boosting the number of Latino Democrats to thirteen, Fresno Democrat Cruz Bustamante garnered enough support in the Democratic caucus to be elected the first Latino speaker of the Assembly. This Latino surge dramatically manifested itself in the 1997 Los Angeles mayoral election, where the Latino turnout for the first time surpassed that of the African American community, reaching 15 percent.[12] Further, in November 1996, 86 percent of Latinos had supported the hike in the minimum wage, and in spring 1997, 82 percent supported the school bond issue in Los Angeles; these issues were hardly part of a Republican agenda.

How Society Abandoned Civil Rights

The death of an idea such as social justice does not happen by accident. Indeed, it is very difficult to reverse public policy and change basic commitments such as civil rights. Generally, there must be forces that mobilize support for this change. In the United States, these forces can only be understood in terms of the American code of values. This value system institutionalizes American behavior. Its image of America is that of a country built by "little guys" of the James Stewart stripe, who have an undying love of fairness. Injustice or inequalities are rationalized as mutations, as anomalies, which will disappear in time because American society provides opportunity for those who want to better themselves. A study of history shows quite a different reality, one of exploitation, racism, and in recent years, a closing of opportunity. Yet although U.S. history is replete with instances of tension between American ethics and American practice, the contradictions are quickly explained away.[13]

Today, almost everyone is repulsed by the frontier saying that the only good Indian is a dead Indian. One would think that it would have been obvious to Euro-Americans at the time that the genocide of Indians violated their ethical system. Instead, they constructed the myth that they were working toward the improvement of the native Americans. Similarly, historian Glenn Price points out that when the United States invaded Mexico, President James K. Polk, like Lyndon B. Johnson and other American presidents, rationalized the breach of Christian ethics with appeals to God. It wasn't the United States' fault. It was Mexico's fault. In dealing with the contradictions between the ethical system and the American habit of discrimination and aggression, American citizens act from a conviction of righteousness and an assurance of "perfect virtue."

Racism and economic discrimination fly in the face of Judeo-Christian ethics. Affirmative action, instead of rationalizing the national sin, recognized that everyone was not equal, and that

people of color and women were not equal because of a historical and systematic racism and gender discrimination present at
every level of society. It sought to put into place remedies that
would ameliorate the tensions between the Judeo-Christian ethical system and American habit of racism. In less than a dozen
years after its passage, the assault on programs to create a more
fair and equitable society was underway. The dilemma was how
to kill the idea without killing the "invented tradition" of an egali-
tarian and just society.[14] As in the case of the Indians or the Mexican War, the response is packaged in rhetoric: ending affirmative
action is actually for the good of the victims.

In order to kill affirmative action, certain myths had to be
socially constructed as truths. First, the argument had to be made
that racial and sexual diversity on public college campuses can be
achieved by judging students on their merit rather than by quota
systems. Affirmative action was discriminating against deserving
white and Asian students, who were being deprived of an education.

The content of the debate over quotas is disturbing. It is a
crass but an effective tool for appealing to the Jewish-American
community. It purposely distorts the issue by equating quotas to
the exclusion of many Jews from prestigious universities prior
to World War II. Bunzel and others allege that they oppose racial quotas to end discrimination in jobs and education because
quotas promote "race consciousness" and deepen racial tensions.
Their logic is that if minorities are all treated as victims of discrimination, the result will be the imposition of racial quotas,
which will cause a decline in the morale of employees (I presume,
white) and harm motivation and self-respect of minority groups.
They argue that the relatively low number of blacks and Latinos
at colleges is not simply a result of invariable discrimination, but
rather of a limited availability of some minorities for college slots.
They will not admit that limited availability actually proves that
there *is* inequality. The Bunzels base their moral authority on the
fact that they are academics, which somehow makes them pure
and disinterested.

A second element of the myth is that quixotic Mr. Smiths
spearheaded the drive to rid society of racial quotas. These were

"angry white males" who weren't going to take it anymore. They just wanted a level playing field for everyone, regardless of the color of their skin. The reality is that mean-spirited people pushed 209, such as the members of Voice of Citizens Together, led by Glenn Spencer, who rants and raves about the Mexican invasion of the United States. These groups very effectively played to white nationalism and fears. Moreover, Proposition 209 was not authored by two quixotic professors but by two disgruntled professors from the California Association of Scholars, an affiliate of the National Association of Scholars, that contributed monies to this well-funded venture. It was hardly a spontaneous revolt against excessive taxation without representation.

In resolving the tension between ethics and the American habit of racism, the campaign to murder affirmative action added a third and a crucial element to its constructed truth. The message was that African Americans and Latinos also supported 209. African American businessmen like Ward Connerly, a University of California Regent who chaired the 209 Campaign, and a few academics were showcased. Black and brown spokespersons like the columnist Thomas Sowell and Linda Chávez, who built careers by pandering to the right, were trotted out.

The 209 campaign effectively used Shelby Steele, a confused African American scholar who taught English at San Jose State University and who is a senior fellow at the Hoover Institution. Steele frequently writes about race. The culture warriors over the years have built Steele into a guru. In a collection of essays, *The Content of Our Character*, Steele describes his dilemma as a black college professor with two sons entering college age:

> Their society now tells them that if they will only designate themselves as black on their college applications, they will likely do better in the college lottery than if they conceal this fact . . . I think there is something of a Faustian bargain in this.[15]

In an interview Steele added that

> In order to achieve a color-blind society, both whites and blacks have to make sacrifices for fairness . . . If something is fair for one group it must be fair for others . . . If preferential treatment

is correct, why not a David Duke Scholarship for poor Appalachian whites?[16]

Aside from providing an ahistorical analysis, Steele misses three essential points. First, poor whites should be given preference to middle-class whites. Indeed, I have routinely written letters of recommendation for poor white students for programs for the disadvantaged. Secondly, Steele is upper middle-class, and should not think of himself as the point of reference. Diversity includes class; indeed, some universities use a number of "preferential" variables, such as age, gender, race, religious affiliation, economic class, military experience, and sexual orientation, in their evaluation of applicants. It is only race that our good bigots choose to pick on. Thirdly, the reality is that in order to have a fully integrated society, it is not enough to seed the very poor; the near poor and the lower middle class also have to step up.[17]

In September 1996 I spoke at the University of Notre Dame. From what I could gather, between five hundred and six hundred Latino students attended Notre Dame. In contrast to California State at Northridge, where 90 percent of my Latino students are first-generation college students, about 50 percent at Notre Dame were second-generation college students, the sons and daughters of Latino professionals. Even though they had lived in middle-class neighborhoods, they found it necessary to group as Latinos at the university and maintain their separate identities.

The rhetoric of the proponents of 209—that rich minorities who do not need affirmative action are the main beneficiaries of special race-based privileges—immediately came to mind. However, upon speaking to the students, I found that most had been excellent students throughout their careers, and their parents, far from being wealthy, were petty professionals such as social workers and school teachers. I did not meet one student whose father belonged to the well-paid professions such as medicine, and the one son of a prosperous businessman that I met was not receiving any financial assistance. Most of them could not have attended Notre Dame without some financial aid. I met a critical mass who had been raised by single mothers and would have never considered going to Notre Dame without the University's outreach program. Strictly from an evolutionary perspective, these second-generation Latino university students will be in a much better position to afford to send their children to elite schools like Notre Dame. Based on my forty years in education, SAT, GRE, LSAT, and other examination scores increase as the generations of college graduates in a family increase.

Another African American prominent in this discourse is economist Glenn Loury. His message is that Americans of all color must find the strength and goodness to overcome their fears and reach out to the most troubled of inner-city residents: first, because as fellow citizens they deserve this help, and secondly, because they are children of God. Loury, a professor at Boston University, is called a black conservative. He has argued for years against the idea of racial preferences and is often quoted by the ultraconservative *Washington Times*. But even he has said that if he had been a Californian and eligible to vote, he would have been reluctant to vote in favor of passage:

> [T]he initiative is flawed both in letter and spirit. Since its underlying premise is that a citizen's racial identity is wholly irrelevant to any proper state interest, CCRI implicitly denies that racial justice is a legitimate public goal. For this reason, I hope it will not frame the national debate on racial preferences in the coming years.[18]

Loury points out that color blindness can, on occasion, be a dumb and dangerous policy. The worst thing about the initiative, according to Loury, is its implicit denial that the government has any responsibility to help "reduce the gap in development between Black Americans and others in the society." However, within the discourse over affirmative action, these aspects of Loury's thought are overshadowed by his thesis that affirmative action has diminished black incentive to acquire skills.

Yale law professor Stephen Carter, author of *Reflections of an Affirmative Action Baby*, argues that affirmative action perpetuates among whites the stereotype that black students or faculty members are undeserving. Carter, a Stanford graduate, applied to Harvard Law School and was rejected. Within a few days, two

Harvard officials apologized for their "error." The university had obtained "additional information"—Carter was black. Carter says that he was insulted. Harvard, according to Carter, had already judged Carter's qualifications, and saw him differently when they realized he was black. Carter viewed Harvard's offer as patronization. Carter, however, took the carrot and went on to a prosperous career, all the while decrying the opportunities given to him. He did not ask whether the Harvard process had been equitable in the first place, or how many of his classmates had received special consideration because they had a surname associated with a benefactor of Harvard.

It is interesting to observe how the words of minority scholars are distorted by the righteous right. Professor William Julius Wilson, an African American economist at the University of Chicago, advocates race-neutral measures to improve the plight of the poor. Author of *When Work Disappears: The World of the New Urban Poor*, Wilson has become an "an academic celebrity" through his stance that white America is not at fault for America's "underclass." Wilson asserts that impoverished blacks contribute to their own worsening situation. In short, they fail to help themselves. According to Wilson's research, the number of working men left in the ghettos has declined precipitously. Wilson underscores the fact that as the nation switched from manufacturing to service jobs in the past few decades, most central city factories closed. Companies began shifting to automated plants in the suburbs as early as the 1950s. More than 1.5 million manufacturing jobs disappeared from 1953 to 1962. Many city residents moved to suburbs, leaving inner-city residents without jobs or prospects. As Wilson correctly observes, the ability to get out of the ghettos is severely hampered by the unavailability of work. Crime increases, and there is no pressure for young men to marry and become breadwinners. The result is lack of hope.

Wilson proposes a costly (but necessary) set of solutions. The issues of employment, education, and family support systems, as well as the relationship between the cities and the suburbs, must all be addressed. Wilson's solutions include setting national school standards, implementing universal child care, and increasing employment by means of "placement centers," with subsidized transportation for workers from inner cities out to suburban factories. Public employment should also be increased.

Wilson's package of solutions is one that intelligent liberals have advocated for decades. It would call for a total commitment of society, and it would benefit all poor people. However, his work has been misquoted. Readers dwell on the concept that the American majority are not at fault for urban blight. Yet indeed they are, because they are unwilling to commit public funds to a solution. Even though Wilson's goal to "get people off welfare and into jobs" seems to echo Clinton's declared reason for signing the 1996 Personal Responsibility and Work Opportunity Act (Welfare Reform), Wilson criticized the signing of the act, a fact that was not widely reported.[19] Self-sufficiency, for Wilson, requires jobs that pay double the entry-level wages of $5 to $6 an hour.

A "bright light" for progressives in the debate for affirmative action is that of former Harvard law professor Derrick Bell, who has said,

> Twenty years ago, I became the first black law teacher not because there were never any blacks before who deserved to be here, but because 20 years ago the students raised cain, insisting it was time they get beyond the all white, all male, so during this whole year, I've been more aware, I was always aware of it, but I was more aware this year of how much I owe what I consider a wonderful job to student pressures. And a part of that is what can I do to pay back.[20]

He added,

> One of the greatest frustrations is to be a black male, and particularly in this situation, to see black women who could be your daughters, if I'd had a daughter, pleading, petitioning, pushing the white man to say hey, this is what we need, and having them respond, we'll do it in our own time. So I decided that I would do something, take some action, take some position that would embarrass them.

Professor Bell took a leave from Harvard until that university hired a minority woman. Of sixty tenured professors at Harvard

Law School, five were tenured women professors and three tenured black professors. None were of Mexican extraction. The law school's assistant dean, Louis Kaplow, responded that the administration would not be pressured into compromising Harvard's standards. Bell, meanwhile, has never returned to Harvard.

Voices among Chicanas/os in academe have not been as clear as Carter's or even Wilson's and certainly not Bell's. Anti–affirmative action voices have largely come from the public sector. The most quoted Chicano on the subject of affirmative action is undoubtedly Richard Rodríguez, author of *Hunger of Memory*, whose discourse has moderated considerably on the subject in recent years. Rodríguez, for all of the criticism directed at him, did not allow himself to be used in the 209 campaign. In contrast, Linda Chávez, author of *Out of the Barrio*, is the Latina celebrity of the right; her main message seems to be that "Hispanics" are doing just fine; it's those immigrants who are dragging down the progress. Even so, Chávez acknowledged that the Republicans, with their strident anti-immigrant message, were alienating the Hispanic vote: "too many Republicans have been quick to fan the nativist flames, blaming immigrants for taking American jobs and increasing crime."[21] She also acknowledged that the welfare bill, which took benefits away from "legal" immigrants, fanned Latino suspicions. Chávez could have easily made the same comment about Proposition 209, which, according to most pundits, alienated Latinos and cost the GOP seats.

While most Latinos in higher education take a politically correct posture in not opposing affirmative action, they also present the contradictory message that there is considerable merit in what critics are saying about Latino and even ethnic studies research and the mediocrity of Latino scholars. One such voice is that of the recently named director of the University of Arizona's Mexican American Studies Center, Adela de la Torre, who was formerly chair of the Chicano Studies Department at California State University at Long Beach. (Her views are more fully critiqued in chapter 5.) De la Torre's message is that Chicanos must insist on rigorous research and Chicano studies must move away from the posture of the 1960s, when "the criteria for entrance into these programs, and scholarly accomplishment meant little." Although not opposed to affirmative action, she does imply that Chicanos as a group are not in favor of standards. Inadvertently, she thereby gives ammunition to those who deny that there is exploitation in the U.S. by asserting that minorities are not victims.

The Changing Definition of Fairness

Affirmative action died in battle. The victors in wars seek to reconcile their motives with the prevailing values and ethical system. Principles such as, We live in a classless society, There is equal opportunity for all, and Work hard enough and you'll make it to the middle-class heaven, are all part of the American myth—and like all myths, they are believed. Propaganda is constructed to justify the war. Since the victors control history, it is important for the losers to put this discourse in historical context in order to understand the tensions and to understand why they lost.

The issue of minority appointments is not only one of fairness but of a sense of fairness. People have to believe that there is equality of opportunity. Without this sense of fairness, the legitimacy and credibility of the whole system would come tumbling down. Americans supported affirmative action because they believed that history had been unfair, mainly to African Americans. Support for affirmative action dwindled as white Americans began to internalize the fear that they would not do better than their parents. In this context, they forgot about past inequities and the present inequality of blacks and others and began to concentrate on how fairness to blacks and Latinos was unfair to all Americans.

Looking back, *Brown v. Board of Education* (1954), which increased expectations and seemed to signal an end to racial inequality, raised the specter of fairness and kept some sort of faith among a critical core of Americans. But this sense of fairness evaporated over the years. The U.S. remains separate and unequal, and most people ignore the fact that cities like Los Angeles are more segregated now than forty years ago. Martin Luther King and many early civil rights leaders believed that they could obtain "equality" through the courts. The logic was that the courts would follow legal precedent (positivist law). This logic is based on the positivist theory of law, that supposedly looks to the original intent of lawmakers for the interpretation of law (and ignores the historical context). What King and others did not count on was the Euro-American habit of reconstructing truth to justify its privilege.

What exactly was the original intent of the lawmakers with respect to affirmative action? President John F. Kennedy said: "There is little value in a Negro's obtaining the right to be admitted to hotels and restaurants if he has no cash in his pockets and no job." Both Kennedy and Johnson recognized that there could be no legal equality without economic equality. President Lyndon Johnson's 1965 speech to the black students of Howard University is generally conceded to be the start of affirmative action as governmental policy.

Affirmative action was supposed be a temporary solution to compensate for the inequality black Americans still suffered. Once equal opportunity was complete for all, affirmative action would no longer be needed. If the measure, then, was one of equality, is it reasonable to believe that equality could be reached in twelve years? In thirty years? Or even more to the point, is the U.S. less separate and unequal today than it was in 1965?

When Johnson delivered his speech, the civil rights movement was already in full swing. The Civil Rights Act of 1964 prohibited discrimination in public education and employment. The 1965 Voting Rights Act supposedly put an end to the systematic exclusion of southern blacks from voting. The Federal Housing Act of 1968 banned discrimination in housing. The idea of racial equity as a national policy was amazing, considering that just two decades earlier, it was government policy to segregate black soldiers, and segregation in schools and in housing was the rule. The intent of the framers of these laws is clear, and so was the context in which they were passed: the late 1960s saw cities burn, from Los Angeles to Washington, D.C. The framers knew that there would be no peace in the nation without a sense of justice, which meant the creation of an equal society. Affirmative action was the remedy for acknowledged discrimination. It was also a means of giving hope to alienated masses of African Americans.

Initially, the lawmakers intended affirmative action solely for African Americans. The courts later interpreted the laws to include Latinos, women, the disabled, and other disadvantaged minorities. As the urgency and tensions between black and white lessened, the idea of a just society faded. Euro-Americans began to have second thoughts. This disillusionment was similar to the love affair Euro-Americans had with integration, which was necessary as long as it was a southern problem but became undemocratic when it meant integrating northern schools. The Euro-American sense of fairness seemed to be satisfied with a de jure end to segregation, even though de facto segregation increased.

Fairness, in the mind of many folk, is synonymous with objectivity, and therefore the definition of fairness must change if indeed objectivity is unfair. Changes in the definition and in the mind-set of society were encouraged by a discourse on the tensions between equality and merit. Politicos skillfully played on white fears, cultivating what has become known as the "white backlash." In my view, the backlash was based more on racial antipathies than it was on a sense of unfairness to whites. John Mitchell in 1968 exploited this tension between the races by playing to white bigotry. Mitchell launched the Republicans' southern strategy by appealing to southern white voters. Up to this point, Republicans had conceded that the South would vote Democrat, but by playing powerfully on white fears, the Republicans gradually shifted the southern vote. The metaphors used by Republican and also, lately, by Democratic candidates are epitomized by Reagan's stereotype of the welfare mom, Bush's Willie Horton, and Pete Wilson's imagery of the invasion of the "illegal alien."

The popular culture has also reenforced underlying tensions between black and white (and between other ethnic and racial groups as well). The intent of the most popular television series of the 1970s, "All in the Family," was to have Americans laugh at "racism" by demonstrating how ridiculous racism really was. However, racism, like sexism and homophobia, is not a laughing matter, and even outright racists identified with the show. Archie Bunker became their hero. Archie looked and sounded like a father, a lovable and harmless racist. This series was followed by a spin-off, the "Jeffersons." Again, this was a genuinely funny show, exploring the life of upwardly mobile George Jefferson, a black businessman who was also, like Archie, a bigot. This was followed by "Sanford and Son," whose star, Redd Foxx, played the part of the original dirty old man, a junkyard dog who hated whites. The message in these two latter series was that there was "reverse racism." (Latinos finally got their niche in "Chico and the Man," in which Chico's employer was a racist but a good-hearted one.)

As popular culture made racism respectable, the courts whittled away at the precise meaning of affirmative action. A shift occurred in ideology from the Warren to the Burger and finally to the Rehnquist courts. Words such as affirmative action, racism, and equality took on new meanings in decisions of the Supreme Court. The most far-reaching of these cases was the 1978 *Regents of the University of California v. Bakke.* The medical school of the University of California at Davis had twice rejected Allan Bakke, age 36, a white male. Bakke's grades were higher than those of some minority students who were accepted. The UC had a quota system, reserving a certain number of spots for nonwhites. The Supreme Court ruled that quotas were illegal, although it permitted race to be one factor in admissions decisions.

Allan Bakke had options. Most experts readily concede that Bakke was denied admission because of his age. At the time, medical schools would rarely admit an applicant in his or her mid-30s. The most logical cause of action would have been to file under the federal Anti-Discrimination and Employment Act and/or California's Fair Housing and Employment Act for age discrimination. But after his second rejection, Bakke chose instead to file a state action for mandatory, injunctive, and declaratory relief to compel his admission to Davis, on the basis that minority applicants were getting preferential treatment. According to Bakke, the special admissions program operated to exclude him on the basis of his race, in violation of the equal protection clause of the Fourteenth Amendment, of a provision of the California Constitution, and of Section 601 of Title VI of the Civil Rights Act of 1964. Bakke won his suit at the state level, where the trial court found that the special admissions program operated as a racial quota: the University of California at Davis

Medical School had set aside sixteen places in the class of one hundred for minority applicants.

The California Supreme Court found that Davis had violated the equal protection clause. Davis could take an applicant's disadvantaged background into account, as long it was applied in a racially neutral fashion. The effect was to make affirmative action unlawful insofar as race was concerned. When the university subsequently appealed the state decision, the U.S. Supreme Court also ruled in favor of Bakke. The U.S. Supreme Court ruling softened the state decision. Race could not be used as the sole factor: "Government may take race into account when it acts not to demean or insult any racial group but to remedy disadvantages cast on minorities by past racial prejudice."

In 1989, after a long judicial history centered around *Bakke*, the Supreme Court dealt affirmative action another blow in *City of Richmond v. J. A. Croson*. The Court held that a law that reserved 30 percent of public works contracts for minority construction companies was illegal, reversing a 1980 decision that had upheld a minority set-aside program.

In state and national politics, affirmative action became a wedge issue. Senator Jesse Helms, during his notorious 1990 re-election campaign, depicted a white worker deprived of a job because an employer hired a minority worker to fill a racial quota. California governor Pete Wilson resurrected a dying political career on the backs of immigrants and minorities, playing to white fears and popularizing the notion that government gave minorities special privileges. The result was that by 1990, more than 70 percent of white Americans believed that it was "very likely" or "somewhat likely" that a white would fail to get a job or promotion when an equally qualified black or Latino applied.

Bakke *and the Color-blind Society*

The political term "color blindness" implies objectivity in matters of race: Americans look not at the color of a person's skin but at the content of his or her character. In the *Bakke* case, Supreme Court Justice Harry Blackmun wrote that "in order to get beyond race, you must first take account of race." It is obvious, based on

Bakke and the history of cases dealing with equal protection, that justices have rarely taken the question of race seriously. Indeed, enforcement of the equal protection guarantee of the Fourteenth Amendment, ratified in 1868, is relatively new in regards to the race question. Before the 1960s it was generally believed that African Americans and other non–Euro-Americans were not equal to Euro-Americans, and therefore equal opportunity had a different meaning for them. During the 1960s, however, the concept of racial equality became national policy and competed, although in the end unsuccessfully, for a place along with what whites call the essential American values of democracy and individualism.

The concept that peoples of color are less than equal has been ingrained since the outset of U.S. constitutional experience. The literature of this country amply proves that Mexicans shared this legacy. For example, the Mexican government was well aware of the popular American view of Mexicans in 1848. It was concerned enough to include in the Treaty of Guadalupe Hidalgo special provisions for the protection of Mexicans remaining in the severed Territory.

The Fourteenth Amendment, passed to remedy the Constitution's legalization of racism, has been watered down by Court opinions that reinterpret the intent of Congress, limit the integration of blacks and others, and subordinate racial equality to the interests of whites. The history of the Fourteenth Amendment in the courts is all too often a history of evasion.

The Supreme Court handling of *Bakke* is a case study of this history of evasion. The details of this evasion are important in understanding how Americans reconstruct the truth. The justices, in their usual fashion, speculated as to congressional intent. They took isolated statements of legislators out of context and concluded that Article 601 of Title VI of the Civil Rights Act was enacted as a color-blind strategy, without regard to the equal protection clause. For example, they appealed out of context to statements of Senator Hubert Humphrey such as:

Racial discrimination or segregation in the administration of *disaster relief* is particularly shocking; offensive to our sense of

justice and fair play. [Italics added] Human suffering draws
no color lines, and the administration of help to the sufferers
should not.

Humphrey, however, was simply applying his metaphor in the
context of disaster relief to argue for relief of minorities suffering from discrimination. Humphrey did not argue that government was discriminating against whites. (It is both relevant and
shocking to recall that during the 1994 earthquake in Northridge,
California, many of the cheerleaders of the *Bakke* case angrily demanded that undocumented Mexicans be denied "disaster relief.")

The problem Congress intended to solve in passing Title VI,
according to the Court, was discrimination against African American citizens by recipients of federal monies. The Court then made
a gigantic leap in logic:

> There simply was no reason for Congress to consider the validity
> of hypothetical preferences that might be accorded minority citi-
> zens; the legislators were dealing with the real and pressing
> problem of how to guarantee those citizens equal treatment.

The justices also appealed to Representative Celler, the chairman
of the House Judiciary Committee and floor manager of the passage of Title VI in the House, who said:

> Against this background, claims that law must be "color-blind"
> or that the datum of race is no longer relevant to public policy
> must be seen as aspiration rather than as description of reality.
> This is not to denigrate aspiration; for reality rebukes us that
> race has too often been used by those who would stigmatize and
> oppress minorities. Yet we cannot—and, as we will demonstrate,
> need not under our Constitution or Title VI, which merely ex-
> tends the constraints of the Fourteenth Amendment to private
> parties who receive federal funds—let color blindness become
> myopia which masks the reality that many 'created equal' have
> been treated within our lifetimes as inferior both by the law and
> by their fellow citizens.

Yet there is absolutely nothing in Celler's statement which justifies color blindness as the Court perceived it, namely, as a prin-

ciple which prohibits race-conscious remediation. Celler merely says that color blindness is an "aspiration" *after* equal protection has been achieved. Representative Celler added:

> words [were used] unequivocally expressing the intent to provide the Federal Government with the means of assuring that its funds were not used to subsidize racial discrimination inconsistent with the standards imposed by the Fourteenth and Fifth Amendments upon state and federal action . . . It [Title VI] would, in short, assure the existing right to equal treatment in the enjoyment of Federal funds. It would not destroy any rights of private property or freedom of association.

The respondents in the *Bakke* appeal (the University of California) argued that the reasoning that

> Congress intended Title VI to *bar affirmative-action programs* [italics added] . . . is also refuted by an examination of the type of conduct which Congress thought it was prohibiting by means of Title VI. The debates reveal that the legislation was motivated primarily by a desire to eradicate a very specific evil: federal financial support of programs which disadvantaged Negroes by excluding them from participation or providing them with separate facilities.

Repeatedly, supporters of Title VI had emphasized that its purpose was to end segregation in federally funded activities and to end discriminatory uses of race in disadvantaging African Americans. Senator Hubert Humphrey, in his speech presenting Title VI to the Senate, clearly stated: "Large sums of money are contributed by the United States each year for the construction, operation, and maintenance of segregated schools."

The Court majority, however, alleged that the Congress which enacted Title VI understood the Constitution to require strict racial neutrality or color blindness. It thus concluded that the concept of color blindness was a rule of statutory law.[22] The Court speculated that Congress would have expanded on its concept of color blindness, if it had taken the time. The Court also justified its conclusion by scattered remarks in the legislative history of Title VII of the Civil Rights Act of 1964, which prohibits employment discrimination on the basis of race in terms somewhat similar to those contained in Title VI. For example, the Court took the phrase "to fail or refuse to hire" any applicant "because of such individual's race, color, religion, sex, or national origin," and concluded that the deliberate attempt by an employer to maintain a racial balance is not required by the statute and might, in fact, violate it.

Previously, no Court decision had adopted the proposition that the Constitution was color-blind. The dissenting minority in *Bakke* reasoned,

> Even if it could be argued in 1964 that the Constitution might conceivably require color blindness, Congress surely would not have chosen to codify such a view unless the Constitution clearly required it. The legislative history of Title VI, as well as the statute itself, reveals a desire to induce voluntary compliance with the requirement of nondiscriminatory treatment . . . It is inconceivable that Congress intended to encourage voluntary efforts to eliminate the evil of racial discrimination while at the same time forbidding the voluntary use of race-conscious remedies to cure acknowledged or obvious statutory violations.

The dissent in *Bakke* found that "there is no indication that Congress intended to bar the voluntary use of racial preferences to assist minorities to surmount the obstacles imposed by the remnants of past discrimination":

> Indeed, . . . this Court has construed Title VII as requiring the use of racial preferences for the purpose of hiring and advancing those who have been adversely affected by past discriminatory employment practices, even at the expense of other employees innocent of discrimination.

Further, according to the dissent,

> Court has also declined to adopt a "color-blind" interpretation of other statutes containing nondiscrimination provisions similar to that contained in Title VI. We have held under Title VII that where employment requirements have a disproportionate impact upon racial minorities they constitute a statutory violation,

even in the absence of discriminatory intent, unless the employer is able to demonstrate that the requirements are sufficiently related to the needs of the job. More significantly, the Court required that preferences be given by employers to members of racial minorities as a remedy for past violations of Title VII, even where there has been no finding that the employer has acted with a discriminatory intent. Finally, we have construed the Voting Rights Act of 1965, which contains a provision barring any voting procedure or qualification that denies or abridges "the right of any citizen of the United States to vote on account of race or color," as permitting States to voluntarily take race into account in a way that fairly represents the voting strengths of different racial groups in order to comply with the commands of the statute, even where the result is a gain for one racial group at the expense of others.

Justice Thurgood Marshall, among the dissenting justices, observed:

I do not agree that petitioner's admissions program violates the Constitution. For it must be remembered that, during most of the past 200 years, the Constitution as interpreted by this Court did not prohibit the most ingenious and pervasive forms of discrimination against the Negro. Now, when a State acts to remedy the effects of that legacy of discrimination, I cannot believe that this same Constitution stands as a barrier.

Justice Marshall then historically dissected the history of discrimination against blacks:

We consider the underlying fallacy of the plaintiff's argument to consist in the assumption that the enforced separation of the two races stamps the colored race with a badge of inferiority. If this be so, it is not by reason of anything found in the act, but solely because the colored race chooses to put that construction upon it. The relationship between those figures and the history of unequal treatment afforded to the Negro cannot be denied. At every point from birth to death the impact of the past is reflected in the still disfavored position of the Negro . . . In light of the sorry history of discrimination and its devastating impact on the lives of

Negroes, bringing the Negro into the mainstream of American life should be a state interest of the highest order. To fail to do so is to ensure that America will forever remain a divided society.

Justice Marshall continued his scathing attack on the majority opinion:

> I do not believe that the Fourteenth Amendment requires us to accept that fate. Neither its history nor our past cases lend any support to the conclusion that a university may not remedy the cumulative effects of society's discrimination by giving consideration to race in an effort to increase the number and percentage of Negro doctors . . . While I applaud the judgment of the Court that a university may consider race in its admissions process, it is more than a little ironic that, after several hundred years of class-based discrimination against Negroes, the Court is unwilling to hold that a class-based remedy for that discrimination is permissible. In declining to so hold, today's judgment ignores the fact that for several hundred years Negroes have been discriminated against, not as individuals, but rather solely because of the color of their skins. It is unnecessary in 20th-century America to have individual Negroes demonstrate that they have been victims of racial discrimination; the racism of our society has been so pervasive that none, regardless of wealth or position, has managed to escape its impact . . . The dream of America as the great melting pot has not been realized for the Negro; because of his skin color he never even made it into the pot.

Andrew Kull, in his work *The Color-blind Constitution* (1992), argues that the framers of the Fourteenth Amendment did not mean to prohibit all forms of racial preferences, only those that were unreasonable or unrelated to legitimate public purposes. Looking at original intent, the framers were specifically concerned about laws like the Black Codes that extended unequal punishments, and unequal benefits, to blacks and whites.

The courts ignored the fact that states in the late 1800s systematically passed laws that separated the races. The Fourteenth Amendment, passed supposedly to end this, was made a sham by judicial review. It was not until *Brown v. Board of Education* (1954), nearly one hundred years after the passage of the Fourteenth Amendment, that the separate but equal doctrine of the 1890s was struck down by the Court. *Bakke* was a return to separate but equal. *Bakke* protected the white majority from the burdens of race-conscious remediation of past discrimination.

The End of Equality

How did we get to the place that equality becomes discriminatory? Proposition 209 has an intellectual precursor in *Bakke*. Nevertheless, if Proposition 209 had been passed in 1978, it would have been declared unconstitutional out of hand. Moreover, it would have been incompatible with the public discourse of the times. Proposition 209 is the product of the gradual promotion of a racist intent on the part of a right-wing elite. The courts, as much as right-wing organizations and intellectuals, have contributed to this intellectual legacy.

The 1978 *Bakke* decision is one of the best-known court rulings in the history of the civil rights movement. Its importance goes well beyond the ruling itself. As bad as the *Bakke* decision was, at least it sanctioned the use of race as a factor in admissions, although race could not be the sole factor. However, the *Bakke* decision set in motion an idea and a language that led to Proposition 209. It literally put to rest the notion of an equal society.

Since *Bakke*, the Court has returned to a legal analysis which reduces racial discrimination to "mere discrimination." First, the Court has chosen to ignore history. In *Bakke* it conveniently ignored the fact that *Brown* had been the law of the land for a little more than two decades and the Civil Rights Act for about a decade. Modern jurisprudence replaced a commitment to equality with a policy of denial and evasion. Through distorted logic it denied the reality of racism and inequality. Fictions such as the separate but equal doctrine, de facto segregation, discriminatory intent, and color blindness are analytical methodologies for avoiding responsibility for racial discrimination.[23]

Brown is clear: constitutional law should be vigorously enforced to guarantee minority interests. Historically, constitutional law and equal protection have mirrored dominant attitudes and priorities. Equal protection serves the interests of the dominant society. The courts, in applying equal protection, use rationality that reflects evasion and denial of racial reality. The outcome would have been different if the courts had used racial discrimination as the norm and made its legal existence intolerable. Instead, they have totally abandoned the concept of effective remediation, which is the essence of affirmative action. Prejudices become aberrations, mere "social blunders," rather than part of the history of American racism.

The concept of equal protection goes against Americans' false sense of justice. The color-blind approach to equal protection trivializes race and rationalizes it to the point that the victim becomes the perpetrator. Indeed, we have come to the point that the term "victim" is negative and insulting to the victim. This is to deny the simple truths that exploitation exists and someone is responsible. The answer is not the mythical pulling oneself up by the boot straps.

The original intent of the Fourteenth Amendment is clearer if it is viewed in the context of both the Thirteenth Amendment, which prohibits slavery, and the Fifteenth Amendment, which secures the right to vote free from racial discrimination. The original intent of these amendments was not to protect whites from blacks. A similar conclusion holds for the civil rights legislation of the 1960s. Yet it took the Court less than a decade to return to a historical policy of denial, evasion, and accommodation.

In case law since *Bakke*, there has been a persistent widening of the concept of a color-blind society. Over the next decade and a half, the rationalization that allowed race to be a factor, but not the sole factor, was transformed into the policy that any consideration of race is discrimination. As a consequence of this rhetoric of evasion, it has become almost impossible to link illegal purpose and overt discrimination. If Proposition 209 is upheld by the U.S. Supreme Court, it will become impossible to obtain a remedy for discrimination.

The present composition of the Court makes it highly probable that 209 will be upheld. The sentiments of Justices Antonin Scalia and Clarence Thomas are evident. They are champions of a new cultural conservatism symbolically represented by the Christian right. A May 22, 1996 *New York Times* article reported,

Repeatedly, Scalia has said that he sees no duty to adhere to precedents with which he disagrees and he has been slashing in his attacks on those who disagree with him.

Justices Kennedy, Souter, and O'Connor sometimes veer in questions of gender and sexual preferences, recognizing that there is a problem in these areas; however, racism and class are another matter. The Court is sovereign, and the denial and avoidance of issues of racism and classism are a central societal feature of the judicial logic. The concept of racism as an evil is at the point of extinction.

In reality, a race-conscious government policy has kept minorities disempowered. The Fourteenth Amendment and other civil rights legislation are window dressing. It has been little more than thirty years since the civil rights legislation of the 1960s was passed, and today it has been largely dismantled. *Brown*, forty years later, has also been dismantled. The Fourteenth Amendment is now being enacted to protect the rights of the majority.[24]

Eight years before the *Brown* case, *Westminster School District of Orange County et al. v. Méndez et al.* had ended the segregation of Mexican children in California schools. Gonzalo Méndez, a tenant farmer in Westminster in Orange County, one of a group of Mexican American veterans of World War II, asked, "If we are good enough to fight and die alongside Anglos, then why are [our] children not good enough to attend the same school as their children?" They filed suit early in 1945 in federal court in Los Angeles, against Westminster, Santa Ana, Garden Grove, and El Modena, seeking an injunction ordering integration. On April 14, 1947, the Ninth U.S. Court of Appeals in San Francisco ordered that there could be no segregation on the basis of national origin.

Fifty years after *Westminster*, Latinos in California public schools as well as in other parts of the country are more segregated than they were in 1945. There are many factors contributing to this state of affairs. The global economy, growing meaner and leaner, has shifted the costs of social production from the rich to the middle class and to older white America, which has enjoyed a monopoly on employment. As a consequence of the downward trend in the pecking order, many white Americans regard people of color as an economic threat.

In order for the U.S. as a society to remediate racism and other forms of discrimination, discriminatory motive must be easily discerned. Based on present case law, it is easily disguised. Uncovering an illicit motive is difficult and expensive, since employers, university officials, and faculty know they only have to conceal actual intent to avoid legal consequences. Motive-based inquiry looks to the intent of the accused rather than the harm inflicted. It shields the review process from the realities and consequences of racism. It is a device for avoiding the charge of racial injustice; it restores the separate but equal doctrine of *Plessy v. Fergusson* (1896), which legalized official segregation as a logical extension of distinctions "in the nature of things." *Plessy* said that laws allowing segregation were constitutional, absent proof of discriminatory intent. As in *Plessy*, the courts today have created a doctrine—the color-blind test—that effectively avoids judgment and defers to the status quo.

The policy of color blindness promotes racial neutrality, prevents race-conscious remediation, and thus encourages racial discrimination. It expresses the concern that affirmative action creates unfair advantages for minorities. Then, paradoxically, it further rationalizes that affirmative action stigmatizes and stereotypes minorities, promoting tribal politics and restricting genuine opportunity.[25]

The argument that race-conscious remediation will narrow rather than widen opportunities is intellectually dishonest and insulting. Remediation is necessary. Its basis is the same as that of the time-honored tradition of scholarships for needy students. Without remediation, there will be no social change and the poor will remain poor. Remediation takes into account inequality, both of race and of class. It recognizes the history of racism in the United States. More important, it recognizes that there has been an accumulated advantage for some, resulting from a long legacy of societal discrimination.

2

It's the Law

When I was growing up, I often heard the aphorism, "it isn't what you know but whom you know." The Spanish word that best expresses the spirit of the saying is *palanca*. It literally means that you know someone with influence who favors you, or you have pull. My grandfather and uncles who worked for the Southern Pacific Railroad would talk about the palancas that they supposedly had with the foreman or someone else in a position of power. When they did not get a job or promotion, they attributed it to the lack of palanca, or in some cases, to the fact that gringo workers had more palanca because of their race. Often they complained that the foreman hired a relative who knew nothing about the job. White workers knew these informal rules of the game, and they were acutely aware of their class and race interests. They would also complain about other whites who knew less but nevertheless got the job because of whom they knew. I haven't heard the aphorism from Euro-Americans for some time, probably because of their belief that minorities are getting the promotions and jobs through their so-called palanca with the government.

This belief that minorities receive preferential treatment is widespread among Euro-Americans who resent minorities getting ahead "at their expense." It doesn't matter to them that the facts show that minorities and women have a glass ceiling. The immediate tendency among people of color is to blame Euro-American racism, which is certainly a factor in our society, for this belief. This explanation is, however, too simple and too clean. There are multiple factors which drive Euro-American judges, professors, and other educated persons to accept the idea that we live in a color-blind society, as well as, paradoxically, the idea that white males are now the objects of discrimination. This essay discusses the American paradigm that justifies these fallacies.

The American Paradigm

The dominant American paradigm provides fertile ground for the courts and politicians who want to deconstruct the civil rights paradigm that made racial, political, and economic equality the centerpiece of policy-making for a brief time in U.S. history. This anti–civil rights movement found expression in the *Bakke* decision of the late 1970s. It did not come about simply through the power of an idea. It was the fruit of a well-organized campaign by right-wing think tanks and organizations to change progressive attitudes inside the American paradigm that had found expression in the 1960s. Right-wing groups launched what Italian political theorist Antonio Gramsci has called political "wars of position," developing ideological stances on topics as varied as "English Only," Proposition 187 and immigration reform, IQ, race and eugenics, affirmative action, welfare, tort reform, sexual preference, and campus multiculturalism.[1]

The New Right began its culture war in the late 1960s, in reaction to what it considered a breakdown of the social order. The culture war took shape in the late 1970s, when William Simon, secretary of the treasury under Nixon and Ford, in his book *Time for Truth*, urged the New Right to form institutions to counter left-wing intellectuals. New Right think tanks cultivated a neoconservative American paradigm, using wedge issues such as religion, family values, and patriotism to sell their ideological agenda.[2] (This theme is explored more fully in the next chapter.) A proliferation of think tanks and organizations sounded the clarion, loudly proclaiming that liberal policies were causing an erosion of American values and institutions. The New Right campaign to change the direction of U.S. policy-making has been extremely successful in the space of only two decades. This success rests on the fact that the New Right's message appeals to and revives what I call the American paradigm.

I am indebted to Thomas Kuhn's *The Structure of Scientific Revolutions* in forming my own definition of the American paradigm, although I differ markedly from him in his later embracement of positivism.[3] Kuhn popularized the concept of "paradigms," arguing that every field of study has an established order of structural guidelines that influence the thinking and actions of its scientists and social scientists. Within these fields, existing paradigms restrict the growth and expansion of new and competing models.

Kuhn likened a paradigm to a textbook which laid out the definitions and the accepted truths in a field—its basic assumptions and methodology. According to Kuhn, these accepted truths and methods could be challenged and in time could change, through what he called a paradigm shift. A paradigm shift must constitute a fundamental and radical change from old to new elements. It involves a transformation in mind-sets, not just those of a few individuals or leaders but throughout the culture. In other words, paradigm shifts include total cultural change in beliefs, values, and behavior.

The validity of a given paradigm has nothing to do with whether it is right or wrong, according to Kuhn. Its validity is determined by its power to bring about results. The paradigm determines the important topics and questions of research in a field. Within the academic universe, paradigm shifts are rare, and indeed little critical enterprise takes place within the paradigm except for instances of "revolutionary science." Scholars believe that they and their fellow scholars make fully informed, rational choices in their research. They insist that the accepted paradigm has been tested by time. The paradigm in their field is constructed from truths that are universal; it is the result of informed, rational choices checked by approved methods of study. They assume that in arriving at the truth, the scholar has made every effort to be objective.

Kuhn has meant many things to many people. He describes a paradigm shift on the analogy of a revolution, which implies a war that ends "with a total victory for one of the two opposing camps." This is a daring and attractive analogy: the "experts" hold a monopoly on a dominant paradigm, which is only overthrown after strife, by a revolution in the accepted ideas. However, Kuhn is more complex than this. He has also argued that a paradigm shift takes place only after a "consensus" develops. In any case, a paradigm shift is difficult and takes a long time.

The concept of "paradigm shifts" is still popular today, and its adherents include academicians, prime ministers, and middle managers. However, many leaders in a field do not fully comprehend the complexities of paradigms or the necessity of radical change when the existing paradigm is incapable of producing solutions to problems. It cannot be overemphasized, in my view, that paradigm shifts only come about through extreme agitation that produces a fundamental shift in mind-sets. More often than not, changes in attitudes are not revolutionary and cannot qualify as paradigm shifts.

Kuhn rather narrowly defined a paradigm as a set of theories, standards, methods, and beliefs which are accepted as the norm by most scientists in a particular field of study. However, Kuhn's theory can be applied beyond particular scientific fields and professions, to academe in general and to the prevailing assumptions and values of a society. While there may be no pure objective truth, Americans tend to believe that their paradigm of society represents the closest approach to it. For example, while admitting that their form of democracy has flaws, Americans consistently dare others to name a better alternative.

The use of paradigms as a mode of analysis has been more common in the physical sciences, management, and even politics than in the social sciences, but it applies there as well. Thus, in the social sciences, paradigms are clearly necessary to search out and understand developments in U.S. society since World War II. The "clash of cultures" taking place in society, for example, cannot be reduced to an understanding of family values based on the public discourse of the 1950s. Alternative modes of analyses must be explored. The fields of ethnic and women's studies advance paradigms for analyzing relations in a culturally diverse society, one far different in the 1990s than it was in either 1900 or 1950. The various ethnic paradigms compete with the prevailing paradigm and with each other to deconstruct culture as static concept and reality.

It is also clear that in any field there are insiders and outsiders. (Outsiders are those who dare to criticize the insiders.) Unfortunately, the insiders control history. As Kuhn wrote, in one of his more quoted passages,

Revolutions close with a total victory for one of the two opposing camps. Will that group ever say that the results of its victory have been something less than progress? That would be like admitting that they had been wrong and their opponents right. To them, at least, the outcome of revolution must be progress, and they are in an excellent position to make certain that future members of their community will see past history in the same way.[4]

The insiders are the current victors. And outsiders are dismissed not so much because what they say is false but because, according to the insiders, it is meaningless and thus cannot be rationally discussed.

Where does Chicana/o studies stand with respect to paradigms? This is not easy to answer. In general, most Chicana/o scholars are not responding to the challenges implicit in this paradigmatic methodology. (After all, who wants to be dismissed as "meaningless" or reduced to a "mere anomaly-monger"?) Indeed, Chicana/o studies at most has kept pace with the semantic shift away from a monoracial, noncultural model of society. However, Chicana/o studies has failed to challenge the dominant cultures and ideas. It has failed to challenge mainstream truths. Its scholars have used old models, incapable of interpreting current social phenomena. Chicana/o scholars mechanically apply the traditional variables such as gender, class, and race, using the outdated methodologies of their individual disciplines. The truth be told, without a new narrative to challenge the old, a paradigm shift cannot take place in interpreting Chicana/o reality.

It is irrational (although rational within the paradigm) for the social sciences to pretend that civilization has stood still since 1900, or that only white middle- and upper-class males are capable of interpreting society. A true understanding of the causes of cultural stresses and strains in society can only be achieved by the inclusion of new knowledge, for example, that of Chicana/o studies, and of new models of interpretation.[5] There is no monolithic American society, and there is no such thing as a color-blind society. The different realities of the citizens in the U.S. demand matching constructs to explain how they think and see themselves and others. Only in this way can we interpret their impact on politics and culture. Diverse cultural norms, values, and ideas are clashing today. It is essential to understand how these clashes affect American values and the interests of the many peoples who make up our society.

Neoliberalism: An Article of Faith

The American paradigm in the broadest sense is multifaceted and includes disparate, even antagonistic currents of thought. It embraces paradigms which are constantly interacting, challenging one another and even the macro-culture. In this, I differ from Kuhn, with his concept of the "total victory" of one camp over another. The differences between Kuhn's and my own understanding of paradigms reflect the differences in disciplines. Resolutions in the "hard" sciences, the exemplars in Kuhn's analysis, are much clearer than in the case of social phenomena. In American society, there is a dominant paradigm which has largely prevailed for over two hundred years, but elements of others survive. American society undergoes pangs of conscience and goes through progressive periods, only to be overcome by the force of the dominant paradigm. There is constant motion, but in the end, the dominant American paradigm is a declaration of faith, like the Apostle's Creed that I recited as a school boy. The dominant American paradigm is fundamentally neoliberal, a concept not to be confused either with the word that Republicans use to describe Bill Clinton or with New Deal liberalism.

The prevailing confusion over the definition of neoliberalism is a result of U.S. politics and its "exercise in evasion." Most people outside the U.S. correctly associate neoliberalism with the positivist theory of nineteenth-century Western civilization. For them, globalization is just another version of the laissez-faire, trickle-down economics that fell into disrepute in the U.S. during the Great Depression of the 1930s.

Neoliberalism takes a different form in the U.S. than it does in so-called Third World countries. For example, there are restraints on the U.S. capitalist system, reflecting moral and social values from the New Deal years and from precapitalist society. The New Deal formula provided for social justice and political community.

Many Americans came to realize that the market does not automatically allocate its prizes fairly. Emanating from these progressive values are Social Security and Medicare, public education, public support of first-time buyer homes for families, and low-rent housing for the elderly—all policies that have been blurred and attacked by the neoliberal rhetoric.

The second laissez-faire era in the U.S. came into full swing with Ronald Reagan, under the misnomer of Reaganomics. Neoliberal writers redefined the American paradigm vis-à-vis the 1960s definition. Like the neoconservatives, neoliberals believe that government is more often a problem than a solution. Their response is to downsize government and institute mandatory low-paid work instead of welfare. They denounce trade unionism, with its protection for workers. For them, entitlements like Social Security and Medicare are problematic and thus merely tolerated because of their popular support.

In the context of neoliberalism, progressive impulses must be neutered. The neoliberal views regulatory schemes to protect society as antidemocratic. According to neoliberal economics, economic growth is sustained by cutting jobs. The neoliberal's creed includes individualism, freedom of contract, the sanctity of property, and a market free of regulation. Neoliberalism rests on complete faith in the capacity of markets to act as optimal economic allocators. The State should have no role as economic actor, planner of economic activity, or regulator.

The demise of the Soviet Union and Eastern Europe saw the surrender of the American left and American progressives to neoliberal politics. Their surrender was based on the accepted truth that the demise of communism proved the superiority of capitalism. Thus, the last half of the 1980s saw an enormous intensification of international capital's offensive. Much of it was aimed at restoring hegemony over the Third World. The offensive was framed as a struggle of democracy against socialism, good against evil, and progress against reaction. The prevailing "narrative" told of an economic contest between socialism and capitalism that resulted in a conclusive victory for capitalism. This message is so strong that the political left in the U.S. collapsed. Few former leftists dare insist that capitalism should be replaced by socialism.

In Spanish there is a saying, "la zorra nunca se ve la cola" (the fox never sees its own tail). This is especially true of North Americans, who are so ready to criticize other countries and point out the flaws in their paradigms. To better understand neoliberalism, a case study of Mexico is useful. It is also of interest because it mirrors U.S. trends. Mexicans recognize the pitfalls of neoliberalism. History reminds them that the *porfiriato*, the regime of Porfirio Díaz from 1876 to 1911, was the heyday of neoliberal policies and resulted in the Mexican Revolution. (In 1994, Mexico's Zapatista rebels deliberately rejected a neoliberal, free-market, free-trade economic model as oppressive and unjust. They were well aware that this had been the model for Mexico's policies under Díaz.)

Under the government of Carlos Salinas de Gortari (1988–1994), and through U.S. pressure, Mexico returned to the neoliberal economic paradigm in an effort to end its economic crisis and to win approval of world banking institutions. The catchall phrase was modernization. To achieve this, the Mexican president put through numerous changes in the Constitution that had been the cornerstone of the Mexican Revolution, privatized state-run and subsidized industries, downsized government, and cut social services. In the process, Mexican wages were programmed to fall under their minimum of $3.00 a day. Mexico also negotiated the North American Free Trade Agreement, which many fear will end Mexican sovereignty and put Mexico under the control of North American multinational corporations.

These actions ran against the accepted Mexican paradigm. Many Mexicans were not fooled by the government of Salinas, whose neoliberal wisdom promised prosperity, economic growth, and employment once inefficient state-run industries were sold off and the market was left to its own devices. Mexicans, conscious of the history of the Díaz era, rejected neoliberalism. So Salinas, as a Mexican president and free-market reformer, hired his intellectual cabal to ideologically revise Mexico's history with a neoliberal slant. The cabal changed official history, rewriting the textbooks. The new texts downplayed past U.S. military intervention in order to make the North American Free Trade Agreement more palatable. Instead of dwelling on the shortcomings of the former dictator Porfirio Díaz, his virtues were extolled. For example, Díaz was portrayed in 1972 textbooks as a corrupt dictator who rewrote the Constitution in order to be "reelected" six times. In the Salinas texts, Díaz takes on the title of "Don," a term of respect or nobility, and is cast in the role of an economic and social reformer. Positive emphasis is placed on his role in creating Mexico's railroad infrastructure and increasing foreign investment.

What Mexico did is no different from what is done in the United States, where the history textbook frames the dominant American paradigm and local, self-absorbed interest groups impose the traditional version of the history of the United States. Criticisms of this paradigm or moves to revise it assume a strict burden of proof, which makes an alternative version of history difficult to sell. This fact is illustrated in academe and the courts. Meanwhile, the American paradigm determines the type of question that is asked in social or legal research, and its answer.

Neoliberalism: Another Word for Positivism

Along with the concept of paradigms, it is helpful to explore positivism, which is at the heart of the American paradigm, because it dictates its theory and its methodology. Nineteenth-century positivism is itself based to a large extent on the eighteenth-century Enlightenment idea of "Reason" and the triumph of "Reason" over superstition and tradition. Reason is the governing principle that regulates the growth of knowledge; it directs and measures the "path of inquiry." Without reason there is intellectual anarchy. At the essence of positivism is the norm of the scientific method, which supposedly ensures rationality. Rationality is based on "the act of *rule-following*, not in the *act of rule-making* or *rule-breaking*."[6]

Neoliberalism is based on positivism. In one form or another, positivism is the dominant theory not only in the legal system but also in higher education and western research in general. It replaced the medieval concept of knowledge, which was based on Aristotelian methods and emphasized the use of reason in exploring questions of philosophy and theology. The assumption of medieval scholasticism was that every problem could be solved by reasoning, even the problem of proving the existence of God. This model gave way to the scientific method of inquiry, which evolved over several centuries. Natural processes could be explained by laws of nature, discovered through empirical observation and expressed in quantitative terms. Mathematics became a model in the organization of natural knowledge. The new way scholars looked at knowledge was a classic paradigm shift. The questions changed from Why? To How? The topics of inquiry changed from metaphysical to materialist ones.

The origins of positivism indirectly stem from Thomas Hobbes (1588–1679), a contemporary of Galileo. Hobbes argued that phenomena consisted of observable facts or events. Using reproducible scientific laws, scholars could predict everything occurring in nature. Central to the analysis was the adherence to the method. Hobbes extended this method to the law and used it to rationalize the authority of the sovereign. Law was nothing other than the "pleasure of the sovereign." Appeals to a higher authority or set of ethics to measure the law were irrational. Hobbes's methodology corresponded with the rise of the bourgeoisie and the preoccupation of this class with the institution of private property. According to the Hobbesian school, private property was entirely a creation of the state. Property rights were nothing more than what the state declared they were, and the courts interpreted the will of the state.

The French nineteenth-century philosopher Auguste Comte (1798–1857) developed a type of scientific positivism which, like Hobbes, he extended to human affairs. He believed in the sovereignty of the scientific method in attaining knowledge. Comte's thought, like that of many contemporaries, is much more ideological than that of earlier philosophers. He was perhaps the first to develop a general science of society. For Comte, like Karl Marx (1818–1883), history and science were themselves instruments of cultural change. His aim was for mankind to think in scientific terms, rejecting the unscientific.

Variations of Comte's method became dominant in American scholarship. The stress on the scientific method was combined with theories of economic policy such as the doctrine of laissez-faire. Named for the French phrase for "allow to do," it literally meant the doctrine of government noninterference with decisions made in an open, competitive market. First developed in the eighteenth century, the concept of laissez-faire greatly influenced later economic thought. It was a linchpin of classical economics introduced by eighteenth-century Scottish economist Adam Smith. It suited the interests of a rapidly expanding industrial economy. It was based on the premise that individuals serve their interests best when they provide the goods and services most wanted by others. The ideas of Comte and Smith combined naturally to justify the idea of a free market.

German scholarship in the late nineteenth century was heavily influenced by positivism and adhered closely to the scientific method. In contrast to English universities, which set out to produce gentlemen first, German universities set out to produce scholars and experts. Part of the process was applying quantitative tests to hypotheses, whether hypotheses were Comtean or Marxist. In the positivist tradition, scholarship was a "technical, specialized, and rigorous pursuit." The chief characteristic of the German legal and scholarly professions was a devotion to Comtean-style positivism, which in turn greatly influenced theory and practice in the U.S. In the field of jurisprudence, positivism holds that the law is complete in the enactments of duly constituted authorities.

The positivist concept of law is based on "moral relativism." Supposedly, absolute or universally accepted values of right and wrong do not exist, at least, none that supersede the law. Appeals to natural law, to the conscience of the nation, and to equity are of little relevance. The expression of the law is "posited" by the legally constituted lawmaker, that is, a legislature, a court, an administrative agency, or a city council. It is their intent that is important, and the role of courts is to stick to the laws intended by the lawmakers.

Positive law is based on a mechanical application of mathematical-like principles for determining the original intent of the lawmakers. The application is systematic, supposedly tested by time. The system's legitimacy is based on making certain that each step in the process meets a positivist standard. According to positivist legal scholars, this method of evaluating the laws results in the common good. Judges and scholars alike go to no end to "sound objective," and as critics have said, "to employ a positivist tone." Positivists claim that the outcome is free of value-laden language.

In short, positivism is not concerned with ethics. Indeed, ethical conduct could very well violate positive law. Ethical principles are not above the law and may, in fact, offend objectivity. Based on deductive jurisprudence, the positivist believes in a coherent and predictable outcome. It is this pretense of scientific objectivity that rationalizes a *Bakke* decision or a Proposition 209. It is part of that basic ethic of American consciousness that says, "It may not be just, but it's the law."

The Mythicization of the Law

Judges and lawyers, like university professors, are primarily upper middle-class males. They are either Democrats or Republicans. A few are liberal and more are conservative. They mirror the interests of the dominant class. What makes them impregnable is that they have been educated to think in what they consider a reasonable manner, holding common truths. Legal scholars reach back to the words of Lord Coke, who said that "the life of the law . . . [is] fined and refined by . . . grave and learned men." The Constitution itself becomes divine revelation. Judges and the courts are not privileged to freely adapt the Constitution to "changed economic and social conditions," which would be contrary to the original intent of the framers of the Constitution.[7]

Conservatives mythicize the law and the courts. They long for crusty old law professors like the fictional Professor Kingsman of the movie "The Paper Chase"—a character based on Harvard's pre–World War II law professor Edward "Bull" Warren—who is portrayed as a Socrates, rigorously probing his students to find the truth.

In certain periods, for example, during the Vietnam War, some law students grew skeptical about many of the nation's "truths" and institutions. With the admission of more women, blacks, Asians, and Latinos to higher education, subtle changes took place. Radicals today are given some political space to express their views. However, except for the occasional radical faculty member, the faculties of the law schools remain overwhelmingly neoliberal. Traditionalists paint the dissident professors as leftist ideologues who want to tear down judicial rationality.

Like university professors, judges and lawyers are the product of the training they receive. The lawyers' education establishes a paradigm which becomes part of their culture. The legal profession trains lawyers to analyze controversies, supposedly preparing them to look at both sides of issues. The attorney is supposed to be objective and to arrive at the truth.

This perception of the law creates a myth that the "rules of law are founded upon principles of right and justice that never change." Legal formalism, a dominant principle of positivism, is the cornerstone of the legal profession's claim to objectivity. Theories of the law are important because they guide the understanding of the law. At different times positivism has been challenged by competing theories—natural law theory, legal realism, and historical, feminist, and critical legal studies, among others—but it remains the controlling mode of looking at the law, very much shaping the conclusions of scholars.

In academe there is a similar mechanical adherence to objective method. Academe mirrors the courts and U.S. common law. Hence, ethical goals in academe, such as hiring qualified minorities, are rejected by faculty governance bodies, who see these goals as violating their "objective" review standards.

Common sense tells us that judges, like professors, are often more guided by their environment than by objectivity. For example, U.S. Supreme Court Justices Sandra Day O'Connor and Ruth Bader Ginsberg played key roles in the case of Teresa Harris (*Harris v. Forklift Systems, Inc.*, 1993), who suffered a pattern of offensive conduct by her employer. The employer called her a "dumb ass woman" and suggested that negotiations for a pay raise be carried on at a local motel. The U.S. Supreme Court held that the Sixth Circuit Court of Appeals properly decided that Harris did not have to show she was close to a nervous breakdown to win her claim. The Court's most conservative justices agreed with Justice Sandra O'Connor's reasoning that sexual harassment cannot be determined on the basis of a single factor or "by a mathematically precise test." The Court applied a standard of what reasonable people would agree upon. Not only did Justice O'Connor write the formal opinion, but Justice Ginsberg wrote a strong concurring opinion. Both were sensitive to feminist issues.

Their reasoning has been markedly different on race questions, and they often fail to understand the interests of minorities. For example, O'Connor, in a North Carolina redistricting case (*Shaw v. Reno*, 1994), joined the 5-4 majority, warning that racial gerrymandering could Balkanize American politics. The case involved a congressional election district that wove its way through ten counties for 160 miles. Clearly, the district had been drawn for the purpose of racial gerrymandering. It packed as many African American voters as possible into a single district. It took into account that previously, only one of the state's twelve congressional districts had a majority of African American voters. Blacks had long been excluded from North Carolina's political process; the state had not sent a black to the U.S. House of Representatives since Reconstruction. Justice Department attorneys, seeking a remedy based on the Voting Rights Act to extend the principles of affirmative action to elective representation, had forced the state to produce a new map that included a second African American–dominated district, the twelfth.

The Court reasoned that racial gerrymandering works against the long-term interests of all voters, black as well as white. The composition of a black congressional district, and gerrymandering in general, serve to perpetuate differences and antagonisms. Justice O'Connor declared in writing for the Supreme Court majority:

> Racial gerrymandering, even for remedial purposes, may Balkanize us into competing racial factions (and) threatens to carry us further from the goal of a political system in which race no longer matters.

Would the decision have been any different with minority judges who share the collective historical memory of their people? Surely O'Connor's legal reasoning as a woman differed when it came to gender issues, compared to her reasoning over issues of race.

The Warren Court, in contrast, was sensitive to a wide range of racial and social issues. Under this Court, there were fundamental legal changes in civil rights law. The Court expanded First Amendment rights. It restructured criminal procedure. It dealt with reapportionment and abortion, and thus became the initiator of social change. In response, conservatives launched an attack on the Court and demanded a return to the role historically played prior to the 1950s, which, according to them, was more "reasoned."

When President Lyndon B. Johnson appointed Justice Thurgood Marshall to the Supreme Court in 1967, Marshall was the first nonwhite to serve on the Court in its 178-year history. Marshall was a persistent supporter of affirmative action and abortion rights. However, he became increasingly isolated as the Court shifted to a conservative majority. He was the dissenting voice in *University of California v. Bakke* in 1978. On his final day on a Supreme Court controlled by Reagan and Bush conservatives, Justice Marshall published a blistering dissent that began, "Power, not reason, is the new currency of this court's decisions," predicting that conservatives would "squander the authority and the legitimacy of this court as a protector of the powerless."

Competing Theories

In jurisprudence one of the persisting theories that competes with positivism is that of natural law. The theory of natural law is the broadest and least popular of competing theories, although it is suggested by the principle, to which most justices adhere on the surface, that the United States is a nation under God. It continues to function side by side with the dominant American paradigm and is even part of the legal reasoning of mainstream scholars. In the natural law tradition, the understanding of right and wrong is grounded in "nature" or in the "laws of reason." The enacted and written law should be judged by reference to natural law. Natural law theory is the opposite of legal positivism, maintaining that if a written law does not conform to ethical principles it may be disobeyed and should be changed. This theory is ridiculed by those with little understanding of the excesses of positivism. Yet the U.S. Constitution's protection of life, liberty, and due process is heavily influenced by natural law theory.

The Senate Judiciary Committee questioned Clarence Thomas extensively about natural law in the context of constitutional analysis during the summer of 1991. Thomas frequently referred to natural law in his academic writings, which his critics labeled "weird" and dangerous. Laurence H. Tribe, a Harvard Law School professor, asserted that Thomas's views on natural law were an unusual and troubling method of constitutional interpretation, more troubling than the conservative views of other recent Court appointees.[8] Under questioning, conservative nominee Thomas recanted earlier statements about natural law and indicated that while natural law made for an interesting academic exercise, "positivism" was the most appropriate analysis for constitutional questions.

Regardless of what Thomas's critics said, the theory of natural law has been popular across ideological lines of left and right. It has been debated since the days of Chief Justice John Jay. In 1798, in *Calder v. Bull*, Jay argued that the legislature did not have the power to enforce laws that violated "all reason and justice." The positivists' response was that "the ideas of natural justice" are too indefinite a basis for legal decisions. Justice Thurgood Marshall invoked natural law in his briefs in *Brown v. Board of Education* (1954). Conservative jurists, for example, Judge Bork and Chief Justice William Rehnquist, have primarily favored positivism, though liberals like Justice Hugo Black have also been positivists. Ironically, most natural law arguments in recent years come from the left.

The natural law argument is often used to justify ideological goals, and in the hands of ideologues, bias can operate totally unchecked. Some advocates of natural law call for the passage of laws that prevent the erosion of basic moral values. At worse, natural law scholars trivialize complex cases concerning underlying values. At best, the natural law theory forces justices to reveal their real reasons for making certain choices. It looks behind rhetoric or legal fiction for competing moral values.[9]

Historically, natural law has been invoked to defend slavery, the subjugation of women, and other unsavory principles. Yet in

1852, a New York Supreme Court judge freed eight escaped slaves in *People v. Lemmon* by an appeal to natural law. The judge ignored the federal fugitive slave statutes, arguing that under natural law, New York state laws were sufficient to deny the former owner a right to the possession of slaves. This ruling was upheld on appeal. In contrast, legal positivism holds that the law makes right. Slavery or murder is wrong only because the law says so, since governments create rights. Thus, positive law distinguishes itself from "morality." Morality requires doing what is regarded as fair and right; it does not require obeying the law automatically.[10]

During the New Deal era, a reform movement in legal theory emerged, called legal realism, that was compatible with the New Deal's political goals. It was led by a group of legal scholars who openly questioned traditional beliefs regarding law. The "realism" of the legal realists consisted of the belief that judges are inevitably faced with a large number of choices, and they choose the facts they want to stress, the precedents they will follow, and the reasons for their ruling. These choices are an innate part of the judicial function. The law, according to the realists, is a social construct, and objective reality is determined by the operating paradigm which guides judges in the "right" way.

The legal realists urged reforms in legal education and in the training of lawyers and judges to deal with legal problems beyond the scope of legal precedent. Legal realists urged that judges consider relevant, reliable social data. They argued that judges should concern themselves with and be guided by the social consequences of their decisions.[11]

The school of legal realism harks back to themes in Oliver Wendell Holmes Jr.'s book *The Common Law*, published in the 1880s. It was a departure from the mechanical process of "logical" deduction from settled principles. It called for the recognition that the necessities of the times are taken into account; conditions, in other words, change. According to the realists, judges filter logic through their own biases, misunderstandings, ignorance, and intentional distortion—their own micro-dimension of the American paradigm. Their decisions reflect their class, racial biases, and other interests.

The main contribution of the legal realists was that they were skeptical. They drummed in the truism that justice is not an automatic process, and they rejected positivism as the basis for the law. As University of Chicago historian Peter Novick puts it,

> The Realists challenged two crucial assumptions of this conception: first, in their denial that one could easily or regularly tell what was or was not an acceptable fit between fact and theory; second, in their denial that judicial rationality and disinterestedness could be assumed. If either of these challenges were admitted, scientific predictability disappeared.[12]

By the 1970s, conservative law professors began another attack on legal realism. This attack was a reaction to the 1960s and what these professors perceived as the liberal trend in national politics, above all, the judicial activism of the Warren Court. The conservatives organized a vigorous campaign, celebrating "neutral principles," "principled decisions," and "the rule of law," as if these principles could only be attained through positivism.

By the late 1970s, Critical Legal Studies (CLS) emerged as the intellectual heir of legal realism. The CLS movement, however, rejects the realists' notion that jurisprudence is coherent and predictable. The realists stressed the judges' social background, prejudices, and psychodynamics in interpreting and shaping the law. CLS scholars base their arguments much more heavily on history. This school has not been successful in shifting the courts' paradigm, but it is quoted in more than 150 federal court decisions. Its skepticism is its most threatening aspect. Traditionalists consider it nonrational, based on emotion rather than reasoned analysis. They accuse the CLS advocates of being subjective and personal.[13]

Within critical legal studies there are several currents; one is critical race theory. Race theory questions the exclusion of race as a factor from mainstream legal scholarship. It challenges the traditional meritocratic paradigm and attacks the pretense of academe and the courts to "objectivity," "neutrality," "meritocracy," and "color blindness." Critical race theorists have drawn from an idea, made popular by postmodernist scholars of all races, that there is no objective reality. There are competing racial versions of reality that may never be reconciled. They put race at the center of their analysis: the law is not race-neutral. Within critical race theory and, for that matter, CLS as a whole, scholars rely heavily on narrative storytelling, which includes the voices of people of color. Their storytelling challenges the versions of reality put forward by the dominant white culture. Consciously, they challenge the existing paradigm.

An important work in this movement is Columbia Law School professor Patricia J. Williams's *The Alchemy of Race and Rights*. Williams blends legal scholarship, memoir, and allegory in this work, which is intended to change perceptions about the substance and spirit of black women. The book was inspired by her discovery of the receipt of sale of her own great-great-grandmother. She uses the document as a springboard for an analysis of "value" and how it is ascribed to individuals, institutions, and events. For instance, Williams points out that miscegenation laws "devalued" blacks, denying them their birth rights as heirs of the white slaveholders who fathered them. Williams's story intertwines threads of commerce law and life. The content of the story is totally political; it challenges mainstream legal theory, not only by giving her side of the story but through her extensive legal argumentation and documentation.

Another well-known figure in the CLS movement is Richard Delgado, a law professor at the University of Colorado. Delgado's best-known book is *The Rodrigo Chronicles: Conversations about America and Race*. According to Delgado, the stories a society tells about itself can be more important than the laws it passes. Stories determine what laws are passed and whether they are seriously enforced. *Rodrigo* is a scholarly novel about two "intellectuals of color": one, a middle-aged law professor who is a civil rights supporter and the other, Rodrigo Crenshaw, a fiery half-brother of the fictional lawyer-prophet Geneva Crenshaw in Derrick Bell's book *And We Are Not Saved*. *The Rodrigo Chronicles* is a dialogue between these two men about the issues of the time.

Critics call the book angry and gloomy. Racism, sexism, and homophobia, according to Delgado, are key elements of "the cultural paradigm . . . the very set of values, ideas, and meanings we rely on to construct, order, and understand the world, as well as communicate with each other about it." Equal opportunity, the professor argues, is a sham. "Neutral" hiring is a sham because neutrality is shaped by America's racist history; neutral hiring is affirmative action for whites. The message in *Rodrigo* is clear: America desperately needs minorities to solve its problems of racial tensions. The legal system is not intended to eliminate racism but rather to keep it at a tolerable level. Prisons are built to warehouse black and Latino criminals, but white crime, a bigger problem, bleeds the economy more than street heists, and corporate malfeasance kills more people than gangs. Delgado rejects law as an engine of social change and endorses two extralegal strategies: storytelling and legal instrumentalism, or black "self-help." Delgado's story contradicts the views of Dinesh D'Souza, Allan Bloom, Thomas Sowell, Shelby Steele, and Charles Murray, who have dominated race discourse.

Critical race scholars argue that the dismantling of the apparatus of formal segregation failed to eliminate racism or to improve the social status of African Americans or other Third World people. This is a claim that is entirely plausible in the context of history. The judges' perceptions of facts are contingent on their racially defined experiences. It is ludicrous to assume that the white majority's racist perspectives can be transcended in one generation, or that neutral laws will not lead to continued white domination.

When CLS first emerged, the academy reacted negatively. Even liberal civil rights scholars, who challenged legal inequality, dissociated themselves from its radical approach. Even some Marxists were offended by what seemed an unscientific tone. However, over time, many liberal scholars have begun to include elements of CLS in their analyses. Liberals, however, have not been so receptive to critical race theory, and they often dismiss the race theorists' arguments out of hand. Indeed, persistent criticism of critical race theory and of the narrative form in particular continues.

The lack of interest in race criticism within the profession is reflected at every level of society. Race theorists are marginalized, and legal scholars shut them out. Liberals and even some radical legal scholars blame this lack of communication on the critical

race theorists, saying it is their responsibility to communicate with the larger academy, especially with "mainstream" civil
rights liberals.

Undoubtedly the critical race theorists are often aggressive.
They reject law as an instrument of racial progress, often advo-
cating extralegal tactics. Aside from the intellectual strategy of
"storytelling," they urge minority empowerment that challenges
the dominant racial paradigms. They thrive on conspiracy theories widely accepted in the black and Latino communities. Some
have even suggested that black jurors nullify certain laws that
send disproportionate numbers of blacks to prison.

Criticism that critical race theory sanctions emotional and
nonrational elements is duplicitous, since these elements are
found in judicial opinions regardless of the theory. Indeed, the
CLS approach in general reveals the nonrational as well as rational elements that infect judicial decisions, raising crucial and
normally unasked questions: Is law an objective reality? Are there
right answers to legal questions? Does the reliance on precedent
in the law justify legal certainty? Are judicial decisions value-free
and politically neutral? Against positivism, it says that judges
cannot depend on science or logic for objective truths. Judges routinely inject their own values into the legal process.

Today's racists are not the crackers of old. White Americans
do not see themselves as racists. They are what race theorists call
"dominative" racists. The skepticism of these theorists is invigo-
rating because its purpose is to solve societal problems. However,
their skepticism toward the Anglo-American legal system makes
them incompatible with even mainstream civil rights scholars,
who are examples of what Delgado calls "the imperial scholar"—
who believe that they hold their sinecures by a divine right.[14]

Truth and Justice

Academe, like the courts, ensures the maintenance of the dominant American paradigm through the designation of official
methodologies and accepted truths. The academy trains the lawyers who become the judges and the professors who teach them.
I never realized how both the courts and higher education are

influenced by the American paradigm, even after working in
higher education for more than thirty years, until I was a plaintiff in a lawsuit against the University of California for more
than five years. Both these institutions are neoliberal, a product of
eighteenth- and nineteenth-century U.S. and European history.
Professors and judges are imbued with a feeling of noblesse
oblige, a sense that they are preserving a "noble experiment" in
democracy for the American nation.

One cannot help but be struck by the smugness of judges
and professors who are part of the myth of the American Dream.
Justice is supposed to be preserved by the courts, as truth is preserved by higher education. The courts uphold the pillars of democracy. The Constitution, a metaphor for the truth, is the beacon
for the noble dream. As Peter Novick puts it,

> Legislative decisions are justified by the legislators' notion of
> their constituents' best interests, but judges' decisions, particu-
> larly when they go against majority views, have to claim to be
> based on something more objective than personal inference.[15]

In academe the beacon is Western civilization.

Illusions are kept alive by myths which, untested over
the course of history, become truths. Chief Justice Marshall, in
Marbury v. Madison (1803), wrote: "The government of the United
States has been emphatically termed a government of laws and
not of men." The concept of a "government of laws and not of
men" is repeated in civic classes and repeated in decisions of the
courts. It is repeated so often that over the course of time even
the mythmakers believe the myth. The Supreme Court in *Planned
Parenthood v. Casey* (1992) pontificated that it was the duty of
Americans to show "respect for the rule of law" by recognizing
the Court as "invested with authority to decide their constitutional cases and speak before all others for their constitutional
ideals."

Although many legal scholars dismiss this idealized vision of
the courts as a meaningless slogan, most lawyers pay tribute to
the rule of law. They pander to federal justices, who assume an
imperial presence. Everyone stands and sits at the leave of the
judge. In this free society attorneys cannot publicly criticize the

judges, and they are sanctioned when they do, even when their criticisms are factual. This aura and this tradition reinforce the myth that the law is a "system of wise restraints that make men free." (Ironically, the scientific method was supposed to rid us of superstition and tradition.)

Higher education enjoys the same sort of exalted status as the custodian of truth. Like judges, professors are supposed to be guided by reason, searching for the truth in an objective manner and putting aside personal biases. As the myth goes, professors are insulated from political and social pressures by the tradition of tenure. By providing a reflective ambience, apart from society, the result of their research is the objective truth.

3

Ideological Combat:
The War over Who Controls History

A definitive analysis of the American paradigm—the dominant paradigm introduced in the last chapter—is beyond the scope of this essay. In its simplest form, the American paradigm is expressed in any eighth-grade U.S. history textbook. It excludes the voices of Chicanos/Latinos and other people of color. The preservation of this paradigm gives the culture warriors a tremendous advantage in the culture war, which is being waged with millions of dollars spent in defense of the most reactionary canons of the paradigm. The strength of the narrative has emboldened the New Right in its attempt to control the curriculum in higher education and the public school system. Strategically, it is taking away legal protection from those who challenge its neoliberal view of the world.

The Political Dimension of History

Those who interpret history, define truth and also define the American paradigm. History, among other things, teaches people about their interests. By controlling historical consciousness, the dominant class weakens the common bonds of working-class people and blurs working-class, racial, and gender identity. Those in control select the common stories that students of all races hear and that are essential to the creation of a historical consciousness.

Presently, the American paradigm merely tolerates gender and ethnic history as a necessary evil that in time, like the evil empire, will go away. The threat of Chicano history is its political dimension, connected with the growth of the Latino population nationally. Currently, this population numbers about 26 million, more than 18 million of whom are of Mexican extraction. Chicano history is seen as a negative force in national politics, a validation that these numbers are changing the American identity. Right-wing critics say that Chicana/o studies programs obscure the attempt to understand the unified concept of an American national identity and to create a historical consciousness among Americans. The New Right wants to preserve Bob Dole's American paradigm of an America that excludes rather than includes new knowledge about the "other" America.

Theory is supposed to clarify matters, not confuse them. Forming a theory requires making assumptions and generalizations. It is, therefore, essential in forming theory to have all the facts possible. "Theory" comes from the Greek word *theoria*, which means "to see," "to look" at something. Theory allows us to look at related phenomena or facts and give the best explanation possible. Theory takes research beyond hearsay, beyond conjecture, beyond the anecdotal, and beyond indoctrination. Generalizations are credible about specific phenomena; they link events to develop answers to specific problems.

Human beings are historical, and it is their nature to participate in history. They remember their experiences. The acquisition of historical consciousness means learning the "discipline of memory." It means identifying your personal and community interests. Through the content of the people's memories, sovereigns maintain power. A false collective memory facilitates subordination.

The interpretations of history, and the right to define truth, are at the base of the culture war, for history is at the foundation of the social sciences and humanities. It controls the decisions of the courts, which base their decisions on the authority of history, interpreting the intent of past lawmakers. Through history, conscious individuals forge bonds with other individuals to form a communal identity. Historical memory creates a sense of unity; the community learns both from its victories and its defeats how to deal with its crises. The dominant classes control the written history of society, which in turn influences historical memory and the continuity and perfection of memory. They ignore the role of the individual, who is often left with only his or her experiences or oral traditions for guidance. Written history is distorted to mold a culture of passivity, establishing values and standards of justice and fairness which favor the ruling class.

In relation to the control of history, Chicana/o studies is both epistemologically and politically opposed to the dominant paradigm. Human change through time is historically constructed. The historian and the social scientist determine people's perceptions of themselves and the world around them. Scholars make distinctions between people and in great part determine the threshold of fairness. They frame the questions and thus the answers. In the United States, it rarely occurs to scholars to ask how the experiences and perceptions of Mexicans differ from those of the dominant society. They almost always isolate Mexicans and the "other" from the social relationships which created them. They presume that Mexicans exist in certain ways; in other words, by restricting knowledge of the Mexican in the United States, options are restricted as well as historical consciousness. Yet this knowledge is essential, not only for the sake of developing among Latinos a historical consciousness, providing them with a filter to understand the past, but also in order to show policymakers how to connect the Latino community to the whole.

In the United States, the only sector that recognizes the importance of a historical memory today is the New Right, whose members know that history can strengthen bonds among the so-called "others." Think tanks like the Heritage Foundation crank out literature attempting either to shape the historical memory of the poor or to erase it. In the United States, only the rich have the right to recognize their class interests. If others raise these interests, they are divisive. The legitimacy or authority of the scholar is lessened by publicly raising these interests.

Ordinary people do not control history. Control is in the hands of professional historians and boards of education. The inevitable consequence is a lack of historical consciousness about the interests of the people. Attempts by minorities and women to take control of their history during the 1960s and 1970s unsettled the New Right, whose response was to make certain that they did not succeed.

Mainstream and right-wing social scientists incorporate the dominant epistemology, which relies excessively on authority. Social scientists create and share meaning and frames of reference. It is logical to conclude that the experience of Third World nations is not like the experience of colonizers. Similarly, the experience of workers is not that of their boss, and the experience of Mexicans in the U.S. is not those of other ethnic and mainstream groups. The challenge of the ethnic scholar is to reclaim these experiences; this is what social history is all about.

Truth and Objectivity in the Culture War

The cornerstone of the New Right's culture war is control of the definitions of truth and objectivity. Objectivity signals to the ordinary person the notion of fairness. Truth is much more of an abstraction, associated with wisdom. The Greek philosopher and mathematician Pythagoras (c. 580–500 B.C.) said that wisdom only belonged to God; the philosopher was a lover, not a possessor, of wisdom. Truth is sometimes evident on its face and at other times, like a cancer, it takes a trained pathologist to find it. The function of the scientific method is to ascertain the truth. The strength of jurists and scholars is their presumption that they possess wisdom, and that through the use of this wisdom in conjunction with the method that ensures objectivity, they arrive at the truth with perfect fairness.

Part of the difficulty in dealing with judges or academics is that they believe in their objectivity and rationalize their fairness. They are not religious or ideological kooks. I would be surprised, for instance, if most members of the National Association of Scholars (NAS) would subscribe to the view of historian Jeffrey Russell of the University of California at Santa Barbara, who, during a deposition in my suit against the UC system, testified that truth could only be found in the mind of God. The members of the NAS who make up the shock troops of the culture war, and whose persistent hacking away at political correctness and multiculturalism helped lay the foundation for 209, think of themselves as "defending science and reason against paranoia, superstition, ignorance and politics." They are not part of the religious right. They are neoliberal warriors in the spirit of the cold war. They describe those critical of their version of truth and objectivity in Western culture as "[people who] promote the image of the scientist as evil and talk about myths and conspiracy theories as if they help us understand the world. Someone has to stand up and say this is not only wrong, but dangerous." They openly call for a counterrevolution against those taking over the academy. "It's time to get nasty—to launch a crusade against quackery," declared a biochemist at a recent NAS convention.[1]

Social scientists have locked arms with the hard sciences in this culture war, which is fundamentally elitist. According to the NAS, "the truth is, there are ways of understanding the world that are superior and there are people who are simply smarter and better equipped to solve problems." Its research director, Rita Zurcher, says, "We should defend the idea that there are elites. That's what students should strive to be."[2]

The NAS has brilliantly tied issues such as alternative medicine to multiculturalism, and the attack on science's ability to find solutions for everything from physical to social phenomena, to the criticism of traditional education. Any deviation from authority is labeled as a flight from reason—as a failure to acknowledge the legitimate criticisms of scientific, academic, and technical elites. The defenders of intellectual orthodoxy accuse their critics of attempting to replace truth and objectivity with political analysis. The NAS portrays such critics as extremists and conspiracy theorists. They allege that the critics' success depends, in large measure, on the public's discontent with its leaders and its nation's course. Thus, skepticism is fueled by the failure of big business or big government.

The struggle over science and reason is focused on academia. Pro-science organizations on campuses are becoming more active in their zeal. Meanwhile, cozy relationships between corporations and universities flourish as universities seek to replace government money by signing contracts with companies that can pay for research projects.[3] Leonard Minsky, executive director of the

National Coalition of Universities in the Public Interest, says, "We worry when corporations use universities to do their work for them. From our perspective, we worry about the search for truth and the search for profits—they collide somewhere."[4]

Are the culture warriors correct that their opponents, such as those in Chicana/o studies and other such programs, politicize education and substitute politics for truth? Education has always been political, as a visit to any board of education meeting or to any faculty senate or university-wide curriculum committee meeting will prove. It is fair to say that anyone seeking a change in the status quo is politicizing the university. California Governor Pete Wilson and the proponents of 209 have radically politicized the University of California system with their heavy-handed elimination of affirmative action.

In general, scholarship has always lent itself to the political. The doctrine of the historicity of the Gospel narratives was a narrative used to foment anti-Semitism. At one time, it was heresy to suggest that the Gospels were the product of Christian imagination and had little or no foundation in fact. Biblical scholars, under the mantle of scholarly objectivity, used passages from the Gospels to vilify Jews. The nature of these narratives was not only religious but political, and they dominated the discourse between Christians and Jews. For centuries Christian scholars forced Jews to accept their truth, citing their authorities. The paradigm only partially changed as the result of the ideas of Jewish scholars— "truth and objectivity" had a minor role in changing the discourse. Blatant and overt anti-Semitism has also been muted by the growing political power of the Jewish community, not by the pursuit of truth and objectivity.

It should be clear by now that the recent assault on affirmative action and ethnic studies has more to do with the political ideology of the culture warriors than with pure scholarship. Changing demographics in places like California have forced some changes in curricula, much to the displeasure of neoliberals. The rise of ethnic and women's studies has been part of this change. The reaction to this change varies, depending on the ideology of the particular community, but it is safe to say that on most campuses, these programs have been "controlled" and inhibited by the authorities.

If pure scholarly objectivity existed, authorities who disagreed would freely discuss their differences, and relative truth
would emerge from the conflict of ideas; that's supposed to be the
nature of scholarly inquiry. But this does not happen within the
American academy, where scholars arrogantly dismiss dissenting
ideas. Chicana/o studies scholars, for example, must take their
ideas outside the academy and to the people in order to get a full
airing. They will not get it within the closed academy.

In the ongoing culture war, the sides are sharply drawn.
Dinesh D'Souza and the National Association of Scholars use
words such as "Balkanization" and "irrational" to describe critics
of the present paradigm. NAS supporters argue that equal time
to everyone is not possible, because not everyone contributed
equally to our nation's history. They accuse ethnic studies of diluting what we have in common. The culture warriors claim that
ethnic studies scholars and multiculturalists are politicizing the
curriculum, when it is their reaction that is politicizing the academy. The struggle is over whose story will be told. The war is
important not only for how it will shape educational curricula,
but also for how it will shape our definition of what it means to be
an American.

The Culture War Ideology

The aggressors in the culture war appear to differ widely in their
ideologies. Important among the many thought-control cadets at
the national level are William J. Bennett, secretary of education
under Ronald Reagan, Allan Bloom, author of *Accuracy in Academia*, and Lynne Cheney, former director of the National Endowment of the Humanities. On the surface, they seem at odds with
radical professors in the humanities and social sciences whose political attitudes and historical memory were formed in the protest
movements of the 1960s.[5] One of the more surprising soldiers in
this culture war is Eugene Genovese, a Brooklyn-born Sicilian of
working-class immigrant origins. A former member of the Communist Party, he was one of the preeminent American historians
of the slave-holding master class of the Old South. His seminal
work was *Roll, Jordan, Roll*, published in 1974, which showed how
slaves, too, shaped this world. In the short space of a decade and

a half he went on to *The Southern Tradition: The Achievement and Limitations of American Conservatism*, where he shows an impatience for critics of Western civilization and the discipline of history; his enemies are postmodernism and political correctness. Genovese and his wife, Elizabeth Fox-Genovese, are on the board of directors of the National Association of Scholars' National Alumni Forum. As Genovese has said, "The Forum is the first organization dedicated entirely to enlisting alumni, trustees, and philanthropists in the battle over ideas."[6] It is headed by former NAS board member and former governor Richard Lamm, and by Lynne Cheney. It is well funded by the Lynde and Harry Bradley, William H. Donner, Earhart, Jewish Community, John M. Olin, John William Pope, and Smith Richardson foundations, all of which are active in fighting affirmative action, immigration, and social welfare.

The best known leader of the culture war is Pat Buchanan. However, his populism and anti-science biases, for example, his refusal to think of himself as a descendant of a monkey, puts him at odds with the scientists of the National Association of Scholars. Apparently what binds all these disparate forces together is love of country—fundamentally, they are Americans—with all of the arrogance that goes with being a so-called American. Their litmus test for going to their heaven is a belief in the superiority of American people and ipso facto of Western civilization.

In the culture war, this Americanism eclipses other differences in ideology. Thus it is common to see Marxists joining forces with neoliberal scholars to defend Western civilization, which is synonymous with that of western Europe. Claims to truth and objectivity become a defense of the U.S. and of Western civilization. It is amusing to listen to the same rhetoric uttered by Lynne Cheney in her booklet entitled *Telling the Truth*, by liberal Arthur Schlesinger Jr., and by Marxist Eugene Genovese. Cheney's rhetoric is singular in its absurdity. Cheney told a House appropriations subcommittee: "Many academics and artists now see their purpose not as revealing truth or beauty, but as achieving social and political transformations . . . Government should not be funding those whose main interest is promoting an agenda." According to Cheney, critics of Western civilization are attempting to create a world "where there is no objectivity, there are no standards outside ourselves by which to judge our work, not scholarly ones and not aesthetic ones."[7] She directly accuses many left-wing scholars of pushing subjectivity under the rubric of multiculturalism.

Joining Cheney on the far right is William Bennett, who also repeats clichés such as "ivory-tower academics, faddish ideologies, and anti-American propaganda crafted to divide."[8] The Bennett-Cheney strategy is to defund the National Endowment of the Humanities in order to dry up one of the few sources of funding for projects deviating slightly from a reactionary viewpoint. In the process, they have effectively succeeded in privatizing research funding. Indeed, the response of the NEH has been typical of President Clinton's administration. In the case of the NEH, as with affirmative action, Clinton has compromised principle by sacrificing dissident points of view. Liberals have allowed the Cheneys and the Bennetts to define truth and objectivity instead of engaging them on the facts. This lack of response by the so-called left of center ensures that only rightist scholars receive support through a chain of right-wing foundations such as the Heritage Foundation and the American Enterprise Institute. An example of the ineffectiveness of the moderates is the National Humanities Alliance, an assemblage of scholarly groups organized to support the NEH. They have appealed to the bankers, industrialists, higher education executives, and other prominent persons serving on boards of museums, libraries, or other cultural institutions, by the use of the cliché, "something's wrong and we're fixing it." In the end, they have excluded leftists.

The abandonment of important political and ideological space by Chicana/o scholars and other progressives has allowed the Cheneys and the Bennetts to pose as the champions of truth. This may not mean much to intellectuals, but it has a great deal of meaning to the populace. The truth, as we know it, exists only in relation to the knowledge available—and only in academe can one get away with substituting theory for facts. The importance of feminism, ethnic studies, and even postmodernism is that they have generated new knowledge and ways of interpreting it. In the study of the American Southwest, for example, the majority of scholars in the field have failed to incorporate Mexican sources. There are exceptions: while I take issue with many of the interpretations of Southern Methodist University historian David Weber, for instance, I acknowledge that he is an excellent researcher who uses archival materials on both sides of the border. He is, however, the exception—and the rule stands that if it's not in English, then it's not worth reading.

The Committee of Scholars in Defense of History

The very name "Committee of Scholars in Defense of History" sounds like shades of the 1920s, when the American Legion controlled historical content in the public school textbooks. That so-called liberals such as Arthur Schlesinger Jr. would promote such an association is amazing. Why was this committee formed? Part of the answer is that the good professor and others were reacting to Afrocentricism and generalizing that all ethnic studies and women's studies programs were in league with Afrocentricism to destroy Western civilization as the basis of study. It is this paranoia that puts many former liberals in bed with the NAS types.

Schlesinger and Diane Ravitch, a former undersecretary of education in the Bush Administration, have accused multiculturalists and Afrocentric scholars of substituting "ethnic cheerleading" for scholarship and of engaging in "social and psychological therapy" instead of teaching history. Schlesinger's often shrill criticisms include repeated claims that there is no need for Afrocentricism; changes have taken place, and increased attention is being given to African American and ethnic studies in general. The Committee of Scholars in Defense of History, led by Schlesinger and Ravitch, issued a manifesto on June 29, 1990, entitled, "NY Should Teach History, Not Ethnic Cheerleading," in which they criticized changes in the New York school curriculum, which now officially included Afrocentric materials. This statement was seconded by historians Thomas Bender, John Morton Blum, Jerome Bruner, James MacGregor Burns, Robert Caro, Henry Steele Commager, Marcus Cunliffe, Frances FitzGerald, David Garrow, Henry Graff, Akira Iriye, Michael Kammen, Stanley N. Katz, William Leuchtenburg, Arthur S. Link, William

Manchester, William H. McNeill, Stuart Prall, Richard Sennett, Hans Trefousse, Richard Wade, and C. Vann Woodward:

> AS SCHOLARS, we are gravely concerned about the proposed revision of the State of New York's history curriculum. We invite the attention of our fellow citizens both to the task force report of July, 1989, calling for fundamental changes in the state's approach to the teaching of history and to the pending appointment by the Board of Regents of a panel to revise the curriculum along the lines demanded in the report.
>
> The history taught to the children of the state must meet the highest standards of accuracy and integrity. We steadfastly oppose the politicization of history, no matter how worthy the motive. Therefore, we have, as the Committee of Scholars in Defense of History, joined together to inform our fellow citizens what is going on, to monitor the revision process and to assess the projected changes in the teaching and testing of American and world history.
>
> The situation is as follows. In July, 1989, a task force on minorities, appointed by the New York commissioner of education, submitted a report to the Board of Regents calling for revision of the history curriculum. The task force did not include a single historian.
>
> The report, a polemical document, viewed division into racial groups as the basic analytical framework for an understanding of American history. It showed no understanding of the integrity of history as an intellectual discipline based on commonly accepted standards of evidence. It saw history rather as a form of social and psychological therapy whose function is to raise the self-esteem of children from minority groups.
>
> The Regents endorsed the report and authorized the revision of the history curriculum by a panel of 21 persons. Of this group six to eight are to be scholars distributed among seven fields; the panel might well end up with only one historian. "Care will be taken," the Regents add, "to ensure that among the active participants will be scholars and teachers who represent the ethnic and cultural groups under consideration"—which sounds like an invitation to each group to write, or veto, its own history.

The members of the Committee of Scholars, are, we believe, well known for their commitment to equal rights and their rejection of any form of racism in the schools and in society. We are also united in our belief in a pluralistic interpretation of American history and our support for such shamefully neglected fields as the history of women, of immigration and of minorities.

We have an equal commitment to standards of historical scholarship. We condemn the reduction of history to ethnic cheerleading on the demand of pressure groups. And we reject as unfair and insulting the implicit assumption in the task force report that minorities are incapable of absorbing a first-class education.

We have a further concern: The commissioner of education's task force contemptuously dismisses the Western tradition. Recognition of its influence on American culture, the task force declares, has a "terribly damaging effect on the psyche" of children from non-European cultures. No evidence is adduced to support this proposition, and much evidence argues against it.

The Western tradition is the source of ideas of individual freedom and political democracy to which most of the world now aspires. The West has committed its share of crimes against humanity, but the Western democratic philosophy also contains in its essence the means of exposing crimes and producing reforms. This philosophy has included and empowered people of all nations and races. Little can be more damaging to the psyches of young blacks, Hispanics, Asians and Indians than for the State of New York to tell them that the Western democratic tradition is not for them.

And little can have more damaging effect on the republic than the use of the school system to promote the division of our people into antagonistic racial groups. We are after all a nation—as Walt Whitman said, "a teeming Nation of nations"—and history enables us to understand the bonds of cohesion that make for nationhood and a sense of the common good: unum e pluribus.

Thus, because of the way this revisionism has come about and because historians have thus far been seriously underrepresented in the revision process, we find it necessary to constitute ourselves as a professional review committee to monitor and assess the work of the commissioner's panel. We will insist that the state history curriculum reflect honest and conscientious scholarship and accurately portray the forging of this nation from the experiences of many different groups and peoples.

The manifesto's portrayal of Western civilization as the "source of ideas of individual freedom and political democracy" is somewhat cynical, in view of the global restructuring of the world economy. The corruption by the U.S. of the meaning of the "democratic world" makes it even more cynical. The U.S. has historically included many a petty dictator in the "democratic" universe. And one only has to look as far as the signers of the above declaration to find examples of the "ethnic cheerleading" of which they accuse minority scholars.

It is instructive to analyze the five points in the committee's manifesto. First, the committee's goal is that "The history taught to the children of the state must meet the highest standards of accuracy and integrity. We steadfastly oppose the politicization of history, no matter how worthy the motive." In fact, for grades K through 12, textbooks were and continue to be published to satisfy regional markets which reflect the political climate of those markets. The adoption of textbooks is surrounded by political maneuvering by conservatives and liberals. What has always been excluded and included in a text is a political act. Further, this debate is usually a white-on-white affair.

Second, according to the committee signers, the Regent's report "viewed division into racial groups as the basic analytical framework for an understanding of American history . . . It saw history rather as a form of social and psychological therapy whose function is to raise the self-esteem of children from minority groups." I agree with the signers that division based on race is not desirable. However, unity based on a history that glorifies those institutions which have historically perpetuated this division will not bring about a lasting peace. Although history or the social sciences should never be used to inculcate nationalism, the curriculum is a powerful tool in the process of cultural and political empowerment and it should lead students to identify with accomplishments, not of a nation but of a community of people. In reality, the signers of the manifesto are reacting to the fact that peoples of color will be a majority in the United States in the twenty-first century. Moreover, race is an important variable in the analysis of U.S. history. History as a form of sociological therapy has always been used by the American public schools to "raise the self-esteem of children" from the dominant class.

Third, the committee criticized the Regent's report for stating: "Care will be taken to ensure that among the active participants will be scholars and teachers who represent the ethnic and cultural groups under consideration." The signers interpreted this as an invitation to each group "to write, or veto, its own history." There is a very fundamental inequality here. Most historians come from the dominant class. What makes Schlesinger and company any more objective than members of the "ethnic and cultural groups"? History should not be used as a weapon for one group to exercise power over the other group. Unfortunately, the lack of objectivity on the part of the Schlesingers has forced ethnic and culture groups to defend themselves and use history as a weapon to lessen the power of the dominant groups.

Fourth, the committee states: "We are also united in our belief in a pluralistic interpretation of American history and our support for such shamefully neglected fields as the history of women, of immigration and of minorities." This statement is hypocritical, given the history of avoidance of these fields by the signers. It can be relegated to the "Some of my best friends are Mexicans" universe. It is a lofty statement, which in principle everyone can support. However, in any political analysis the past history of the signers is relevant. In the face of this history, it is difficult to assume good faith.

Fifth, "Western tradition is the source of ideas of individual freedom and political democracy to which most of the world now aspires. The West has committed its share of crimes against humanity, but the Western democratic philosophy also contains in its essence the means of exposing crimes and producing reforms. This philosophy has included and empowered people of all nations and races." The West has committed more than "its share of crimes against humanity." There were 25 million to 38 million indigenous people in what is now Mexico and Central America at the time of the so-called "discovery," and this number fell to a little over a million in the next eighty years. Many of the great holocausts have been perpetrated by the West. Indeed, one of Schlesinger's icons, Andrew Jackson, committed more than his share of "crimes against humanity." Lastly, the statement that Western philosophy has "included and empowered people of all nations and races" defies history.

The statement of the Committee of Scholars that there has been "progress" is relative to who is counting. The status of people of color has not changed significantly over the past several decades, and there is evidence that the gains made during the 1960s and early 1970s are eroding. In 1992 I spoke at a plenary session of the American Historical Association in Washington, D.C. While the theme was a reevaluation of the profession and the status of minorities, the plenary sessions were poorly attended. More significantly, the program did not list one panel on Chicanos. Very few Chicano or Chicana scholars were in attendance, and the number of black scholars was disproportionately small. What's more revealing, no one seemed to care—the fad had passed.

Even more perplexing is that Schlesinger, Ravitch, and their ilk couch their chauvinism in terms of a sticky liberalism that recognizes that past injustices existed, thus making chauvinism sound reasonable. After issuing this report, they took their political battle to California. They succeeded in getting their point of view adopted in the recently reformed California curricula. (African Americans do not have the political clout in California that they have in New York, and reactionary forces are very much entrenched in California.) Their agenda was used as the basis for the new Houghton-Mifflin social studies textbook series (which part of the cabal was involved in developing, and from which they profited). In its consequences, the campaign launched by objective scholars such as Schlesinger is more political than scholarly.

One of the few reasoned critiques dealing with Schlesinger's defense of history was published in the *Phi Delta Kappan* of December 1994 by Alan Singer, entitled "Reflections on Multiculturalism." Singer argues in reference to the Committee of Scholars in Defense of History,

> If educators want to respond to what they feel are historical mis-
> representations and prejudices in Afrocentric and other ethno-
> centric philosophies and if they expect young people to hear
> them, they must also address what is happening in our society.
> Silence on societal issues suggests complicity and discredits calls
> for reason, academic scholarship, and the value of learning.

Singer criticizes statements made by Ministers Louis Farrakhan and Khalid Abdul Muhammed regarding what the Nation
of Islam has termed "the secret relationship between blacks and
Jews," but he differentiates his concerns from those raised in
the media.

> For me, the primary issue is not the validity of their claims
> about Jewish involvement in the subjugation of Africa and Afri-
> can peoples—which I believe are gross historical misrepre-
> sentations—or even the Nation of Islam's anti-Semitism. What I
> am more concerned about are the reasons causing many young
> African Americans to accept the plausibility of these charges.

A primary reason, for Singer, is the fundamental failure of our society to include African American heritage in the curriculum in
the schools.

Singer criticizes the Schlesinger/Ravitch position that, "in
their 'objective' view," past injustices are aberrations outside the
democratic American consensus and have largely been elimi-
nated. Schlesinger and Ravitch present a "progressive" model
of continuing improvement that defines all American people as
immigrants and views the United States as a country offering
unlimited possibilities. They perpetuate traditional myths about
American culture which are fundamentally Eurocentric.

Culture is a dynamic force that is reshaped through experiences generated in political and social struggles and through
group interaction. Immigrant groups in the U.S., for example,
have continually redefined how they see themselves, sometimes
aiming for assimilation into a broader American society and at
other times trying to preserve distinct ethnic identities, languages,
and communities. They don't practice a "condescension that assumes that some histories are less political than others, that some
cultures are healthier than others for the pluribus unum."

It would be foolish to deny that some minority scholars have been excessive in their criticism of American society. However, without their critiques, the American paradigm of the Committee of Scholars in Defense of History would go unchallenged. Schlesinger, Ravitch, and their supporters are promoting their respective ideas about the nature of U.S. history and multicultural education. It is a political war with economic consequences. And, in the last analysis, Schlesinger and Ravitch have a broader access to the media and to audiences at all levels of government than most minority scholars. They are political activists. It is interesting, however, that this has not dismissed them as scholars.

The War and Its Resources

In order to understand the real dimensions of the culture war, it is necessary to follow the money.[9] The names which are most frequently mentioned in support of this war are the Bradley Foundation, F. M. Kirby Foundation, John M. Olin Foundation, Smith Richardson Foundation, Sarah Scaife Foundation, Alcoa, Henry Salvatori Foundation, and the Wiegrand Foundation. In the area of affirmative action alone, the following think tanks, representing a large investment of money, actively push their line: the Hoover Institution, the Heritage Foundation, Washington Legal Foundation, Center for Individual Rights, Mountain States Legal Foundation, Manhattan Institute for Policy Research, Center for Equal Opportunity, American Enterprise Institute for Public Policy Research, the Cato Institute, Rand Corporation, Hudson Institute, Heartland Institute, Lincoln Institute, Institute for Justice, Independence Institute, and the Pacific Research Institute. These think tanks serve as residences for right-wing scholars who are paid to conduct the "war of position." For example, Frederick R. Lynch, author of *Invisible Victims: White Males and the Crisis of Affirmative Action*, is a Sarah Scaife Scholar at the Salvatori Center at Claremont College. The Heritage Foundation helped fund *The Bell Curve*. The Hoover Institution at Stanford sponsored the work of John Bunzel, one of the intellectual godfathers of the anti–affirmative action movement in academe. Dinesh D'Souza is the recipient of an Olin Research Fellowship for $98,400 and received another $20,000 to promote his *Illiberal*

Education while a fellow at the American Enterprise Institute. The list does not stop there.

At the center of the war of position is the NAS. It says that it is reacting to the excesses of the 1960s, but it goes further than that. It is leading the war for control of theory and curriculum. Among its allies is the Madison Center for Educational Affairs (MCEA). MCEA grew out of a merger between the Institute for Educational Affairs (IEA) that was founded in 1978 by Irving Kristol and William Simon, the head of the Olin Foundation, and the Madison Center, founded in 1988 by William Bennett and Allan Bloom, author of *The Closing of the American Mind*. The Smith Richardson, Olin, and Scaife foundations played leading roles in this merger. MCEA has been extremely active in funding right-wing student newspapers and training cadre.

The effectiveness of MCEA and its Collegiate Network, which coordinates its various activities, cannot be overestimated. The Collegiate Network (CN) has a toll-free hotline for writing, editing, or business advice. It places its students in internships with *The New Republic* and NBC News, even publishing a quarterly, *Diversity and Division*, on race and culture. The CN has established conservative campus newspapers such as the *Dartmouth Review*. D'Souza, for example, is a former editor-in-chief of the *Review*. Others fostered by the MCEA bore from within at newspapers such as the *Wall Street Journal*. As Table 1 suggests, MCEA receives wide support from foundations:

Table 1.
Foundations Supporting MCEA, 1992

Bradley Foundation	$150,396
JM Foundation	25,000
F. M. Kirby Foundation	17,500
John M. Olin Foundation	220,600
Smith Richardson Foundation	195,000
Sarah Scaife Foundation	100,000
Walton Family Foundation	15,000

Source: Data from Jean Stefancic and Richard Delgado, *No Mercy: How Conservative Think Tanks and Foundations Changed America's Social Agenda* (Philadelphia: Temple University Press, 1996), p. 113. Their source is the *Foundation Grants Index* 1995, ed. Ruth Kovacs.

Aside from money raised from these foundations, the Madison Center runs aggressive mail fund-raising campaigns.

The MCEA has established other groups. One of the most active is the Leadership Institute, which offers leadership seminars and trains young conservative organizers. The Coors Foundation played a leading role in establishing the Institute. Its budget of $1.2 million in 1992 rose to about $4.2 million in 1994. In 1992, foundations supplied about a quarter ($263,500) of its budget:

Table 2.
Foundations supporting the Leadership Institute, 1992

M. J. Murdock Charitable Trust	$115,000
Salvatori Foundation	28,500
Carthage Foundation	65,000
McCamish Foundation	25,000
Kirby Foundation	20,000
DeVos Foundation	10,000

Source: Data from Jean Stefancic and Richard Delgado, *No Mercy: How Conservative Think Tanks and Foundations Changed America's Social Agenda* (Philadelphia: Temple University Press, 1996), p. 115. Their source is the *Foundation Grants Index* 1995, ed. Ruth Kovacs.

The NAS interfaces with these groups as well as a host of other groups. It publishes its own journal, *Academic Questions*, funded in part by a gift of $100,000 from the Smith Richardson Foundation. The Sarah Scaife Foundation alone gave the NAS $375,000 in 1992 for general operating expenses and for its accreditation program.

The Center for Individual Rights, founded in 1989, funds litigation in the area of property rights and anti-regulation, challenging speech codes and affirmative action programs. It has close ties to the NAS. It created the Academic Freedom Defense Fund. It has been very active in universities, and led the fight against affirmative action admissions programs in *Hopwood v. Texas*, filed against the University of Texas Law School in 1992. In that year, for example, the Center received $100,000 from the Smith Richardson Foundation, $150,000 from the Carthage and Bradley Foundations, and $125,000 from Olin. It also received $30,000 from the Pioneer Fund.

The Center for the Study of Popular Culture was established in California in 1988 by David Horowitz and Peter Collier, formerly radicals and publishers of the left-wing *Ramparts*. The culture it "studies" through its conservative journals, such as *Heterodoxy*, includes universities, the public media, and the legal system. It founded the Individual Rights Foundation in 1992 to challenge campus speech codes and fund litigation. In the first two years the Foundation won more than forty cases dealing with First Amendment rights.

These facts and figures are just the tip of the iceberg that is fully exposed in Jean Stefancic's and Richard Delgado's *No Mercy: How Conservative Think Tanks and Foundations Changed America's Social Agenda*. Clearly, as the authors point out, liberals, let alone radicals, have no institutions to equal these lobbying and leadership training groups.

The impact of the right-wing groups is enormous. The money and resources at their disposal[10] dwarf the money and resources available to the Left, including the "clueless" liberals. Their propaganda that minorities and their study programs are politicizing education is a staggering exercise in hypocrisy.

The attack on Chicana/o studies, among other targets, is political. For Chicana/o scholars to accept the myth that the academy is not political, and to accept the concept that Chicanas/os are not victims, is suicidal. The assault on academic freedom is not being led by a cadre of dissidents clamoring for political correctness. It is led by well-funded think tanks and academic organizations claiming to be the gatekeepers to a heaven of "truth and objectivity."

Another Conspiracy Theory

An important concept of historical materialism is that nothing happens by accident; there is always a cause. In the first chapter I explored the concept of affirmative action, hoping to lay out the importance of the question to the ongoing struggle to democratize society. My premise is that the American paradigm has built-in antibodies, for instance, racism and xenophobia, that reject the inclusion of foreign elements and ideas. In the second chapter I discussed how culture and theory, through a paradigm, determine the questions we ask and the answers to them. In this chapter I introduced the "culture war" in more depth and demonstrated how the paradigm is manipulated to produce the intended answers and preserve the status quo. In concluding this chapter, I return to the issue of affirmative action and posit that, in the light of the activity of the New Right, the passage of 209 was not the result of either an accident or a grassroots effort, but rather was the product of a conspiracy of the right.

The official story is that two quixotic professors in northern California were concerned that the 1964 Civil Rights Act had gone too far and was now discriminating against white males. So they, at personal expense, drafted the Proposition almost singlehandedly and, joined by other unselfish volunteers, pushed through the California Civil Rights Initiative. It was passed above all because of the unselfish work of a black businessman who simply wanted to be measured by the content of his character.

It is too early to discern the whole story. The whole truth may never really be known. But this campaign was just too perfect and too well orchestrated. It needed money and technical knowledge far beyond the capabilities or resources of Thomas Wood and Glynn Custred. The ultraconservative Smith Richardson Foundation gave at least $25,000 (in 1992) to the California Association of Scholars, of which Wood and Custred are prominent members. How much the CAS received from other right-wing foundations is a subject that deserves study.

The question of money and where that money came from is critical. Publication of *The Bell Curve: Intelligence and Class Structure in America Life*, passage of Proposition 187, and the debate over affirmative action crystallized at about the same time. A common pattern of funding also emerged. The ultraconservative, racist Pioneer Fund, for example, underwrote much of the research for *The Bell Curve*, and has also contributed to the Federation of American Immigration Reform (FAIR), and other right-wing projects. Are events like these, and the pattern of funding, coincidental? Is it McCarthyism to point to a community of interests? Is it wrong to quote FAIR leaders to demonstrate this community of interests? For example, Otis Graham, professor at

UC Santa Barbara and one of the founders of the zealously anti-immigrant FAIR, blamed Latinos shortly after the Rodney King uprisings for the disturbances; he is quoted by the *Arizona Republic* of April 30, 1995, as saying:

> We're quickly learning what the Israelis learned about borders and citizenship. We're going to have to get awfully tough, and it's going to be unpleasant. But that's the consequence of living next door to a failed society with a bunch of failed societies below it.

Or is it wrong to dwell on the ranting of Glenn Spencer, founder of Voice of Citizens Together, who was a supporter of 187 and 209 and who accuses Mexico of invading the U.S.?

It is unfortunate that the arguments of many of the opponents of Proposition 209 were weak, adding little to the debate over affirmative action. They were designed not to offend anyone, while attempting to win over white women (which they failed to do). The legal debate was warped by politics. But it has been a political fight from the beginning. Consider the principal actors. Governor Pete Wilson, whose political career has been forged by wedge issues, embraced 209 as a key part of his presidential campaign. He twisted enough arms among the University of California Regents to get them to abolish all race and gender preferences in UC admissions, hiring, and contracting. Republican majorities in Congress seized the issue; they held hearings and threatened to attach prohibitions against race preferences to every appropriation bill in sight. Ward Connerly, a black businessman with ties to Wilson, pushed the issue, making him the darling of the right wing as well as strengthening his own business ties. Another principal actor was Attorney General Daniel Lungren, no champion of minority interests, who determined the title and label of the initiative. What the voters got was false and misleading. Lungren's broadening of the original language was deceptive, presenting an insurmountable problem for courts in interpreting voter intent

It is ludicrous to claim that the campaign for 209 was a grass-roots movement. Connerly encountered problems gathering the 700,000 signatures needed for the proposition to appear on the ballot. The campaign was forced to pay commercial signature-gatherers at premium prices to complete the petitions. Then there was the question of the ballot description created by Lungren. For supporters of proposals that would end race- and gender-based preferences in public programs to call their measure the California Civil Rights Initiative, and for them to quote Martin Luther King, especially when his closest family members opposed the measure, was repugnant as well as hypocritical. Opponents went both to the legislative analyst's office and to court, asking that language about the possible discriminatory effects of the clause be included on the ballot. They lost both times. If the measure was about affirmative action, why were the proponents so vehement about not calling it what it was?

The reality is that the New Right is waging the affirmative action war at the ballot box rather than in the courts. It has won the war of position and is now going on to the war of maneuver. And it is masterfully manipulating language. For example, Section (a) of Proposition 209 says:

> The state shall not discriminate against, or grant preferential treatment to, any individual or group on the basis of race, sex, color, ethnicity, or national origin in the operation of public employment, public education, or public contracting.

What does "preferential treatment" mean? There is a long case history on the meaning of discrimination, but there is no precedent on the meaning of "preferential treatment." Even the California Court of Appeals refused to say anything other than they were words of "common understanding." Not so! Discrimination and preferential treatment are not synonymous. They are not interchangeable. The words are wrought with possibilities, like the term "reverse racism," which the right has so adroitly exploited. You can bet that the meaning of "preferential treatment" will be one of those code words for limiting remedies and opening the door for litigation. The wording of the initiative is well thought out. (Why isn't the category of religion included?[11])

The supporters of 209 have specific targets in mind. For example, the views of Connerly regarding ethnic studies are well known. After I spoke at a Chicano graduation at the University of

California at Santa Barbara in June 1996, he called the UCSB administration and asked why they were having Chicano graduation.[12] Connerly has been persistent in his criticism of diversity courses as having little academic or professional value. Glenn Spencer told me that the issue of ethnic studies would be settled by 209, and he wrote letters to this effect to the administration of the California State University at Northridge. Thomas Wood, one of the framers, wants to eliminate employment outreach programs. Under the vague language of 209, programs commemorating the Holocaust or a holiday such as Cinco de Mayo may be prohibited under "preferential treatment." The lack of precision functions to evoke confusion.

It is clear that Section (a) has threatening implications for academe. Chicana/o studies and African American studies courses fall outside the federal protection of Title VI of the Civil Rights Act of 1964 and the Fourteenth Amendment as presently interpreted. California law is therefore controlling. People of color are far from paranoid in predicting that opponents will use 209 as a launching pad to eliminate these programs.[13]

Section (c) of Proposition 209 states,

> Nothing in this section shall be interpreted as prohibiting bona fide qualifications based on sex which are reasonably necessary to the normal operation of public employment, public education, or public contracting.

This language evoked the bitterest exchanges during the campaign. For the proponents the clause is a legal safeguard. Proponents contend that they borrowed the terminology from similar language in the Civil Rights Act of 1964. Section (c) was included to allow sex-based distinctions in narrow circumstances that nearly everyone supports. The state constitution should not require the state to let male prison guards conduct body searches of female inmates, for example, nor should it forbid single-sex sports teams in public universities. Neither should it mandate unisex bathrooms or sanction men working in girls' locker rooms.

Such harmless interpretations of Section (c) are, at best, naive. Everyone knows that the California Supreme Court is a Deukmejian-Wilson court and that this clause would supersede

California's current equal protection clause. The California Supreme Court has construed the state's equal protection clause to mean that sex discrimination should be treated just as suspiciously as race discrimination. In general, California's standards of proof in race and gender cases are better from the standpoint of plaintiffs than those imposed by the federal government. It is not farfetched to speculate that Wilson-appointed courts would alter and undermine "highest scrutiny" protection against race and gender discrimination under the state constitution, supplanting it with a flimsy "reasonableness test" operative in federal cases. Thus, as sterile and harmless as Section (c) may sound, it signals the erosion of all the hard-fought gains of women and of ethnic groups who have historically suffered discrimination.

The proponents of 209 got just what they wanted. They won the election and established the will of the electorate. What was once an extreme position is now the "vital center." Proposition 209 also opens the door, at the very least, to an assumption that California's model discrimination laws no longer control. Most important, the right is much better prepared for the war of maneuver than the left.

4

The Culture of the Academy

This chapter addresses academic culture within the context of the American paradigm, and in particular, the culture of faculty and its reactions to ethnic studies programs. In the previous chapter I discussed the American paradigm in relation to the culture war, pointing out that the purpose of any national paradigm is to preserve its textbook version of itself. The American paradigm is no different. Despite the contradictory forces within it, one of its chief characteristics is its defense of Western civilization and institutions. Its authority supposedly rests on science and the legitimacy of Western rationality.

The linchpin of any societal paradigm is culture. Culture gives meaning and context to a group of people or situation. It holds a group together; it creates individual and collective identity. Culture gives society a sense of history. Culture is a collective endeavor that rewards members for believing and acting like others in the culture, and sanctions them when they don't. It is more often emotional than rational. Culture gives meaning to its members, helping them cope with political and/or social insecurities.

In the last chapter, we saw how both liberals and conservatives share basic values that lead them to defend a culture. The basic reaction of these defenders of Western culture, when ideologies and cultural practices are challenged, is emotional; their defense goes beyond rationality. This is natural, since culture builds allegiance to core values and consequently to the paradigm. In short, culture is historically based and unique to the historical experience of a specific group. It comprises and defines the group's ideas and practices.

The Ahistorical Perspective

I have argued that no one understands better the importance of the control of history and historical memory than the New Right. New Right historians laud the virtues of truth and objectivity in their profession. Yet a basic problem with the New Right's own critique of education is that it is ahistorical. Historian Lawrence W. Levine of the University of California at Berkeley, in his *The Opening of the American Mind: Canons, Culture, and History*, posits that the best way to counter the culture warriors is through the history of the American university itself. He traces that history and the many curricular changes brought about by social pressures and economic changes.

The concept of a "Western civilization core curriculum" so praised by the New Right is itself a construct of their ideology. The curriculum, in the long run, has been a fluid rather than a static entity. A typical American college education a century or two ago could seem remarkably narrow or even foreign to today's eyes. In the nineteenth century most colleges offered few if any courses on science, modern language, or history. A college education might consist of studying the "classics," concentrating more on grammar than analysis of the content. As Levine shows, the two world wars greatly influenced the rise and decline of "ideal" curricula such as the so-called Western civilization core courses. Indeed, at one time American literature itself was highly controversial, and as late as the 1920s, specializing in American literature was "professional suicide."

Throughout the history of the American university, there have been several subcultures which interact and lead to conflict over core issues of the goals of the institution and the structure of the education it should offer. The British tradition was defined by the liberal arts and the education of the total person. It tended to deemphasize specialized and scientific knowledge. The German tradition placed greater emphasis on the sciences and specialization, elevated the status of faculty, and tended to deemphasize undergraduate education. The mission of faculties to educate upper-level and graduate-level students as researchers and scholars in their own particular field of study was more important in the German than in the British system. Thus, British tradition is reflected in the content and scope of the undergraduate curriculum; German tradition more heavily influences the nature and purpose of faculty research and scholarship.

Because neither British nor French universities conceded the legitimacy of academic research in "applied" subjects, it followed that their business and engineering education focused on teaching what was practiced. German academics, by not blocking the creation of research faculties in engineering and business economics, made way for the development of "industrial scientists." This marriage gave the German university influence beyond that of the British or French, and its industrialists were given valuable space within academe. American higher education was heavily influenced by the German model and the marriage between industry and higher education.

Before World War I, medicine and law first gained their footholds and acquired legitimacy within the university. According to David O. Levine's comprehensive study of the history of higher education in *The American College and the Culture of Aspiration, 1915–1940,* World War I cemented the marriage between higher education and government, binding them together in ways previously unheard of; for example, colleges provided army training through the Student Army Training Corps program, which increased enrollment and institutionalized professional training such as engineering. After the war, business education consolidated its position. The business community gave research and endowment funds to universities as incentives to subsidize the emerging profession. During these years, 1915 to 1940, the links were forged between education, government, and the economy, and a large sector of the public accepted the relationship between college attendance and individual mobility, thus binding the American culture of aspiration to institutions of the university. The market in this context became a source of opportunity not only for the individual but also for higher education; this, in turn, drove institutional change within higher education.

The massive influx of immigrants through long periods of American history also drove curricular change. The large immigrant population was interested in upward mobility. Professionalization brought respectability. Universities were especially important in urban centers, where they were often the only route to respectability. Although the more prestigious colleges long excluded Jews, other immigrants, and the working class, junior colleges adjusted to the changing economy and offered new practical curricula, and eventually, others followed suit. Higher education responded to the vocational aspirations of its clients.

Economics, wars, immigration—a multitude of factors—led to curriculum fights within and outside the academy. In the short run, proposals for change were often bitterly resisted. In the long run, the curriculum offered to students was transformed. Lawrence Levine's conclusion in his study is that the underlying fear of the neoconservatives is not that the university is too closed, but that it is too open.

In spite of the past history and its attendant conflicts, historians of education still generally conclude that the faculty of today's American university are more similar than dissimilar in their attitudes toward educational assumptions, values, and goals. They propose that faculty have similar criteria for institutional excellence, and that faculty and institutional culture produce conformity. A critical notion is that of "quality." Universities are very concerned with their images, their rankings, and the "quality" of their students, departments, and course offerings. Important distinctions are drawn between research and teaching universities, and between four-year and two-year colleges. Harvard, Yale, Stanford, and other private universities often advertise the superior quality of their institutions, especially in preparing students for graduate work. Faculty members and students, in turn, take on the identity and aspirations of their institutions.

Faculty Culture

In speaking about faculty culture, let the reader beware. All generalizations have exceptions. Each university, although similarly conforming, also has its own personality. There are some 3,000 institutions of higher learning in the U.S., with an enrollment of around 12 million students, and employing 700,000 to 800,000 part-time and full-time faculty members. Most of these faculty members, however, share the experience of advanced study at only 100 to 150 leading graduate institutions in this country. What are their common values?

Graduate training socializes students. It forms their roles and expectations. Graduate school conditions students to accept "the culture of the discipline." It teaches them to master metalanguage specific to their field of study, to subscribe to specialized journals, and to attend conferences. There they learn how to act like professionals, present papers, and meet colleagues. Socialization continues when the candidate interviews and becomes an assistant professor. Afterwards the "scholar" submits articles to accepted journals and becomes a "good citizen" on the road toward tenure.

Within the university the various disciplines compete for resources. The young scholar is conditioned to value research as an end unto itself. Even at teaching institutions, as distinguished from research institutions, the reward system promotes scholars on the grounds of research. "Publish or perish" is deeply rooted in the university culture. Specialization becomes a cult. Scholars learn loyalty to the discipline, and interdisciplinary work loses academic credibility. The theoreticians enjoy the same status as the surgeons of medicine and rank highest in the pecking order. Practical, soft, applied disciplines are at the bottom in the pecking order.

Although the main justification for a public university is teaching, the norms for judging teaching are for the most part nonpedagogical. They suffer from an over-reliance on student evaluations, even when reviewers know that students are afraid to accurately evaluate their instructors, or that some instructors actively seek out good evaluations. Evaluation of good teaching also suffers from hearsay evidence. Good teaching resembles an optional extra-credit essay. The Association of American Colleges, in a 1985 report entitled *Integrity in the Curriculum*, wrote: "If the professional preparation of doctors were as minimal as that of college teachers, the United States would have more funeral directors than lawyers."

Faculty culture produces the conviction that teaching is an art, not a science, and that to be an effective teacher, a scholar merely has to know his or her subject matter. Teaching is informational at best. Most university teachers don't have the foggiest notion of how people learn. Still, faculty members demand complete autonomy in their classrooms. They determine course content and instructional procedure, and they gauge student achievement. Professional autonomy is mysteriously linked to academic freedom.

Too often, the professor remains unchanged in the course of his or her career. Faculty culture resists experiment and innovation. The portrait of the professor carrying a set of yellowed note papers from which he reads a lecture is more than a stereotype. It takes too much effort to change; it demands too much time away from the "scholar's" specialty. New knowledge demands change, which threatens the knowledge base of the professor.

Faculty governance makes change all the harder, since it usually involves some sort of consensus.[1] Faculty culture fosters skepticism of what it knows nothing about. On one hand, faculty are resistant to new ideas, and on the other, faculty have absolute power to evaluate scholarship. This power converts the faculty into a privileged caste. Professors become accustomed to this power and behave like sovereigns. It is easy for them to think of themselves as meritorious and of others as below their level.

Professions form monopolies; they are self-regulating, controlling the production of new practitioners. They produce conformity and resistance to change. Law schools, for example, discourage undergraduates from taking law courses outside law school; medical schools make them take a series of courses which in most countries are taken at the college preparatory level. The social sciences and other disciplines control graduate programs that confer terminal degrees, giving graduates the union card to work at a university. This is all done in the name of professionalization. In effect, bishops ordain other bishops. Professionalization, according to the bishops, ensures meritocracy.

Ironically, professionalization avoids one of the canons of the American paradigm, the free market. University professors operate in a closed market where conformity is rewarded in the name of quality. This professionalization reinforces the culture of academe, producing insular, arrogant, and politically motivated individuals, who cultivate the image that they are disinterested seekers of knowledge. Any criticism of them is condemned as anti-intellectual.

The Faculty Review Process

The cult or, better still, the myth of a meritocracy is reenforced by the reward system driven by a peer group review, which varies from campus to campus. For the sake of example, I concentrate on the University of California system, which probably has one of the most intense peer group reviews of any institution of higher learning. Indeed, I observed in reviewing approximately three hundred personnel files of professors at the Santa Barbara campus that it was usual for professors at other colleges and universities to refuse to write letters of support for a UC faculty member's file, on the grounds that the UC was carrying the process to a ridiculous extreme.[2]

The process at UC is somewhat similar whether it involves appointment or promotion. As in most university systems, the tenured track positions are divided into assistant professor, associate professor, and full professor ranks. Each rank has a series of salary steps, and moving from one step to the next is a result of the recommendation of the department and successful completion of what is called a "merit" review. For appointment of a candidate, outside letters from experts in the field are solicited, the number varying from three to twelve. Letters from experts in the candidate's field are also sought when moving between the ranks, up to Professor Step VI, the distinguished professor level.

When a file leaves the department, it goes to the Committee on Academic Personnel (CAP), which is a creation of the faculty senate, consisting of professors from various disciplines. Before formally reviewing the file, CAP sends it to the provost of the School or in some cases to the dean or associate dean over the department, who reviews it and sends it back to CAP. In special cases, CAP also sends the file for review to an ad hoc secret committee, whose members are recommended by CAP and who are supposed to be from fields related to that of the candidate (but not from the candidate's own department).

The ad hoc committee makes its review and sends it back to CAP. Once CAP has both the ad hoc and the provost (or dean's) reports, it makes its own review and then sends it to the associate vice chancellor. The latter makes his or her review and then gives it to the vice chancellor, who sends it to the chancellor for a final decision. Throughout this process, the candidate's file is supposed to be confidential. Decisions are allegedly based solely on the file. Confidentiality is supposed to ensure objectivity.

While this process seems fair, objective, and likely to ensure merit by subjecting the candidate to various tests, in reality it promotes a tremendous amount of conformity, especially in the social sciences, humanities, and the arts. Reviews are made every two to three years, and rewards are given to the "good citizens." The choice as to who writes the outside letters is determined by the candidate's department, which takes great care in selecting outside reviewers who are compatible with the candidate. Moreover, the interpretation and weight given to the outside letters is at the discretion of the university reviewers, who can discount negative reviews or interpret them in any way they want. In most cases, the only experts evaluating the candidate are those at the internal department level, those solicited for outside letters, and to a much lesser degree, the members of the ad hoc committee. The administrator in practice only pretends to review the files.

Why does the UC go through this elaborate scheme? For a simple reason: it justifies less teaching and more pay. It is usual for a professor to be paid around $100,000 at the UC, teach four courses annually (on the semester system), and receive additional money for research in lieu of teaching summer classes. At the University of New Mexico, which is also a research institution, there are full professors who are paid only $50,000 a year with a slightly higher teaching load. In the California State University system, where review is not nearly as intensive, in fact is almost nonexistent, full professors are paid $65,000 and teach eight classes annually. Meritocracy is supposed to justify the rewards. Under the UC review process, research production eclipses all the other categories of review, which include teaching, professional activity, and university and community service. Although these categories are supposed to be equal in importance to research, in practice they are ignored.[3]

The Pister Report: Academic Resistance to Change

In June 1991 the University of California officials unveiled policy changes aimed at encouraging and rewarding excellent teaching, applied research, and other forms of service in the University of California system. Dr. Karl S. Pister, subsequently named chancellor of UC Santa Cruz, chaired a faculty task force which recommended new personnel rules. The task force was formally known as the University-wide Task Force on Faculty Rewards. The task force argued that too many UC professors are trapped in a "vicious circle" of chasing research grants and publishing research papers. The report concluded that many faculty members are so pressured for research results that they "find insufficient time and little encouragement" to pursue teaching and public service. Pister almost apologetically said that the panel's report calls for "a modest change in the culture of the university, but a very important change." He then admitted that there was already opposition from some professors whose careers had been based mainly on research and who feared additional scrutiny of their teaching skills.

The thirteen-member task force recommended that faculty be encouraged to become mentors to minority students and to help reform curricula. While stressing that public service should not replace pure research, the task force urged the UC system to broaden its criteria for awarding faculty pay raises and promotions. In addition, the committee urged that evaluations by a professor's peers of his or her teaching should be given the same weight as evaluation of research. The report's most dramatic recommendations affected promotions to the highest salary steps for a UC professor. Previous excellence in teaching, research, and public service, plus national or international distinction in research were required, although de facto research was "the" determining factor. The new guidelines built in more flexibility in the acceptance of applied research, which was widely interpreted as a "goodie" to ethnic and women's studies.

The Pister Report offended many professors, who felt it was too extreme and that in the quest for equality, the quality of the UC would be diluted. The debates over the report, although guarded, indicate that many professors viewed it as an affirmative action measure.[4] A controversial point concerned promotion of assistant and associate professors. The proposed policy allowed more flexibility for professors who devoted extra time to teaching or public service over research, and it specified rewards for good counseling of students.

The task force followed the recommendation of Ernest Boyer of the Carnegie Foundation that the scholarship of teaching, as well as the traditional scholarship of discovery, be rewarded. The changes in the reward system would encourage faculty members to devote more time and energy to creating better classes. It would also encourage them to be more generally informed about the discipline, counteracting the trend toward over-specialization.

The Pister Report recognized that the university often encouraged esoteric scholarship, published in highly specialized books and refereed journal articles, while it devalued anything written for the general public. The rationale of the report was that a well-crafted article written for ordinary people is far more demanding than adding footnotes to Plato. It advocated rewarding a political scientist, for example, who used his knowledge to improve the quality of his community.

The scholarship of integration is generally accepted in such fields as law, engineering, literary criticism, and urban planning. The report aimed at broadening the concept of scholarship in all fields. Its intention was to encourage research that would seek solutions and tie the university to various facets of the community—to foster changes that have been normal throughout the history of education, for example, linking higher education to business and engineering. If adopted, the Pister Report would have changed the concept of research to include applying scholarship to the classroom and to the world.

The arguments for the adoption of the report seemed compelling. The value of research as it was traditionally defined meant that the pivotal factor was published research in technical books or journal articles written expressly for other scientists and scholars. Philosopher David Glidden of UC Riverside, in a November 1991 article in the *Los Angeles Times*, observed:

> scientists and scholars increasingly write more and more about less and less and, as a consequence, know less and less about more and more. The discipline of specialization requires reading deeply instead of widely. Yet, often it is better to be well-read, especially where the humanities and social sciences are concerned, since they address the ways we think and live, the values we have.[5]

According to Glidden, knowing everything in the university is knowing all there is about a narrow subject. For example, in my case against the UC, one of the reviewers, anthropologist Donald Brown, was an expert on penile implants among members of a tribe in Southeast Asia. This is his claim to fame.

Glidden argued that during the entrepreneurial 1980s, UC professors in the humanities and social sciences advanced their standing by almost exclusively concentrating on specialized research, aping the model of the natural sciences. He called them

> free-agent marketeers hawking innovations of their own erudite subdisciplines, building reputations within the university for what's hot and au courant, and generating a secondary form of pedantry devoted exclusively to the work of fellow scholars.

As a result, salary wars ensued for superstars, while classes became more overcrowded and fees escalated.[6]

In the end, the faculty senates of the various campuses emasculated the Pister Report. To be fair, UC President David P. Gardner had sponsored the task force and had pushed for adoption of the report. Pister himself did not go against the culture of the university, satisfying himself by stating, "The most important thing is the reaffirmation of the importance of teaching in the university." The actions of the faculty senates demonstrate the opposite. Even so, the UC claimed that it was joining a national trend to give undergraduate teaching more importance in research universities. UC officials claimed that review policies had been amended to go beyond student evaluations of teachers and to require supplemental evidence of teaching skill, preferably reviews by other professors.

The debate over Pister is important because it reflects the UC culture, and faculty culture in general. It underlines the values that are held by professors. Faculties at research and teaching universities are similar, rather than diverse, because of their culture of avoidance of change and of criticism. Even enlightened administrators hesitate to implement necessary reforms in academe, where professors determine what they do, what they want to do, and what they want to reward. In the case of Pister, the pretext was that they did not want to undermine academic standards under the guise of reform. The truth is that they wanted to capriciously maintain their little fiefdom, doing business as usual with the minimum of scrutiny as to their teaching or other activities. The losers are the students, since providing the general knowledge they need in the classroom is neither a value in the minds of the faculty nor is it rewarded by the system. As Glidden put it,

> The university is an allegory for the larger society. Both suffer from an obsession with self-interest, at the expense of common interests, common causes, common good. The Pister report tests the goodwill of the faculty. Public support for the university is hanging in the balance.

In the end it was clear that campus leaders were engaging in a public relations stunt. They had no intention of changing the academic culture of the academy. The Pister Report came and went, and life goes on as usual.[7]

Studying Aliens

Gunnar Myrdal's *An American Dilemma* argued in 1944 that the race problem stood not only as a challenge to America's democratic principles, but as a moral dilemma at the very heart of the nation's democratic ethos. For Myrdal the key solution was education. Education was a vehicle for combating racism and improving the standard of living of most blacks. Education would break down class differences and end segregation. Chicanas/os

and other Latinos owe an intellectual debt to Myrdal and black intellectuals who have kept this issue alive as an important part of
the public discourse.

Today there are basic problems with Mydral's blueprint, although parts are still viable. The changing economy has removed
numerous stepping-stones from the path leading to the middle
class. The cultural ethos of the country still denies that economic
progress is tied to educational attainment, although the evidence
is overwhelming. At the same time, education is no longer as
open to minorities in many cities as it once was. In the immediate post–World War II era, the future held hope for most white
Americans. Today, however, the younger generation know that
they will not have it better than their parents. Their fear has
heightened racism and nativism, which spills over onto the campuses. Few would have predicted that the official historian of
Camelot, Arthur Schlesinger Jr., would be leading the charge
against the aliens.

We have already discussed at length society's evasion of
the Civil Rights Act of 1964 and the Fourteenth Amendment. This
evasion raises obstacles to integration and acceptance of knowledge about minorities on campuses. No less of an obstacle is the
culture of higher education, which is dedicated to the preservation of the American paradigm. It is telling when more faculty
members attend a faculty senate meeting at Berkeley to discuss
ethnic studies requirements than to discuss the invasion of Iraq.

The question of ethnic studies must be clearly distinguished
from identity politics. Certainly, the initial thrust for ethnic studies was a matter of identity. One cannot discount the need of
Mexicans, Salvadorans, Guatemalans, and others to express pride
in their accomplishments. Ethnic studies was also a response
to the racist politics which labels people "illegal aliens," evoking
the image of criminals from outer space attempting to invade our
bodies. The response of many Chicano youth that "We didn't
cross the border, the border crossed us," takes on new meaning in
this context.

Normally rational Euro-Americans go berserk when they see
Chicanos carrying the Mexican flag during a march. People unconsciously reject the alien. Higher education is no different. Why,

critics demand, would anyone want to learn anything other than Western tradition? In a discussion of ethnic studies, critics almost always dwell on the extremes; they do not bother to look at well-functioning programs which have kept their intellectual integrity while maintaining ties with students and community.

Identity politics has become the bogeyman. Dissent, according to critics, is viewed as betrayal. Ethnic studies departments are portrayed as "enclaves of group think and separatism that have nothing to do with actual thinking or learning."[8] Gross generalizations are made by normally rational scholars such as Schlesinger about the status of ethnic studies.[9] They have thus heightened racial and ethnic tension by trivializing the accomplishments of the various ethnic studies programs in theory, research, and curriculum development. They characterize ethnic studies as an entitlement program and curriculum movement for African Americans, Latinos, the poor, women, and other downtrodden groups.

Another bogeyman is the theory of multiculturalism. According to its own advocates, multicultural education is designed to restructure educational institutions. Its aim is for all students, including middle-class white males, to acquire the knowledge, skills, and attitudes needed to function in a diverse world. Multicultural education is, however, *not* an ethnic or gender-specific movement. It is a movement designed to "empower all students to become knowledgeable, caring, and active citizens in a deeply troubled and ethnically polarized nation and world."[10]

Proponents have never meant multicultural education to be exclusively for people of color or the so-called disenfranchised. Teachers in multicultural programs teach in predominately white schools and districts, and very few of them are minorities. Nor is multiculturalism a new movement in education. Its predecessor was the intergroup education movement of the 1940s and 1950s. This movement failed because intergroup educators never persuaded mainstream educators of the need for all students to have this experience. Mainstream educators saw intergroup education as not for whites but for "them."

Opponents have cast multicultural education reformers as critics of Western tradition. Multiculturalists vehemently deny this accusation, knowing full well that this is the kiss of death in American society. Dr. James Banks, an African American educator from the University of Washington, writes that multiculturalism "grew out of a civil rights movement grounded in such democratic ideals of the West as freedom, justice, and equality. Multicultural education seeks to extend to all people the ideals that were meant only for an elite few at the nation's birth."[11] Multiculturalists

> demand that the truth about the West be told, that its debt to people of color and women be recognized and included in the curriculum, and that the discrepancies between the ideals of freedom and equality and the realities of racism and sexism be taught to students. Reflective action by citizens is also an integral part of multicultural theory.

Multiculturalism is alien to the American paradigm because it is in large part postmodern. It challenges positivist assumptions about the relationships between human values, knowledge, and action. For positivists, knowledge is objective and beyond the influence of human values and interests. For the multiculturalists, knowledge is "positional . . . it relates to the knower's values and experiences, and . . . implies action."[12]

Critics have linked multiculturalism with the breakdown of social order in the Balkans, Northern Ireland, Lebanon, and Burundi. Schlesinger, in his book *The Disuniting of America: Reflections on a Multicultural Society*, perpetuates the myth that multicultural education destroys national unity, as if the multiculturalist divided the nation along lines of race, gender, and class. In this work, Schlesinger identifies African American and Chicano studies with multiculturalism.

In reality, ethnic studies and multiculturalism are often at odds,[13] not so much because of their goals but because of their clientele and the color of their leadership. While multiculturalism is strong in grades K through 12, it is not unified in higher education outside schools of education. Tensions between the camps are heightened by very real turf battles. Many members of ethnic studies departments see multiculturalism as solely a white movement that encroaches on their domain. They ask why multiculturalists have not been proactive in their support of minority hiring on campus and ethnic studies programs, and why most multicultural instructors are white. With a bit of exclusivity, some faculty members of ethnic programs also view multiculturalists as having few ties with the ethnic communities.

Another millstone around the necks of the multiculturalists has been the accusation that they have launched a political correctness attack on other faculty members to diversify the curriculum. The threat of "PCism," in my opinion, is greatly exaggerated. It is one of those wedge issues, like immigration, that are exploited by opportunists. No one will deny that in the matter of speech, there are overzealous members of any faculty who want to impose standards of collegiality; however, to bill their zeal as a conspiracy is a bit much, and to bill it as an effort to take over higher education is absurd. PCism can go too far, but at the same time, some standards of civility and respect must be maintained or the streets will come to the academy. Unfortunately, many white multiculturalists are endowed with the same white chauvinism as their mainstream brethren.

The ironic part of the PC debate is that the right-wing conservatives who complain about PCism are the sector that has most persistently demanded conformity and purity of ideology. Many leftists, on the other hand, support codes that outlaw racist and hateful speech and conduct, although this sector has traditionally championed free speech and First Amendment rights. There is no doubt that the right, with its organizational superiority, has manipulated the news media and promoted the PC issue. On campus this issue has also won over to the right many professors, who have strung a series of aberrations into a generalization. The PC issue hits at the heart of academic freedom and of tenure in academia, which is linked with the right of faculty to choose candidates of any color and to choose curricula of their own design. The right brilliantly cast it in terms of a defense of academic freedom. Their rationale is that the quickest and surest way to the truth is to encourage the expression of diverse points of view and promote active discussion and debate of different views—as if, for example, the "freedom" to call someone a greaser, nigger, or bitch is necessary to arrive at knowledge.

Ethnic Studies and the Struggle for Parity

Ethnic studies programs and departments are products of the 1960s and early 1970s. While it is true that they came about largely because of the struggle of students, it is not true that they have a homogeneous thrust. For example, in the best known ethnic studies department in the country, at the University of California at Berkeley, there are profound differences among the different ethnic components. Ethnic studies departments and programs also differ from race- and gender-specific programs. In many cases ethnic studies programs have been a creation of the administration and have been resisted by African Americans, Chicanas/os, and other scholars of color, who accuse the administration of trying to phase out their individual identity.

As of the mid-1990s there were more than seven hundred ethnic studies programs and departments in the United States. Out of this historical process, at least six established professional associations have developed: the National Council of Black Studies, the National Association for Chicana and Chicano Studies, the Asian American Studies Association, the American Indian Studies Association, the Association of Puerto Rican Studies, and the National Association of Ethnic Studies, formed in 1992.

Certain broad values united the early ethnic studies programs. The individual programs such as Chicana/o studies, which grew out of student and community grassroots movements, challenged the Eurocentric curricula of higher education. Hence, from the outset they were viewed as insurgent programs. A white faculty member in 1969 accused me of blackmailing my way into the institution because the creation of Chicano studies was the product of student protest. The ethnic studies programs are still seen as illegitimate programs to be tolerated rather than respected, in spite of the fact that scholars in these areas have produced a sizeable corpus of literature in the past two decades.

Almost all of the ethnic studies programs were culturally nationalistic in the early years, and nationalism persists in various forms today. What cultural nationalism was or is has never been adequately defined by even critics of color. For example, I find many Chicana/o scholars accusing people of being cultural nationalists because they don't agree with them. Many younger scholars also react to criticisms that they cannot speak Spanish, or that they come out of a middle-class background and so cannot identify with community interests, by calling their critics "cultural nationalists." I have known many cultural nationalists who are at the same time nationalist and socialist. Others favor national liberation but have little affinity for the national culture. I have found chauvinists among both so-called nationalists and so-called internationalists. The faults of the early ethnic studies movement should not be ascribed to something as complex and amorphous as cultural nationalism.

According to professor Evelyn Hu-DeHart of the University of Colorado, "most ethnic studies scholars today adopt a relational and comparative approach, looking at questions of power through the prisms of race, class, and gender."[14] As we have discussed elsewhere, this flies in the face of the positivist model of academe. Cultural tensions are acerbated by turf battles. Sociology is not going to concede the study of race to ethnic studies departments, for example. Traditional scholars are full of preconceptions about the illegitimacy and inferiority of ethnic studies programs.

These tensions are played out in power struggles. The various proponents for race- and gender-based programs naturally want a measure of parity on campus. The backbone of the university is still the department. Departments control budgets, hire their own faculty members, and, determine the course of study. In order to be respected and to define a field, "setting standards for pedagogy, research, and publication," autonomous departments are necessary. Thus far, with few exceptions, universities have resisted establishing race- and gender-based departments with full-time appointments rather than joint appointments.

This was the major struggle during the 1993 Chicano student hunger strike at the University of California at Los Angeles. Students demanded a department of Chicano studies. Even to the end, UCLA Chancellor Charles Young, undoubtedly supported by Associate Vice Chancellor Raymond Paredes, refused to give them a department with equal parity with traditional departments. Instead, the students were given a "center" with all of the functions of a department: tenured faculty with sole appointments in the center, the right to generate courses, and so on. The fiction in the name was necessary because up to the end, Young and Paredes did not think that the model of a full-fledged department was viable. It was also a case of capriciousness and of the arrogance of believing they were right.

One of the problems in the creation of a new department is that it requires extensive review by the faculty and by other oversight agencies. Contentiousness is inevitable because the culture of the faculty resists change, especially when the programs deviate so drastically from their paradigm. Because programs (and centers) can exist by administration fiat, ethnic studies units tend to be programs rather than departments. When they are departments, most are ineffectual because the university administration and governance units keep them that way. The departments usually have few faculty members, most of whom are untenured. They are thus easily marginalized and manipulated. Unfortunately, the various racial and gender groups within ethnic studies and in race- and gender-based departments are often played off against each other by the administration, weakening what clout they possess.

Gradually, institutional paradigms do change in response to structural changes, which in turn produce changes in the institutional culture. Studies, as well as personal observation, show that student outcomes are affected by the number of ethnic studies courses and women's studies courses taken during the undergraduate years. Cultural awareness and commitment to promoting racial understanding are heightened. One study of the results of such courses showed "positive effects on participation in campus protests, political liberalism, listening ability, foreign language skills, and attending recitals and concerts." Ethnic studies and multicultural approaches make a difference, though in ways often hard to measure: they help shift the paradigm.

Nevertheless, the picture is gloomy. Ethnic studies is viewed with suspicion and there is enormous internal resistance to its operation. As we have seen, this resistance goes beyond color or gender. Most multiculturalists are white, yet even they still encounter resistance. Faculty culture—the institutional culture of higher education—resembles society. It operates and maintains a cultural paradigm that discourages dissent.

5

Chicana/o Studies and the American Paradigm

This chapter deals in more depth with higher education's reaction to Chicana/o studies, and its manipulation of the concepts of truth and objectivity to justify the maintenance of the American paradigm. It builds on the last chapter, where I examined the role of faculty culture in retarding change and rejecting alien cultures and ideas such as ethnic studies programs. As I have argued throughout, the "system" rejects diversity and affirmative action, and basically tries to eliminate or marginalize any voice, whether of professors or students, which challenges its way of seeing the world. This rejection of alien voices is not new.

In the 1960s, Latin American, American, and Asian studies were frowned upon by traditionalists, even though these programs comprised traditional disciplines.[1] (This was before Chicana/o studies, African American studies, and Asian American studies were even conceived.) Scholars disapproved of mixing disparate disciplines. In part, today's antipathy toward ethnic studies programs is a legacy of this past. Ethnic studies, like their predecessors, remain illegitimate disciplines to most positivist scholars. The methodological eclecticism of most works in ethnic and women's studies offends purists. To them, these new disciplines lack a consistent theoretical framework, "borrow" from other fields, are opportunistic, and worse, journalistic.

The Status of Chicana/o Studies

Today there are Chicana/o studies programs at two-year colleges, teaching and research institutions, and even some high schools.

The discipline itself is divided into teaching and research fields. The teaching field is much more developed than the research field, partly because research fields evolve from teaching fields and partly because of the failure of research institutions to initiate doctoral programs in Chicana/o studies. Many institutions offer courses in Chicana/o studies and a few confer bachelor of arts degrees in the field. The total number of departments in Chicana/o studies is fairly limited, whether in teaching or research institutions.

Among the research institutions in California, Chicana/o studies programs exist at various stages, ranging from departments to centers. The UC is important because more than 50 percent of the doctoral degrees received by the nation's Chicanas/os in the various disciplines are from the UC system. As mentioned in chapter 4, the University of California at Los Angeles has a quasi-department, the César Chávez Center, which performs teaching functions, hires and fires faculties, and initiates curricula, but is not formally a department. This unit has about five tenured faculty members and offers a bachelor of arts degree. It also has a separate research center. The University of California at Santa Barbara has a Chicana/o studies department and is planning a doctoral program in the future.

Since 1991, thanks to the initiative of Dr. Yolanda Broyles-González, new hires at Santa Barbara have been sole appointments. Previously, the appointments were held jointly, both in a traditional department and in Chicana/o studies. However, the UCSB department is still disabled by a lack of a critical mass of professors and by political baggage that it has been carrying for two decades. It has only three core appointments, and because of a liberal leave policy, only one full-time faculty member was teaching in the fall of 1996, for example. The University of California at Davis has made efforts to establish a core department, yet all but two members of the faculty are from traditional disciplines. Both of the latter programs confer bachelor of arts degrees. The rest of the UC campuses have, in varying forms, ethnic studies programs. The best known ethnic studies program is at the Berkeley campus, which confers Ph.D. degrees. UC San Diego and Riverside also have ethnic studies departments and at San

Diego there have been rumblings about a Ph.D. program in ethnic studies.

Of the private California colleges, only Claremont College has what can be termed a Chicana/o studies department. Its members come from various departments and colleges. Chicano visibility has come from the Tomas Rivera Center, a think tank. In recent years, because of an excellent group of Chicana/o professors, Claremont has attracted a large number of Chicana/o students pursuing doctorates. No other private universities in California have the capability of training graduate students in Chicana/o studies. Some schools, such as the University of Southern California, allow specialization in Chicana/o studies within the graduate programs of other disciplines.

Among the California State University campuses, only the following campuses have functioning Chicana/o studies departments: San Diego, Long Beach, Fresno, Fullerton, Northridge, and Los Angeles. San Francisco State has La Raza Studies, which includes Chicano and Latino studies. The rest of the campuses have small programs, each with fewer than five faculty members. The state universities play an important role in Chicana/o studies as a teaching field, although their faculty are also increasingly producing scholarly articles and books.

There is little doubt that California State University at Northridge is the leader among the state universities and has institutionalized Chicana/o studies as a teaching field. Its program is interdisciplinary, incorporating humanities, social sciences, arts, community studies, and education. The goal is to produce a universal student, who can apply methods in each of these areas to Chicana/o studies, similar to the goals of the pre-1960s Latin American and American studies programs. In the pursuit of this goal, courses on Mexican experiences in Mexico and the U.S. have been created. Professors have been developing teaching strategies and bibliographies in the field for more than twenty-seven years. The CSUN department has become a community of teaching scholars. It has twenty-two full-time positions in Chicana/o studies, of which fifteen are tenured.[2]

The advanced state of the teaching field at CSUN marks it as a pacesetter. Now other universities have developed this teaching field, which many curriculum experts maintain is vital to the development of a research field. The course work has been time-tested in the classroom laboratory. The evidence clearly shows that Chicana/o studies challenges the prevailing paradigm in higher education of traditional-based disciplines.

Within Chicana/o studies there is considerable discussion of the issue of gender. The debate is prevalent during the annual conferences of the National Association for Chicana/o Studies. There is also a great deal of dialogue regarding gay and lesbian studies within the discipline. In recent years scholars have discussed incorporating Central American Studies and the concept of a Meso-American identity. The growing Central American population has made many within the discipline much more sensitive to the need for inclusion. Reflecting this concern, three programs have changed their names to include the word "Latino": the University of California at Berkeley, California State University, Long Beach, and Fresno State University.

Within California there is also a trend toward more Chicano-oriented programs within the community colleges. For the most part, these courses are offered within existing departments; however, as in the case of San Diego City College, there are also a few departments of Chicana/o studies. The growth of these programs has been limited by the dearth of programs in Chicana/o studies conferring a master of arts degree, which is generally the requirement to teach at a two-year college.

Except for Arizona State University, most of the universities outside California do not have Chicana/o studies departments. Arizona has a first-rate research center and a developing department. It is rapidly becoming the leader in the field. In a three-year period it added twenty-two professors of Mexican extraction to its faculty and had two dozen associates attached to its Hispanic Research Center. It has hired a director of its Chicana/o studies department and is presently developing curricula and offering courses. ASU is in a position to dominate Chicana/o studies by building on the experiences of other universities in developing both teaching and research areas. Other well-known programs outside California are the research centers at the state universities of New Mexico, Texas, Austin, Houston, at Michigan State, Minnesota, and Illinois at Chicago Circle. There is also a growing Mexican American Studies Center at the University of Texas, Arlington, which has been put together largely by the energy of José Angel Gutiérrez.

A Question of Identity

It is very difficult for new fields and paradigms to penetrate academe. One factor is the cultural arrogance of the custodians of the accepted truth. But another very important factor is that it takes a critical number of scholars to whittle away at the prevailing paradigm. Over the past decade I have become increasingly skeptical of the ability of Chicana/o studies to gain acceptance within academe without surrendering the community's interests. Part of the problem rests in the development of the discipline itself as an interdisciplinary approach to teaching and research, which is alien to the present curriculum design within academe.

Inherently, the present paradigm pits different disciplines and methods against each other. Most scholars are schooled in single disciplines. They study an area of knowledge through a specialized viewpoint of the field, whether it is in history, literature, art, or sociology. The general rule in universities is to base Chicana/o professors in mainstream departments and then artificially bond them into a Chicana/o studies program. This dispersal has had disastrous effects and has retarded the development of the teaching and research fields in Chicana/o studies. The tendency for scholars based in mainstream fields is to adopt the paradigms of those fields. A Chicana/o specialist who hails from the history department is likely to become a historian with a traditional positivist approach to that area of study. A historian based solely in a Chicana/o studies department, in contrast, is much more likely to develop a different paradigm, one which is more inclusive of other disciplines.

The problems in developing the discipline are exacerbated by the dearth of doctoral programs. With no terminal degree in Chicana/o studies, the training of Ph.D. candidates necessarily occurs in other fields. This has prevented an organic development of a unitary discipline and instead, resulted in interdisciplinary rivalry. The field develops haphazardly. Knowledge is accumulated and refined by scholars in disparate disciplines, with very little shared communication and very little opportunity to debate their differences in order to create a synthesis. There is a lack of loyalty to a unique field of Chicana/o studies, or a lack of commitment to building one. The consequence is that Chicana/o studies has failed to adopt canons or even a set of ethics. The situation is inherently divisive. In reality, there are no traditions and scholars are "on their own." Most of the "young scholars" who were graduate students in the 1960s have dropped out of active participation in the National Association for Chicana/o Studies (NACCS). Most have accepted the canons of "positive" knowledge and, with age, have returned to their primary disciplines.

Since the 1970s the knowledge base known as Chicana/o studies has rapidly expanded. A substantial number of books have appeared about persons of Mexican extraction in the visual and literary arts. The body of knowledge about Chicanas/os has grown considerably from the days when the only two books available seemed to be Carey McWilliams's *North from Mexico* and Octavio Paz's *Labyrinth of Solitude*. As in any other field, the quality of the material is spotty. One problem, as suggested above, is that many Chicana/o social scientists replicate the weaknesses of mainstream scholars and, in particular, fail to reflect their own experiences in their work. For example, I question how a Chicana/o scholar who has never grown up in a Mexican family, who does not have contact with working-class Chicanas/os, or who does not speak Spanish, can make generalizations about the group based on a limited sampling of interviews. This flaw in Chicana/o research is produced by the system, which puts a premium on being a scientist.[3]

Who is a Chicana/o expert? This is another problem confronting Chicana/o studies. Most Chicana/o scholars seem to believe that they are entitled, by virtue of their Spanish surnames, to teach Chicana/o studies. Others are the victims of this attitude. For Euro-American scholars in traditional departments, all Chicanas/os, regardless of their training, are qualified to teach a Chicano content course. Numerous Chicana/o scholars who have visited me at Northridge have told me, "I was just hired at so-and-so university; I don't know anything about Chicano studies, and the department makes it a prerequisite that I teach a class in Chicano history (or political science, and so on). Please help me!"

Unfortunately, there is scant literature analyzing the discipline of Chicana/o studies itself. Two recent critiques of Chicana/o studies are Ignacio M. García's "Juncture In The Road: Chicano Studies Since 'El Plan De Santa Bárbara,'"[4] and Adela de la Torre's "Perspective on Ethnic Studies: Activism Isn't Enough Any More; Scholarship and Intellectual Rigor Are Required If Programs Are to Move into the Academic Mainstream."[5] These critiques represent opposite poles of the discussion and merit close attention.

García is a historian with roots in the 1960s who wrote about the Chicano Movement as a journalist. While both García and de la Torre come from the same generation, García's formation differs from de la Torre's in that he has always enjoyed close links with the Chicano community. He posits that the field of Chicano studies

> as a field of inquiry and a stimulus for social and political change is nearing a critical juncture, which will determine both its direction as an academic discipline and its contribution to the struggle for civil rights in the Mexican American community.

He describes three main options: (1) Chicano studies becomes integrated into the larger ethnic studies programs, or its courses are cross-listed with core departments, or become diffused by Chicano scholars having joint appointments; (2) the status quo continues, namely, Chicano studies programs remain understaffed, underfunded, and marginalized, or, (3) Chicano studies fights for departmental status, providing the needed autonomy to develop as a discipline. This third option includes the building of departments that are problem/solution oriented.

García's article traces the development of Chicano studies,[6] from the Plan of Santa Bárbara to the founding of the National Association for Chicana/o Studies (NACCS). It includes a narrative of the student movement, Movimiento Chicanos de Aztlán

(MECHA). A basic flaw in his narrative, however, is that his focus is generally outside California; the article also suffers from the lack of primary sources.

García's view of Chicano studies is definitely activist and nationalist. According to García, the shift from activist scholarship has been challenged by

> Post-modern sectarianism—lesbian feminism, neo-Marxism, and a militant form of Latinoism . . . Many centers find themselves challenged by non-Chicano Latino scholars who want to promote their scholarly interests. They argue that all Latino groups have a common experience with racism and poverty in American society.

García argues that neo-Marxism offers little in terms of a workable paradigm. The issue of class is not central. While he compliments Chicana scholars for being more tenacious and militant on their issues than Chicano scholars, García criticizes those who have limited themselves to attacking Chicanos, and he criticizes some feminists for moving away from the community. The theme of community-centered research is at the nexus of García's critique.

García is especially critical of NACCS for failing to combat opportunism or Hispanic revisionism. He points to opportunism in many Chicano studies programs, which he attributes to the "'lure' of tenure, promotion, and success in academia." He promotes identity politics, calling for a regaining of the perspective of the Plan of Santa Bárbara, which called for the establishment of Chicano studies programs that were linked to the barrios and produced applied research to solve problems in the community. The Plan called for community oversight of research; the spirit of the plan was reflected in the preamble of NACCS.

García correctly points out that most young scholars today come out of a different experience than that of the politically active "founders." He seems to be calling for a reeducation of these scholars to make them more sensitive to community concerns. He advocates a separation of different Latino groups into their own programs. García would restrict the knowledge base of

Chicano studies to Chicanos/Mexicans. If, for example, Central Americans wanted a program, his response would be that they should start a separate Central American studies program.

De la Torre's perspective on Chicano studies has almost nothing in common with García's. She is an agricultural economist by training, with a decided neoliberal outlook. Although she did her undergraduate studies during the movement years, she chose not to participate. She came to Chicano studies at California State University at Long Beach via the department of economics. De la Torre's work betrays an air of elitism and a break with the principles of the NACCS preamble. Her article suggests the existence of tensions at the University of Arizona, where she is now director of the Mexican American Studies Center:

> As my first semester ends at the University of Arizona, I have just begun to understand the depth of the perils faced by directors of ethnic studies programs. Unlike more traditional departments, these programs emerged from the civil rights unrest of the 1960s and reflect, more often than not, the rhetoric of that era. It was a time when ethnic and racial authenticity were the criteria for entrance into these programs, and scholarly accomplishment meant little. Unfortunately, this legacy has created a fundamental contradiction as new scholars emerge with sterling credentials and academic legitimacy.

Unfortunately, the article was written for a mass audience, addressed to a public that is hypercritical of Chicana/o studies and, in the aftermath of 209, poised to launch a campaign to eliminate it.

Although de la Torre has a thin publishing record, she compared herself, in good positivist fashion, to more established scholars:

> People like Henry Louis Gates at Harvard, Ronald Takaki at UC Berkeley and Renato Rosaldo at Stanford are significant scholars involved in academic centers devoted to ethnic and racial issues. But at other such centers, many of those in charge chafe at the mention of scholarship having more weight than activist authenticity.

Her article launches an attack on ethnic studies and its students:

> When I became director of the Mexican American Studies & Research Center here, the curriculum and lack of full-time faculty meant there was little structure or accountability to either the students or the administration . . . My own review of student records found that more than 40% of the majors in this program could not pass the minimum writing requirements for the upper division, and these students were graduating without remediation or recommendations for writing intervention . . . Critics of ethnic studies programs are correct when they assert that curricula do not reflect the intellectual rigor of established disciplines. This is because of lack of expertise and scholarship in the area during the 1960s and into the 1970s.

De la Torre makes some exceptions, stating that there are

> academic concerns over the issues of multiculturalism, diversity and race relations [which] created a dynamic dialogue across traditional disciplines and ethnic studies programs. This was captured symbolically when Harvard University established a highly visible African American studies program with Gates and other top scholars in the field.

Most damning, de la Torre dismisses the importance of the history of racism in higher education. This is implicit in her call for change:

> It is not surprising that administrators across the country have begun to review their ethnic studies programs. Yet often, as here at the University of Arizona, the path to transform a program from mediocrity to excellence requires challenging the status quo of political brokers from the past so that the program could meet the demands of an elite institution.

De la Torre, among other things, seems to have forgotten that the University of Arizona and California State University at Long Beach are not Harvard, and that most state universities admit a high number of students with remediation problems, whether brown, black, or white. In addition, there are enormous class differences among students. Yet de la Torre persists:

If ethnic studies is to achieve credibility in academia as well as in society, leaders must shift away from the rhetoric of the 1960s to the substantive merit of the scholarship. Minorities are not victims of the system but masters of their own destiny. We must develop a scholarship and understanding of the issues that face minority populations so that we can provide students and faculty with requisite skills to work together.

The problem is that de la Torre adopts the neoliberal rationality that affirmative action stigmatizes students. She carries it one step further—Chicano and black students have *not* been exploited by racism. Her arguments echo those of Schlesinger.

De la Torre continues,

The battle for the soul of ethnic studies is between those who want to maintain isolation, cultural nationalism and the litmus test of authenticity based on political values and others who view diversity of opinion, diversity of scholars and academic rigor as keys to success. In the context of many ethnic studies programs, this latter point of view is seen as threatening because it implies that "outsiders" may gain entry to the insiders' politically gained spots.

De la Torre is assuming that every activist got a job in ethnic studies programs. The reality is that most of the activists did not benefit from Chicana/o studies, since their education was often delayed or terminated by their activism. Positions for the most part went to persons like de la Torre, who contributed very little to the struggle. For her to argue that "if ethnic studies programs do not open their intellectual doors, the promise of intellectual equality becomes merely an illusion in the academy and we will continue to tokenize our scholars," is disingenuous. Her article, although calling for "critical dialogue," is elitist. It naively assumes that her generation needs no struggle; it will make its arrangements with the administration, who will act differently toward those who do not have the burden of having come from the 1960s—who are not "tenured radicals."

García and de la Torre represent extremes. The truth, I think, lies somewhere in the middle. As García argues, the nexus for any

Chicana/o studies program must be the community. The status quo is intolerable and the blame for the failure of most ethnic studies programs rests with the academies, not the few Chicana/o professors at the institutions. Both the teaching and research fields of Chicana/o studies will never fully develop until structural changes are made and programs become full-fledged departments. And ultimately, these departments should function for the public good. On the other hand, the model should not necessarily be the Plan of Santa Bárbara. Few programs were founded on this very idealistic plan, written in 1969, that inadequately addresses many of today's issues. Students and Chicana/o scholars should write their own plan if that's what they want.

The National Association for Chicana/o Studies is not the appropriate vehicle for activism. If a national organization subdivided into smaller units to advance political and social goals is desired, another should be constructed on this model. NACCS should be a free forum to discuss differences, introduce new ideas, new knowledge, and both challenge and defend the neoliberal American paradigm (whose virtues many of our brethren still adhere to). It should be a neutral place where the de la Torres and the Garcías can exchange their views.

This commitment to open discussion also implies that, contrary to García, the arguments of lesbian feminism have a rightful place at NACCS and similar forums. If Chicanas/os are supposed to deal with the issue of race, how can they talk about racial equality if they shut out other voices in the community who are discriminated against? As for neo-Marxism, for which García has no use, its critique of capitalism is essential for demythicizing the American paradigm. From a personal point of view, Marxism still offers "workable paradigms." And it would also be wrong to exclude a Marxist from a dialogue.

As García points out, opportunism exists in many Chicana/o studies programs, and the "lure" of tenure, promotion, and success in academia are principal factors. I disagree with him in the tendency to blame the young scholars in their twenties who are attempting to grasp situations of struggle that we were fortunate enough to experience first-hand. García is also correct that identity politics are a part of Chicana/o studies; however, should this be the sole focus? Take, for instance, the reality of places like Los Angeles, where there are large numbers of working-class Central Americans who share a history of colonialism with Mexicans. If García's argument were accepted, they would be excluded from Chicana/o studies. This is the late 1990s, not 1970, and the times dictate a reevaluation of the old paradigm of Chicana/o studies. A dialogue should be opened, not ruled out.

To be fair to de la Torre, we must admit that the development of Chicana/o studies with respect to teaching has been uneven. With respect to research, most universities are in the dark ages. The practitioners do not agree as to what should be done. NACCS, which should provide a forum for debate, fails to do so. Very little intellectual socialization takes place, and every year fewer senior scholars attend its meetings. Senior scholars prefer to attend sessions in their "real" discipline. A few years back, for instance, NACCS held its convention in the same month as the American Sociological Association Convention—and that is where Chicana/o sociologists ended up, revealing through their choices the power of the university's reward system and of the culture of academia.

Every discipline forms its own culture, as a result of interaction of the members of a community of scholars. Unfortunately, with few exceptions, Chicana/o studies is not forging that culture, either intellectually or spatially. There are few Chicana/o studies *departments* in the U.S. and those few, like the department at Northridge, are limited in influence because the primary focus is usually the development of a teaching discipline, not a research discipline. This makes the shifting of the American paradigm all the more difficult.

Purging the Nonbelievers

The American paradigm presumes that it represents the truth, or closely approximates it. What is the truth is more a philosophical question than a scientific one. In his excellent book *What Is History?*, a must for historians of all colors, Edward Hallett Carr readily admits that there is no "objective" historical truth. History represents a point of view. He criticizes nineteenth-century

German historian Leopold von Ranke for his mechanical retelling of the past, and for the positivist claim that history is a science. Carr advocates a "common-sense view of history. History consists of a corpus of ascertained facts," he says, which in itself presents a challenge to the historian since "the historian is necessarily selective."[7] The historian's life experiences play a determined role in the selection of the facts, which may prevent him or her from understanding the truths of others.

Despite very clear admissions by scholars that they do not have a monopoly on truth or objectivity, the pretension continues. In Oscar Handlin's *Truth in History*, the author commits all of the sins that he accuses others of making. Although he admits to the human limitations of the historian, he thinks of himself as the custodian of truth. Handlin begins his book with a first chapter entitled "The Abuses of History," where he writes, "Historians, like other scholars in the United States, long occupied themselves in self-justification." In the next breath Handlin laments the dissolution of the sense of community of academe, because unqualified minority scholars were being foisted on the profession: "I was surprised in 1968 at the request that I recommend teachers not according to ability but according to race and political orientation."[8] While Handlin admits the inability of scholars to escape the limitations of their culture, he himself does not recognize his own limitations.

The contradictions in Handlin's work are even more evident on the topic of truth and objectivity in a historical context. One of the best works on this theme is historian Peter Novick's *That Noble Dream: the "Objectivity Question" and the American Historical Profession*. The title is borrowed from Charles A. Beard, who adopted it for one of two essays repudiating his faith in objectivity in historiography. Novick's work is a history of American historiography and the idea of objectivity. Novick writes that it was not until the 1880s that scholars accorded professional status to historians. The leaders in this new field controlled the profession for many years, resisting new ideas and changes.

Novick describes history as an Anglo-Saxon enterprise, showing that the biases among the early historians was "near unanimous." They resisted the entrance of Jews and immigrants into the profession; Novick documents the overt anti-Semitism in the correspondence of leading historians. According to Novick, the American concept of historical objectivity is firmly rooted in a bad translation of Leopold von Ranke's phrase, *wie es eigentlich gewesen* ("as it really was"), and a translation of the word *Wissenschaft* as "science." The new historians borrowed from the prestige of empirical science. In one swoop, they were no longer *cuentistas*, mere storytellers or propagandists, but social scientists. At John Hopkins a historical seminar was pretentiously described as "a laboratory of historical truth." The founding fathers of history built the doctrine of empirical objectivity into methodology.

The foremost challengers of "that noble dream" of historical objectivity in the 1930s were Carl L. Becker and Charles A. Beard. They held that historical interpretation was, and always was, relative to the historian's time, place, views, prejudices, interests, and circumstances. For their heresy, the professionals called them "relativists."

The cold war, according to Novick, strengthened the defenders of objectivity, as did the optimism generated by the history boom in the universities. Many historians joined the cold war purge and unfairly associated Beard with fascism (Beard had opposed American intervention in World War II). Lewis Mumford, Allan Nevins, and Samuel Eliot Morrison were among those who castigated him. They jeered Beard, a former president of the American Historical Association, at AHA meetings. Handlin ridiculously said that Beard "had no students" and that his "influence upon subsequent scholarship was slight." Historians drew an illogical link between Beard's isolationism and his relativism, while cheerfully celebrating the objectivity of their work.

The decades following World War II, considered a "boom period" for the history profession, show dramatic change. The 1960s, driven by the post-war baby boom, saw the demand for new historians soar. The stress of the baby boomers on the infrastructure, as well as the increased cynicism about truth and objectivity brought about by the Vietnam War, shook the confidence of the professionals. According to Novick, the inability to screen the new historians with the same vigor as in the past brought unconventional currents of thought into the profession, to wit, those of new black historians who were separatists, nationalists, or scornful of assimilation, of white radicals, and of feminists. The public discourse encouraged the hiring of these new elements. The number of bachelor degrees awarded in history reached the all-time high of 44,663 in 1971, but then rapidly plunged over the next fifteen years to a low of 16,413 in 1986. Faculties grew older and the lessened demand allowed them to more closely scrutinize candidates. A crisis in objectivity had spread to all the disciplines in the academy, including the sciences. The defense of objectivity came from the right, which associated its maintenance with the status quo.

From my vantage point, the most devastating aspect of Novick's work is his account of the way historians appeal to truth and objectivity in order to purge others. When Handlin attended his first meeting of the American Historical Association in 1936, he wrote in reverential tones about this professional experience. Handlin, a Jew, was not aware that the year before, his adviser, Arthur Schlesinger Sr., noted in a letter of recommendation that Handlin had "none of the offensive traits which some people associate with his race." Schlesinger's colleague Roger Merriman, in recommending Daniel Boorstin, said that he was "a Jew though not the kind to which one takes exception." Even non-Jewish historians with Jewish-sounding names were suspect. In a letter recommending Wallace Notestein for a post at Yale, Charles Hull of Cornell wrote that "his family are Presbyterians, very much so, except Wallace himself, who is a somewhat straying sheep."

Novick's book is the historiographic and epistemological opposite of Handlin's book, *Truth In History*. Novick simply argues that there is no such thing as "truth in history." Historical objectivity is an "incoherent" and "dubious" goal. Novick writes, "Most historians generally write about their colleagues the way Arthur Schlesinger Jr., writes about the Kennedys." They ignore their flaws and their racism and ultra-patriotism. Novick proves that professional, political, psychological, and cultural pressures influence and even determine the epistemological interpretation of historians, and their philosophical and professional biases.

The history of American higher education is full of Galileos who were symbolically tried for their deviance from the American paradigm. The isolation of so-called revisionist historians is not new; the experiences of Chicana/o and other scholars of color, or for that matter, of feminists are not aberrations. William Appleman Williams, author of *The Tragedy of American Diplomacy* (1959) and *The Contours of American History* (1961), was hounded by his colleagues. Oscar Handlin, the cold war historian, tried to ruin Williams's career, writing a scathing review of his work. Williams had dared to question the objectivity of the cold war historians. Williams feared the irresponsible nation-state and the triumph of an American corporate liberal state intent on economic growth as a way of life. He challenged the cold war paradigm, which justified expansion through open-door imperialism.

Williams challenged the liberal apologetic that allowed hysterical anticommunism to justify acts of Realpolitik. Williams was a leader among the revisionists, whose elimination Schlesinger Sr. demanded before their attack on America went any further. He accused Williams of being a "procommunist scholar." Williams was harassed by the House Committee on Un-American Activities, which demanded to see the manuscript of *Contours*. In a cry that is all too familiar, the defenders of objectivity charged that the *New Left Review*, led by Williams, was politicizing the discipline of history.

Rewards and Assimilation

Chicana/o scholars would not be human if they did not respond to the American paradigm. The deviance of Becker, Beard, and Williams is heroic, but they were giants who could stand up to the system. Most young scholars, including Chicanas/os, are middle class by virtue of their education and share middle-class values of material success. They soon realize that they are vulnerable. They learned as students that you write to please the teacher, which in part explains their scholarly success. This principle is transferred to their careers. And their writing is for those who review them.

Like other institutions of society, the university has a life of its own and a culture of its own. As I have discussed in the previous chapter, scholars in research institutions are very well paid and rewarded. They maintain autonomy over what is taught and control the resources of the institution by staying out of the political arena. They have lifetime appointments called tenure. They bolster their claims for promotion by building in review processes to justify merit increases. This review takes place at almost every step of the way, from a lowly assistant professor to the majestic full professor rank. Universities say that their review process ensures that scholarly integrity is maintained.

At research universities professors typically live in university towns in close proximity to each other. They socialize with one another and intellectually banter with one another at social events. They eat at the faculty club, their children date, and in the process, they recycle each other's ideas, biases and even worse, tolerate and shield each other's prejudices. These incestuous intellectual affairs often cross over class, race, and even gender lines. Faculties become institutionalized and professionalized. In other words, they bond.

The university review process is more closely linked to the rewarding of a faculty member than ensuring merit. It promotes conformity, opportunism, and intellectual incest. Down the line you know you are going to be reviewed, so it is to your advantage to be "collegial"—a "good citizen," as some reviewers like to say, especially as you approach the upper limits of the professorial ranks. As historian Page Smith once commented: candidates were commonly applauded for their "objectivity" when they opposed reform and, therefore, agreed with the bias of the majority of the reviewers.

Within the halls of academe, scholarship is thus a political weapon. The universities reflect the attitudes of the dominant ideology. In recent years, as the faculties have gotten older, universities have also grown more conservative. Indeed, a goodly number of 1960s scholars who opposed the Vietnam War and bled for Third World people are today's nativists, defending Western civilization. The overwhelming majority of these professors are white, male, and come from middle-class or upper-class families. Most have been educated in U.S. or European academies. They look at the world through the same lens as their colleagues—their knowledge is derived through common sources—and it seems consistent to them to have a text on "World Literature" with 90 percent of its selections from Europe, or to have a Spanish department staffed entirely by Spaniards. They look at societal themes through a Eurocentric prism.

Chicana/o studies, embracing history, sociology, literature, and so forth, is suspect because it is alien to American academic culture. In the end, like the general culture, the university operates to control scholars (and the public), who are conditioned to believe prescribed definitions of truth and objectivity. Scholars insist that "knowledge" is constantly revised through a process of peer criticism and review that keeps its distance from the world. But it never occurs to them that by excluding "different" knowledge, their results are tainted, or that the peer group process in fact ensures conformity. The search for truth in academe is a con job.

Chicana/o academics have, for the most part, assimilated into this academic culture. It is natural. No one likes to be marginalized. In life you learn not to say anything when a racist or sexist joke is told: it's harmless fun, so turn the other way. Thus it is with Chicana/o studies; you don't make an issue of the false and often racist assumptions that your colleagues make. It's not collegial.

Because of this culture, which is driven by faculty governance with peer group review at its center, you don't rock the boat. Thus, the direction of Chicana/o history is shaped by the peer group review process in universities, which rewards the type of scholarship that the reviewers believe is compatible with their kind of truth and their kind of objectivity. They defend their view in the name of science, in effect promoting the dominant ideology which dissidents call neoliberalism and sometimes Eurocentricism.

Black historians have better coped with these pressures than have Chicana/o historians and scholars. In all probability this is because of the long historical tradition of the black community in this country, dating back to W. E. B. Du Bois, who in his lifetime was spurned by academe and never offered a permanent position at a prestigious white university, but who challenged the prevailing paradigm that explained the black experience in the U.S. His works have been a beacon for generations of black scholars.

Chicana/o scholars and activists often complain that most of the public discourse on politics and education is in terms of blacks and whites, and that at almost every level, Chicanos and

Latinos are excluded. This is also true in the field of history, where Chicana/o history is largely dismissed or devalued. This lack of presence may be due to the lack of a critical number of historians of Mexican ancestry. But just as important is the lack of a Chicana/o tradition within the profession, and the "me-too-ism" of Chicana/o scholars who, unlike black scholars, are more diverse and a critical number of whom criticize their own discipline. Despite the racism in society and the antipathy toward black historians, they are not easily dismissed. The thrust of the criticism of Chicana/o scholars has been that they are not getting their individual shares of the pie, and that there should be more Chicana/o representation on professional boards and panels. Currently there is almost no criticism of the paradigm. Why bite the hand that feeds you?

6

A Case Study:
Acuña v. The Regents of the University of California

In the fall of 1996 a debate took place at California State University at Northridge on Proposition 209. David Duke, the former Klansman turned American politician, spoke for the Proposition. Duke said, among other things, that affirmative action is not needed because there are already anti-discrimination laws on the books. He claimed that lawyers are lined up eager to take discrimination cases on a contingency basis. Duke's statement reflects the general ignorance of society on the topic of employment discrimination. I shopped my case to a half dozen legal firms, who told me that the UC had unlimited resources and that it would bankrupt them to take the case. They said that the UC had the deepest of pockets and overwhelming influence with judges and politicians, and therefore, the average UC professor does not have the resources to sue the UC. The average citizen, for example, does not have $25,000 to put down as an initial retainer. Indeed, it is easier to sue and get a judgment against Chrysler than against the University of California.

Before I filed the suit, then Alumni Regent Ralph Ochoa warned me that if I sued, the UC had several dozen lawyers as well as the ability to hire outside counsel. They would bankrupt me, smear my name, and in the end I would lose. At that time I was still naive enough to believe that justice was possible through the judicial system. I was also naive enough to believe that large public interest firms would be knocking down my door for the chance to defend my rights. The five-year struggle against the University of California shattered all such illusions that I had about the judicial system and, for that matter, academe.

I applied for a position in the Chicano Studies Department at the University of California at Santa Barbara in December 1990, at the urging of El Congreso students and my wife. After twenty-two years at California State University at Northridge, I wanted the challenge of helping turn around a troubled department and of supporting the new leadership in establishing a Ph.D. program.

The department submitted my name as its sole candidate after a series of meetings. I was so busy readying myself to go to El Salvador that I did not read the political situation at UCSB, where an attempted coup of the chair was underway,[1] shifting the original unanimity. When the official vote took place, three professors strongly supported my appointment and three abstained. The administration, according to discovery documents, abetted this division and intentionally undermined the authority of the chair. The administration blatantly violated its own procedures, frequently meeting with dissidents and others, and engaging in the type of backroom governance which historically has kept Chicana/o studies weak and divided on numerous campuses. (Four previous searches by the department had been unsuccessful. Members of the department rarely agreed on anything. The department operated like a revolving door, unable to retain a critical mass of professors. As a result it only had the equivalent of 3.5 tenured-track appointments, all of which were joint appointments with other departments.)

On June 20, 1991, two students called me and told me that they had heard that I was turned down. I then called Vice Chancellor Gordon Hammes, who refused to give me details other than coldly telling me that I could not cut it in the UC. At my request, the administration on July 30 sent me an aggregate summary of the comments of various review committees. According to Martha Cody-Váldez, the analyst processing the case, she had called attention to the emotional and angry tone of the reviews to Associate Vice Chancellor Julius Zelmanowitz, who cavalierly dismissed the warnings. (Cody-Váldez, who may have been under duress by the administration, later testified for management.)[2]

The aggregate summary of July 30, 1991, contained passages such as:

> [Reviewing agencies] must, therefore, adopt the strictest kind of scrutiny, in a case like this . . . [Acuña] would be the first in that department not to have a joint appointment, involving periodic peer review in an established discipline and department, since he would be full-time in Chicano Studies.

> *Occupied America* [one of my books] is a "cult book"—and certainly, as [this reviewing agency reads] in the comments of outside evaluators, it has had an immense impact on the conceptualization and teaching of Chicano history. So too [this reviewing agency concludes], Acuña himself may with accuracy be termed as a "cult professor."

> *Occupied America*, which appeared just at the time Chicano Studies was emerging as a teaching field and therefore when it was in great need of a core book, lifted Acuña from relative obscurity to the position of almost solitary intellectual leadership in the Chicano movement and community.

> A person of Professor Acuña's stature and experience would stand so far above the rest of his colleagues that his position could verge on being dictatorial . . . This would have a potentially dominating influence on the kind of research and writing that would be smiled upon, or rejected as wrong and unacceptable.

> As the output of a 23-year career, the scholarly substance and significance of the materials accompanying this case are very meager. Much of the work does not fall into our usual basic research category, and more than some does not appear to be of major scholarly significance.

> Professor Acuña has produced an angry special-pleading, moralizing work entirely lacking in distanced, critical stance toward his subject.

[Acuña is] an inveterate polemicist and pamphleteer who ignores the rules of evidence, fills his work with angry pronouncements on a wide array of subjects, and flagrantly, openly, and
apparently on purpose shapes his analyses and narrative to serve
a political purpose.

Believing that such a person [Acuña] might be insulated in a
large established Department . . . in a field so inchoate as Chicano Studies, that kind of appointment would be an error, and
one difficult to correct.

Although, according to the academic personnel manual, the reviews of outside experts carry considerable weight, the UCSB
administration and the faculty senate committee summarily dismissed the favorable reviews provided by experts in the field of
Chicana/o studies, calling them nonanalytical and implying that
they were written by my political cronies. Instead, they relied on
their own uninformed and biased assumptions.

I requested a meeting with UCSB Chancellor Barbara Uehling. She refused. UCSB administrators, in fact, defied me to sue.
Naively, I sought the advice and support of UCLA Alumni Regent
Ralph Ochoa, then chair of the Regents' Affirmative Action Committee. Unknown to me, soon after the original denial, Ochoa
began helping UC officials, with whom he had personal and business relations. Throughout the litigation Ochoa lobbied heavily
on behalf of UC within the Chicano community.

On October 3, with the support of El Congreso students, I
helped organize a march and rally on the UCSB campus. Discovery documents later showed that police surveillance was heavy
during the march. The documents also showed that an under-
cover police attended a lecture I gave in Dr. Ramón Favela's class,
and they suggest that the campus police used student, staff, and
faculty informants to keep tabs on me.

In late November I filed a claim with the California Department of Fair Employment and Housing and received the right
to sue. Three months later, Chicanos marched down State Street
in Santa Barbara in the largest protest to date, numbering more
than 3,000. In March 1992, through the intervention of Leonard
Minsky of the National Coalition of Universities in the Public In-

terest, the Center for Constitutional Rights, which had a reputation as an aggressive advocate for civil rights, took the case. On September 25, 1992, my complaint was filed in Alameda County Superior Court.

During the fall of 1992, in a series of legal maneuvers, the UC removed the case to the federal court in the Northern District and filed a motion for dismissal of the suit. Eventually, the federal court kept the ADEA (age discrimination) claim and remanded the state causes of action back to the state. The defendants' legal maneuver cost money, ate up time, and suffocated me in paperwork.

The UC hired as outside counsel Corbett & Kane, a defense firm that claims to be female-run and specializes in defending management against victims of employment discrimination. Corbett & Kane is run by self-styled liberals, who pride themselves in employing a sibling of former State Supreme Court Justice Joe Grodin. Judith Droz Keyes, one of its partners and the lead counsel in my case, is one of the top pro-management labor lawyers in California. She was also active in the anti-209 campaign. The firm is absolutely ruthless. It let the proverbial taxi meter run wild. The strategy was clear—to spend us into the ground.

Frank Acuña, my son, joined the case as local counsel, as did Lisa Honig. Beth Minsky of the National Coalition was, by this time, the driving force behind the case. UC counsel and Corbett & Kane successfully moved to change the venue to southern California: they wanted to get rid of Frank Acuña, an experienced litigator, who spent some 100 hours in two months answering motion after motion. They did not like the idea of trying the case in Alameda County. It had too many working-class African Americans, Latinos, and progressive whites, in contrast to Santa Barbara, which historically had all-white juries. The move also increased travel time for attorneys and made it a billing Disneyland. The plaintiff (Acuña) decided not to appeal the change of the venue because of the cost of defending.

The move to Southern California forced Frank Acuña and Honig out of the case. At the time this loss seemed devastating. In the end, the move proved the best thing that could have happened, because my base of support was in the Los Angeles and Santa Barbara areas.

Armando Durón, a good friend and adviser, joined as local counsel for the federal case; he recruited Moisés Vázquez as local counsel for the state case; and Beth Minsky of the National Coalition assumed an even greater responsibility.[3] The defendants knew the weaknesses of my attorneys; they were solo practitioners. To offset this we recruited ten other attorneys as well as the American Civil Liberties Union, which played a limited role until the last stages of the case.

Defendants' (UC's) counsel hit us with a whirlwind of demurs and motions. Santa Barbara Superior Court Judge Ronald Stevens, a conservative, played it straight and ruled strictly on the law. We had hopes that he would control the defendants' abuse of the court through their extravagant waste of money. His most important ruling was that the *University of Pennsylvania v. EEOC* applied in my case. He reluctantly ordered defendants to hand over confidential documents, since according to the Pennsylvania case, confidentiality does not apply in discrimination cases.

Over the next year and a half, plaintiff's counsel plodded through more than twenty depositions. It received confidential reports which clearly showed that the UC had denied me employment because of my politics, my race, and my age, and had conspired to do so, intentionally attempting to destroy my reputation. Even so, the UC frustrated the production of documents. At this point we should have had a full-time attorney pressing the defendants with court appearances. As a consequence of limited resources, we missed opportunities. The court appointed a referee to manage discovery.[4] He ordered the UC to produce system-wide documents, which the defendants frustrated by legal maneuvers. The referee failed to control Corbett & Kane. Meanwhile, the presiding judge granted defendants' motion to subject me to psychiatric tests. (We filed two writs to the appellate court to stop the examination but lost.)[5]

Corbett & Kane also hired an investigator to look through twenty-five years of student newspaper articles at California State University at Northridge to dig up dirt, not only on me but on the Chicana/o Studies department and the Chicano community on campus. The investigator was on the campus for more than eight weeks, using the California State University Legal Counsel to obtain access to materials made nearly inaccessible by the earthquake. C&K attorneys also called Chicano and Chicana scholars throughout the U.S. in an effort to get them to testify against me. In one case they attempted to intimidate an associate professor at UC Berkeley into testifying. The C&K attorney asked the Chicano professor whether he was loyal to the system. The UC even attempted to hire a Chicano attorney, a partner in a large firm, to serve as a front. (To their credit, Latinos in the UC General Counsel's Office declined involvement.) Corbett & Kane and the UC also set out to deliberately assassinate my character and destroy my legitimacy.

In June 1994 Corbett & Kane won a court order forcing me to produce my unpublished manuscript, *Anything But Mexican*, all research notes, and research documents for future publications. My research consisted of some thirty years of document accumulation, much of which is on microfilm. My concern was that the ideas, the secrets within these notes, would be exposed to a large body of defendants and experts who had demonstrated that they wanted to win at any cost, and who intentionally distorted information during the discovery stage. When I admonished the referee after court that it was harassment and it violated academic freedom, the judge told me that he didn't care about academic freedom or fairness. He only cared about employment law.

The ownership of intellectual property is considered a fundamental academic freedom right. The protection of intellectual property is jealously guarded by scholars. It involves more than just a property right; it is recognized as principle in "common law or in equity; to prevent copying, publication, or use of such intellectual property without his [the owner's] consent, and to obtain damages thereof." In the developmental stage, before publication, the protection of this intellectual property is even more critical.

The summer of 1994, when UC handed over more than twenty-two boxes of documents under court order, marked a turning point in the state case. My attorneys by this time were exhausted by the incessant paperwork. Law is not a matter of justice. It is a matter of who can outspend the other side. For example, Corbett & Kane set depositions in Puerto Rico, Madison,

Wisconsin, Kansas City, and Austin, Texas, in the course of a week. We did not have the resources to attend the depositions, and made motions to quash them since they were after-acquired evidence (which means evidence acquired after the final review had been made). My attorneys mistakenly believed that the judge would follow current case law and not allow the depositions into evidence.

The University of California, one of the largest public corporations in California, has unlimited funds to spend on legal fees to defend its malfeasance, and no one questions either the practice or the sums spent. The *San Francisco Chronicle* reported that in 1992 the UC had a staff of thirty-five attorneys at its Oakland headquarters and another twelve lawyers based at several campuses and other locations, earning from $70,000 a year to more than $100,000. UC general counsel James Holst then earned in excess of $168,000. This legal staff is not enough. The UC employs more than a hundred outside firms, paying them anywhere from $100 to $300 an hour. In 1992 the UC paid these firms some $23 million. This figure does not include the millions of dollars paid in settlements intentionally hidden from the public and their elected representatives by "gag" orders. Nor does it include the costs of inside UC staff.

Members of review teams know they can discriminate with impunity. They are assured that the UC will dig deep into the taxpayers' pockets to defend them. The UC's assault prevented me from doing effective political work, since I had to help the attorneys. Nevertheless, we began a campaign to get the legislature to intervene. Assemblyman Richard Polanco wrote to UC President Jack Peltason. Later, Assemblywoman Hilda Solis and Assemblyman Antonio Villaraigosa also wrote letters. On the whole, however, the so-called Hispanic Caucus did not effectively support us. They allowed the UC to get off the hook, partly because I am not a political insider and partly because I had stepped on toes with my political columns. The inability to garner sufficient support from Latino politicians allowed Assemblyman Jack O'Connell and State Senator Gary Hart to lobby openly for UC Santa Barbara, which was in their districts. It also took pressure off then Assemblyman Tom Hayden, who chose not to support me.

We learned from the documents that there was considerable internal manipulation of the review process. For example, the Committee on Academic Personnel (CAP) nominates the members of a secret ad hoc committee, supposedly in fields related to that of the candidate, to "objectively" review the candidate's qualifications. In my case, Phillip Hammond, a Religious Studies professor, was assigned by the CAP chair, Jeffrey Russell, to shepherd my file. However, we learned in deposition that Russell himself took over the case, writing the final draft of the report. Cynically, Hammond and Russell originally nominated UCSB historian Otis Graham Jr. to chair the ad hoc committee. Graham, as it turned out, is one of the founders of the Federation of American Immigration Reform (FAIR), one of the most zealous anti-immigrant organizations. Graham considers himself an expert on immigration, although he has never published on the subject. Graham was surely my ideological opposite, a fact which Russell, who is in the same department as Graham, and others must have known. As I noted in chapter 3, Graham blamed Latinos for the Rodney King uprisings, and the *Arizona Republic* quoted him as saying,

> We're quickly learning what the Israelis learned about borders and citizenship. We're going to have to get awfully tough, and it's going to be unpleasant. But that's the consequence of living next door to a failed society with a bunch of failed societies below it.

In normal circumstances no one would know who CAP had nominated to this crucial committee. However, under *University of Pennsylvania v. EEOC*, I was entitled to know; as noted earlier, in cases of discrimination, the defendants waive their rights to confidentiality. Ultimately, however, Graham was not appointed to the ad hoc committee.

Instead, historian Robert Kelley, a close friend of Graham, became the chair of the secret committee. Kelley himself testified in a deposition that I had lied about the Mexican-American War—everyone knew Mexico was to blame for the war with the United States. Moreover, Kelley claimed that he knew Mexican-American history and had published on the subject in his textbooks. On

close scrutiny we found that Kelley used the term "wetback" with
impunity in his 1986 text. Graduate students also told us that he
was intolerant of any dissent and that most minority graduate
students had dropped out of his graduate seminar. The members
of the ad hoc committee, CAP, and even the chancellor deferred to
his alleged expertise on a topic of which, in fact, he knew little.

The two other members of the ad hoc committee were no
better. Giles Gunn, an English professor, went to great lengths
to establish that my methodology was incorrect (and also that
he was not a racist), even though he had not read the bulk of
my works and knew almost nothing about Mexican Americans.
Wallace Chafe, a renowned linguist, an expert in Native American languages, and a former member of the Central Intelligence
Agency (CIA), was in many ways the most dogmatic of the ad hoc
reviewers. For example, during his deposition the following exchange occurred:

Miguel Caballero: "Do you consider Noam Chomsky a
scholar in linguistics?" Chafe: "Yes." "Would you consider some
of his work polemical?" "His non-scholarly work that is to say his
work outside of linguistics is extremely polemical. His work
within linguistics, yeah, it's kind of polemical within the field as
he takes very strong positions." "Is his polemical work scholarship in the linguistics fields?" "I suppose you know that I disagree with him violently on a number of things and one of them is
the way he presents things." "Is his work scholarship [*sic*] in the
linguistics field polemical work?" "I know what you are getting
at. I actually think that—I hope he is not going to read this—some
of it is not responsible scholarship." "But some of the polemical
work is scholarship?" "Well, you see I have very strong feelings
about this work and I know what you'd like me to say, that his
work is scholarship and it is polemical at the same time." "I'd like
you to tell me the truth." "I think in some ways he is kind of a
charlatan. I don't want that passed around." "Do you have scholars in the field of linguistics who believe that his polemical work
is scholarship?" "Yes."

This same eminent scholar stated that the committee was
very flexible in evaluating my work. The following exchange occurred when Chafe was questioned by my counsel as to why the

committee completely disregarded extramural letters from some of the most knowledgeable scholars in the field:

Caballero: "If the entire Chicano Studies scholarly community said that Dr. Acuña's work was scholarship, you have stated that you still would have reviewed the work and made your own determination on it?" Chafe: "That's exactly right."

Consistently, the depositions revealed that the internal reviews were simply a matter of following the leader. The internal reviewers admitted that their reviews were not supposed to be scholarly. Only one of the dozen or so internal reviewers claimed any expertise in Chicana/o studies, and his claim is highly questionable. Indeed, the custom was to defer to someone on the committee who claimed expertise.

Provost David Sprecher, whom everyone also cited as an expert, was a mathematician. During his deposition he changed his testimony, attempting to delete his earlier references to my political activities. The defense of the review process sometimes verged on the ridiculous. For example, Ian Ross, a biologist, insisted that in order to be objective, both sides had to be given. My counsel then asked whether when writing about the Holocaust, both sides had to be given. Ross answered, yes. The ramifications of this go without saying.

Enter the Federal Forum

The referee had ordered the defendants to produce all promotion and hiring files at the Professor V and VI level dating back to 1981, and all personnel files of Chicana/o professors during this same period. By August 1994 the defendants had given up a portion of these documents to which we were entitled. The documents were heavily redacted, and my attorneys were certain that the state court would compel the defendants to produce unredacted files, as well as other documents necessary to prove that I had been treated disparately and that the policies of UCSB had a disparate impact on Chicanas/os.

The defendants suddenly changed tactics: faced with having to comply with full discovery, Corbett & Kane switched to the federal forum. Unknown to us, the defendants had a pipeline to the new federal judge managing our case. UC counsel David Birnbaum knew Federal Judge Audrey Collins, a recent Clinton appointment and an African American, and had written a solicited letter of recommendation for her when she was appointed to the federal bench.[6] Before we had this information, my attorneys were ecstatic, because most of the federal judges are arch-conservative and white. I, however, had my reservations from the start; Collins, a former Los Angeles deputy district attorney, was also a graduate of the University of California at Los Angeles Law School. Almost certainly she had been a student of Murray Schwartz, a criminal law professor who was acting UCSB vice chancellor and then acting vice president for the system during the early years of the case. By this time I was wary of the UC's power.[7]

Events moved quickly. Judge Collins propelled the case as if the state court had no life. Federal Justice Hupp, Collins's predecessor, knowing that the state court was the logical forum, had offered the defendants the option of staying the federal case; it was obvious that Collins was more "motivated" to try the case herself.

The pace stressed the legal team further. Beth Minsky had other cases, and we had grown over-dependent on her.[8] When she could not stretch herself any further, more and more of the work fell on Moisés Vázquez, who emerged as lead counsel. The review of the personnel files produced in August fell into the cracks of our operation. Simply finding out what we had on hand took about three months. In November the defendants hit us with a motion for summary judgment. We had expected the motion, but we also expected to go to trial in the state court where all of the discovery had taken place. There was a lot of discovery outstanding, and we never imagined that Collins would disregard the history of the case or show utter disrespect for the state court. Robert Racine organized the response to the motion for the summary judgment, which was a major undertaking. Judge Collins then arbitrarily ended discovery in the federal court. She did refer the matter of the heavily redacted files to the magistrate, who found in our favor, and the defendants were ordered to produce unredacted files. We received the last batch of these unredacted

documents on the last days of January 1995. We were in the process of writing a supplement to our response to the summary
judgment motion, submitting twelve additional comparative files,
but less than three weeks later Collins granted a partial summary
judgment.

Collins dismissed our charges of discrimination on the basis
of race and national origin.[9] She acknowledged that we had established a prima facie case as to disparate treatment. Nevertheless,
she dismissed the claim on the ground that we had failed to produce evidence that defendants' reason for denying employment
was a pretext for discrimination. (A jury later found that these
reasons were pretextual.) Incredibly, Collins ruled that the file of
Jeffrey Russell (which we had submitted as evidence of disparate
treatment) could not be used as comparative evidence, on the
ground that the 1981 decision on his promotion was too remote
from 1991. This action was arbitrary because it was within the
boundaries of the discovery dates set by the state court.[10] She also
ruled that we could not use promotion files since my case involved an appointment. My attorneys were livid.

The judge let our ADEA (age discrimination) claim stand, the
only one remaining of the original charges. Earlier, we had lost
our political discrimination, i.e., free speech claim under state law,
because the Center for Constitutional Rights, although warned
repeatedly, exceeded the statute of limitations by two months.
Naturally, we were disappointed. In particular, we had believed
that our race discrimination claim would be the easiest to prove,
after political discrimination. A crisis resulted, and we called a
legal team meeting.

From the beginning, this was a political case. We knew that
affirmative action was under attack and that employment discrimination law would be one of the few vehicles left to protect
the interests of the "other" on university campuses. Should we
appeal the summary judgment? What was the political thing to
do? We decided not to appeal at this time, because the remedies
were the same in the age and race causes of action. There would
always be time to appeal at the end. Next, in federal court we
were not entitled to a jury trial under the race claim, whereas in
an age claim, a jury would be the trier of fact. No one by this time

trusted Collins. The important point at this juncture was to show that the reasons for the denial were pretextual. Lastly, we could not financially afford a delay.

Meanwhile, Superior Court Judge Stevens's health took a turn for the worse. His cases were distributed among the other judges, and our case was transferred to Judge James Slater, known as "Slater the deflator" because he let the air out of the tires of a vehicle belonging to a disabled person who parked in his reserved parking space. The scandal of deflating tires would eventually lead to Slater's retirement. Vázquez had always gotten along with Slater, but I was hesitant about the change. Vázquez and others still had the illusion that because Slater was liberal, he was somehow fairer. The judge had been a Santa Barbara county supervisor, representing the district which included UCSB. From my perspective, this surely meant that he had ties to UCSB, which is the largest employer in Santa Barbara County. I grew more uncomfortable as time went by, especially when I saw him wave to one of the defendants in court.

Collins scheduled a court date. Slater did the politically expedient thing and stayed the state trial, which we were pushing to take place before the federal trial. From the beginning we wanted a state trial. The remedies and burden of proof were more flexible in state court. In a federal trial the plaintiff must get a unanimous jury verdict of 6-0, whereas in a state trial, a 9-3 verdict is sufficient to win. Moreover, only our age claim would be heard by the jury in federal court.

The power of the UC goes well beyond money. Its network of alumni and legislators is formidable. Even public interest firms which are supposed to be fighting for minority rights are beholden in indirect ways, for example, when the UC picks up blocs of tickets at $250 apiece for fundraising banquets for Latino civil rights advocates. Business ties are cemented at alumni affairs, where the objective is to create a network of "family" support. The *Los Angeles Times*, the state's most powerful newspaper, has close ties to the chancellor of UCLA. Once I filed a suit against the UC, I was all but blackballed from the editorial pages of the *Times*. I first attributed the censorship to the bias of an editor, but when the discovery documents showed a memo from Marilyn Lee to a

UCSB administrator congratulating him on how the institution was handling the publicity in my case, I grew suspicious. Lee is a vice president of the *Times*, a former chair of the UCSB Alumni Association, and a former Alumni Regent. Also, a goodly number of the law clerks in the state and federal courts come out of UCLA, an advantage that became very evident in Collins's court.

Technically, the courts are supposed to control litigation and prevent the parties from abusing the process by making frivolous motions or confusing issues of law. Collins never made any attempt to control Corbett & Kane. In fact, she abetted their behavior. She did everything in her power to give the advantage to the defendants. She ordered us to purge every document that had any mention of politics, race, or gender, and ordered us not even to utter those words in court. She then restricted each side to twenty hours to present opening and closing arguments as well as our case in chief, although we had the burden of proof. She narrowed us to one hundred documents in all. Finally, she limited the number of witnesses that we could present, and allowed only one of the outside reviewers to testify as to the meaning of his or her letter, although all of the outside letters were admitted into evidence. This denied us the opportunity to rebut defendants' misrepresentations of what the review letters said.

I spent most of my sabbatical leave in Moisés Vázquez's Whittier, California, office. By this time Beth Minsky was extremely busy on other cases. Logistically, it was impossible to coordinate a case of this magnitude out of Washington, D.C., where she was based, and we were in danger of losing the case on grounds of failure to prosecute it. Secondly, we did not have the funds to fly her out. An additional burden fell on Vázquez, the lead attorney. The case severely strained his resources, and it is fair to say that there would have been no case without him. Also very involved was Jesús Cruz, a paralegal, working out of Vázquez's office. Much of the work on the case was done between 9:00 P.M. and 4:00 A.M., since Vázquez had other cases and trial appearances.

Over the summer of 1995 we continuously reduced the list of documents offered into evidence. At the same time, the defendants, with the court's collusion, tried to break our backs with frivolous motions *in limine* (motions to exclude evidence). They challenged documents which clearly reflected on the credibility of the defendants and their witnesses, and Collins rubber-stamped their motions. As mentioned, Collins would not let us use any comparable files if they did not concern appointments, and she moved the cut-off date to 1985. Essentially, we were not allowed to use 95 percent of the files produced in discovery.

During jury selection, Collins refused to exclude persons challenged by plaintiff for cause, including the husband of the faculty advisor to the UCSB student newspaper, the *Nexus*, until he admitted at a side bar that he would be biased. Another juror was dismissed essentially because he had a Spanish surname. The judge blatantly used her discretionary powers in favor of the Regents in regard to the jury instructions, which were weighted to make a guilty verdict nearly impossible; for example, she instructed the jury that for conviction, age must be *the* determining factor among others rather than *a* determining factor. In her jury instructions Collins also denied liquidated damages, despite case law precedent to the contrary. Finally, Collins intentionally made it difficult to get the unanimous verdict which was necessary to win. Collins stated that we needed six jurors (with two alternates). Then Collins, without informing the plaintiff, impaneled all eight jurors. The effect was to slant the unanimous jury from six to eight, making it considerably more difficult for the plaintiff to prevail.

Collins initially denied the plaintiff the right to submit *Occupied America* as three separate books, solely on the representations of defendants' counsel Ian Fellerman. Only after two weeks into the trial were these three books allowed into evidence. This was offset by more latitude for the defendants and wholesale elimination of other evidence. The judge denied the plaintiff the right to offer in evidence written works of Robert Kelley which made racist and anti-Mexican statements, although these works undermined his credibility as an "objective expert."[11] Collins also denied me the right to submit a manuscript of *Anything But Mexican: Chicanos in Contemporary Los Angeles* (Verso, 1996) into evidence, although I had mentioned the book on my vita and I had been forced by the defendants to produce the rough draft in dis-

covery. Through the course of the trial, Collins failed to sanction
or admonish defense counsel even when, as the facts show, they
clearly misled the court or were wrong about factual issues.

Spectators filled the court room, which made Collins nervous.
At one point, Collins threatened to clear the largely Chicano/
Latino audience from the court. She removed several spectators
for wearing "Justice for Janitors" tee-shirts, which she allegedly
thought read: "Justice for All." Throughout the court proceed-
ings, Collins treated our Latino supporters with disrespect, while
allowing *ex parte* communication between her clerks and the defendants. Her attitude was so antagonistic that observers attributed it to an anti-Mexican bias.[12]

Three faculty members of the Chicano Studies department
had abstained in the department vote on my application. These
three, Denise Segura, Rosalinda Fregoso, and Francisco Lomeli,
testified for the defendants.[13] As it turned out, their testimony
hurt the defendants more than it did us. Fregoso was inarticulate,
and Segura was caught in contradictions. Segura, to whom the
administration had given an administrative and unadvertised in-
ternship after the case began, was asked by Vázquez whether she
had received $30,000 for research support from the University.
She answered that she didn't remember. Next, Vázquez questioned Segura's academic credentials, asking her whether she had
based her dissertation on interviews of twenty women; she responded that it was forty. He asked if the interviews were in
Spanish, to which she responded affirmatively. Vázquez then
asked her how she could have conducted the interviews, since she
did not speak Spanish. This exchange was personally distasteful
to me, and I had done everything possible not to criticize Chi-
cana/o professors at UCSB,[14] to the point of admonishing supporters who did. However, sides were now drawn.[15]

Moisés Vázquez's closing remarks to the jury were masterful.
It was a hard-hitting critique of the case. The essence of the sum-
mation was that the defendants' case was based on four pretexts:
excuses equal pretexts; pretexts equal lies. Of the four lies, the first
was the defendants' claim that I was not qualified to teach in the
University of California system. Vázquez laid out the case: the defendants conceded that I was qualified in three of the four areas of

review: teaching, professional, and university and community service. Three of the top Chicana/o scholars in the field testified that
I was more than qualified. Associate Vice Chancellor Zelmanowitz conceded that I had three scholarly books (my count was five,
with two foreign editions and three popular books). Secondly, the
defendants claimed that that since I had never supervised Ph.D.
students, I thus did not meet the criterion for employment. This
was false: UCSB did not have a Ph.D. program in Chicano studies,
and as of October 1995, no proposal had even been submitted. In
contrast, I was the founding chair of the Chicana/o Studies Department at California State University, Northridge, which was
the largest Chicano studies program in the nation, offering bachelor of arts and master of arts degrees. UCSB did not even have a
master of arts program, and its premier Chicana/o professor had
only one Ph.D. student in twenty years. Vázquez highlighted the
opposing testimony of Dr. Ramón Ruiz. The third lie was that the
abstentions mattered. The truth was that reviewing agencies were
comprised of full professors who didn't care much about what
junior professors thought, and only paid attention to them because it fit their interests. The administration abetted the departmental dissension. Fourthly, the defendants claimed they did not
take age into consideration. Vázquez ran through the wording of
the reports. He mocked the argument of the defendants that they
could not have discriminated on the basis of age, since many of
them were above fifty.

When the jury entered with the verdict, marshals swarmed
into the courtroom. One of them told me that Collins had ordered
them there, because she feared a disruption if and when an
unpopular verdict was reached. Collins added to the tension by
allowing a shackled Mexican-American prisoner to be brought
in while the verdict was being delivered. The judgment caught
Collins and her clerks, as well as the defendants, off guard. Clerks
and defendants groaned when the verdict was read; Collins sat in
shock, and did not admonish them for this behavior.

The jury was a working-class panel. There were four Latinos,
one Filipino, one African American, an elderly white woman, and
a mixed Asian-white male. They listened attentively throughout
the trial, taking copious notes. In the course of the trial, defense

attorney Keyes made every attempt to cultivate the jury members. In the end, the jury found the defendants guilty of age discrimination. The defense had began its excuses early, complaining that four of the jurors were Latinos and inferring that they could not be objective. Once they actually lost the case, they complained that many of the jurors were more than fifty years old and thus biased. In a report to the Regents, they said that none of the jurors had a college education and most barely had a high school education, so they could not understand the abstract issues of the case. Our experience is that working-class juries in general are more apt to look at the facts and look for justice. They do not accept authority blindly, which was the opposite of what the defendants' counsel expected. They are also more apt to have experienced discrimination and injustice in one form or another.

From the beginning, my attorneys and civil rights supporters had said that if we got the case before any jury, we would win, since working-class jurors judge circumstances through a different vantage point than professionals. They perceive that the system must work for all. Fairness weighs on their minds. They assume there are injustices, and that it is the role of the court system to correct injustices. Their experiences teach them that life is not always fair, and that it does not always work in their interest. The presumption of fairness is greater among white middle-class professionals, for many reasons, although this presumption is breaking down.

Following the trial, and hidden from public scrutiny, Collins denied the plaintiff procedural due process rights by not holding an open court hearing on the instatement issue (the issue of the preferred remedy, namely, getting the job). Defendants and other UCSB employees submitted declarations that were libelous. The judge refused to allow us to cross-examine the declarants, as well as hearing oral arguments on any of the post-trial motions. The court had *ex parte* communication with defendants.[16] Collins allowed inflammatory statements to be made by Giles Gunn, who claimed that Mexicans in Santa Barbara were calling over the radio for retaliation against anyone who voted against Acuña. She allowed unsubstantiated declarations by Ray Huerta and Francisco Lomeli that they would be afraid for their lives if I were given the job at UCSB. Associate Vice Chancellor Zelmanowitz swore that I knew what his car looked like, that he had found tacks near the tires of his car, and that I or my supporters must have put them there in order to flatten his tires. This character assassination was orchestrated by Corbett & Kane, who have used similar tactics against plaintiffs in other cases.

All in all, however, the trial verdict represented a tremendous victory for our attorneys and for the Chicano/Latino community. The enormity of the victory will become clearer in the years to come, despite the efforts of the judge to tilt the scales of justice in favor of the UC.

Some nine months after the trial, Collins once more showed her bias by reducing our attorney fees by 80 percent. In a civil rights case, the losing party pays the prevailing party's attorney fees and costs. Even though the UC paid $2.5 million to Corbett & Kane alone as of December 1996, the judge found that my counsel was entitled to only $500,000 for attorney fees. Presently this decision is being appealed.[17] Collins has dramatically sent the message that attorneys can defend these types of cases, but "don't expect to get paid for your time."

Cultural Compatibility

The defendants' case was based on a classic neoliberal model. The rationale behind their case was that I was evaluated by a time-tested process, designed to be objective and to seek the truth about my credentials to teach at the University of California, and that after a fair and objective review they found me to be unqualified. While I met three of the four criteria for a distinguished professor at the University of California, the reviewers alleged that I was deficient in research because the works that I produced were popular items and not scholarly. Indeed, they went so far as to allege that I did not use archival sources in my research. A stream of administrators and faculty flaunting their credentials laid the foundation for the credibility of the defense's narrative. The message was that Acuña was good at organizing marches, but that this was the august University of California. The strategy was to convince middle-class white male jurors who had been conditioned by the American paradigm, and they prepared their strategy to conform to this model.

In contrast, our strategy was simple. We had to penetrate the neoliberal rationality, and show that the university reviewers were not experts in the field of Chicana/o studies, that they were not objective, and that they treated me unfairly. We put Acuña into evidence. The assumption in the defendants' strategy was that the jurors would not find me as impressive as their witnesses. So I had to put on a demonstration. I did what I have been doing very effectively for forty years—I lectured to the jury. The narrative was that I taught in the public schools, received my Ph.D. at night, worked in community organizations for forty years, helped organize the first Latino headstart program in the United States, was the founding chair of the largest ethnic studies program in the U.S., conceived a teacher training program that produced some two hundred Latino teachers, wrote ten books, close to a hundred op-ed pieces, more than fifty book reviews, and had been a reviewer for major academic presses and journals. In recognition of these achievements, I had received awards from NACS (National Association for Chicano Studies) as their distinguished scholar and other national and international prizes.

We offered the testimonies of three of the most distinguished scholars in the field of Chicana/o studies, which helped us immeasurably. The first was Dr. Ramón Ruiz, a founding chair of the history department at the University of California at San Diego. He countered the UC's argument that I never taught Ph.D. students, and that this was an essential requirement for the position. Dr. Ruiz testified that he hadn't taught Ph.D. students before joining UCSD, but since then had trained more than a hundred. Dr. Ruiz cast doubt on the credibility of Kelley's version on who was at fault for the Mexican-American War. The next witness was Dr. Carlos Vélez-Ibáñez, dean of humanities at UC Riverside, who testified that in his opinion, I was one of the top experts in the field and I qualified as a distinguished professor. At Northridge we had one of the few Chicana/o studies graduate programs in the U.S., and I was a moving force in its development. The third witness was Dr. Raymond Padilla, professor of education at Arizona State University, who testified as to the unfairness of the process. Our appeal was not to some positivist claim to legitimacy but to the basic issue of fairness. And this was easier to "sell" to a working-class jury than to a jury of "professionals."

In retrospect, I often wonder why the UC reviewers who evaluated my candidacy were so emotional. There is no doubt from their language that they went beyond the scope of a normal academic review.[18] I also readily admit that once the controversy began, I contributed to some of the antagonism. My actions were justified. In order to gain support, I had to go to my support. I had to go public in my criticisms of what had happened at UCSB. This was my constitutional right. The criticism stung the "imperial scholars," and it became a personal crusade to the defendants: keep me out at any cost.

My own background was not unique. My father was a tailor; he was Mexican and barely finished the sixth grade. My mother was legally blind and never finished the first grade. I attended a Jesuit Prep School, after which I volunteered for the military draft, was inducted into the army, married young, and had two sons. I worked sixty hours a week, carried eighteen units, and received a B.A. and M.A. from a state college. While teaching at a high school and then a community college, I attended a non-prestigious evening Ph.D. program in Latin American studies at the University of Southern California. Throughout this period, I volunteered in community activities, ranging from establishing a volunteer preschool to registering voters. Naturally, I was against the Vietnam War. The 1960s formed much of my political perspective, but not all. My preference was much more applied than it was ideological. As I have mentioned, I carried this attitude into my curricular work in Chicana/o studies, as well as my research.

My fundamental approach in establishing Chicana/o studies was that students have a right to fail, that Chicana/o and Latina/o students have the right to attend college, and that their success or failure is partially determined by how much we motivate them. A population has to be seeded, and in the case of most immigrant groups, success does not come in the first generation. I expected a large dropout rate, but I also expected a substantial success rate. Indeed, many of our students have become medical doctors, lawyers, teachers, and even Washington bureaucrats.

Presently, the daughters and sons of both the successes and the dropouts are attending CSUN. These students come up to me and tell me, for instance, "My mother attended CSUN in 1970, do you remember her?" I always say, surely. These students, for the most part, will succeed, as will a whole network of family relations who will follow their example.[19]

My experiences have imbued my writing with a sense of impatience with what I consider stupidity. Ramón Ruiz told me once, "I just reread *Occupied America*, and I agree with everything you say, but couldn't you say it in another way? The way that you say things is what gets you in trouble." I agreed, but the way I say things should not take away from the validity of what I am saying, nor should it excuse the bias of the defendant reviewers. This writing style in itself is part of the challenge to the American paradigm, even though it brands me as a bad citizen.

Lastly, because I made a full professor at thirty-five in Chicana/o studies, I had a sense of freedom not normal to others in my profession. I was able to experiment. I was above the peer group process and at the forefront of the field itself. *Occupied America* was a challenge to the existing paradigm, and it didn't matter what the so-called scientific community said. Interestingly, the Chicana/o studies curriculum I developed was and is fairly traditional in form, as is most of my research.

What role did my incompatibility with academe and the American paradigm play in the review process? Probably quite a lot.

Being a Good Citizen

In order for the American paradigm to shift, a critical mass of scholars would have to accept the premise that the American paradigm is wrong and agree to change it. In all probability, this will not happen. During my suit, I read through the infamous personnel review files, and one phrase sticks in my mind. Reviewers kept on referring to candidates that they liked as a "good citizen," in a way very reminiscent of my daughter's middle-school report card. "Good citizenship" refers to deportment, which generally means conformity. I found a pattern in the files: good citizenship was the overriding factor in promotions, especially in the case of marginal candidates and minorities. Indeed, throughout the litigation of my case, Associate Vice Chancellor Zelmanowitz made the point that new appointees were not judged by the same standards as promotions—merit did not have the same meaning—although the academic personnel manual did not distinguish between the two. In the case of internal candidates for promotion, being a "good citizen" was a determining factor.

The candidate's deportment thus plays a central part in the review. This reality forms part of the consciousness of the scholar. And it is safe to say generally that a minority scholar would have to take the views of critics such as Arthur Schlesinger Jr. into serious consideration, before the candidate advocated multiculturalism. For Chicana/o scholars, the choice is often whether to abide by the interests of the academic or the Latino community. The choice is political and it has nothing to do with scholarship. The outcome is determined by the paradigm adopted by the scholar as much as it involves bonding with either community. This normative commitment is influenced by the degree to which social control and authority are operative in each of these communities. In the case of Chicana/o scholars, there is a strong predisposition toward following the rules of academe—being "good citizens." Throughout their education, from kindergarten through the doctorate, they are conditioned to follow rules and incorporate the biases of the system. They are motivated by a fear of social disapproval along with the professional commitment to excellence as defined by the institution.

Conformity with the academy is consistently rewarded. In contrast, the influence of the minority community is diluted. The rewards and punishments available to the community are limited. Family members take pride in the individual successes of relatives who are educated and make few demands on them. Minority scholars are only left with a historical memory of what "good citizenship" means within that universe. In the case of the African American community, ostracization means a great deal more than in the Latino community. African Americans have more intricate networks interrelating black scholars. In the case of Chicana/o professors, elitism develops, and it often seems to them that their only duty is to be a good professional—a good citizen.

The choice of the kind of research for the Chicana/o scholar is a social act, which is often at odds with the interests of traditional scholars. The ability of the Chicana/o scholar to resist the social control or peer group pressure of these scholars and of the institution over his or her research determines his or her moral authority in the community. Yet the Latino community does not have the moral authority to protect its interests within academe. It is almost impossible for the lone Chicana/o scholar within a universe of white male scholars to have any moral authority or to affect a quantitative or qualitative shift. He or she is thus easily controlled.[20]

The scholar's judgments are often driven by his or her socioeconomic interests. It is easy to rationalize that you have to get tenure or promotion in order to be independent. The scholar incorporates the culture of the institution and is not conscious that he or she is making choices within the narrow confines of the prevailing paradigm. In the case of the Mexican Americans who testified in court, they made a choice. In the end, these scholars, some of whom were once shouting *Víva la Raza*, said whatever the university wanted them to say, even to the point of denying the presence of systematic racism in the reviews of Chicanos at UCSB—something that they had admitted to me outside the courtroom. For them too, the issue of compatibility with academe and the American paradigm was critical.[21]

A court order prevents me from referring to the files of individual Chicanas and Chicanos to illustrate my points. Ironically, even though they have been "good citizens," white reviewers don't hold them in the highest esteem. These files are, however, part of that knowledge that I have engraved into my historical consciousness and that of my attorneys. From what I read in these files and from a review of the careers of many of the scholars who cooperated with the administration, I would say that my case was a boon to their careers. By testifying for the UC, they proved once and for all that they were "good citizens."

I walked away from the trial with a great deal of skepticism. The power of seduction cannot be underestimated.

Peer Group Review: The Myth of Fairness

At present, right and wrong in higher education are determined by those who control the review process on the various campuses. They are the sovereigns. They resolve questions of choice. They determine whether there is sufficient evidence to prove that minorities and women are treated equally; they determine whether a written work is scholarly or not scholarly. Since they define what "meritorious" means, it is almost impossible to prove that the vast majority of the professors at research universities are either mediocre teachers or mediocre researchers.

The stamp of approval of the reviewing body is extremely important because association with a research institution gives the candidate authority within his or her field, regardless of whether the reviewers had the expertise to evaluate the scholar. The reviewing agency receives license to judge even those in other fields. Within an institution, these bishops also have the authority to anoint themselves as most distinguished in the world in terms of research productivity, even if they are actually mediocre. Needless to say, they are also likely to spend little time and energy on teaching, particularly of undergraduates.

The basic tenet upon which the peer group review is based is the myth of a meritocracy. The labels "liberal" and "conservative" mean little. The faculty and administrators of both stripes[22] see themselves as meritorious, and they act the part. Yet in reviewing the files of professors at the Professor V and VI level at UCSB, I did not find a single Nobel prize laureate among them. As far as I could determine, less than 5 percent ranked as world-renowned or had international reputations. The reality is that the definition of merit is determined by the particular body of reviewers and applied particularly, not universally. The concept of merit is arbitrarily applied to the admission of students, the hiring and promotion of faculty, and the allocation of other forms of reward and recognition in higher education.

In my study of the personnel files, for example, I found Euro-American candidates, some with no teaching experience, others with student complaints of sexual harassment, who nevertheless were appointed or promoted because of merit, defined narrowly in their cases as so-called excellence in research. In my case a great deal was made by the reviewing committees of the fact that the departmental vote was three for and three abstentions. In the case of another recent appointment, sixteen voted for the scholar and twelve against him, with eleven other faculty members abstaining. The reviewing agencies took scant notice of this split vote. The review process is flawed with inconsistencies at every level, from candidate to candidate.

This review is subtle: the process of peer-reviewed publications and peer-reviewed assessments of quality of scholarship actively works against opportunities for "outsiders" to become "insiders" and allows the system to weed out nonbelievers.[23] Racial, class, and gender differences affect how people see the world. The fact that those who control academe are white and male makes a difference. Moreover, most reviewers lack competency to review minority scholars, not because they are white, but because they do not permit themselves to work outside their deductive mode. This lack of expertise turns into ignorance in times of stress. Patterns of budgetary change simply expose the patterns of faculty biases. The expansion of the research university has slowed down markedly in the 1990s. With the competition among mainstream scholars intensified, the consequences for members of minority groups are devastating. The insiders have clamped down on ethnic studies and the hiring of scholars of color in their own departments. Faculty governance thus becomes an excuse for the absence of change.

During my thirty years in academe, I have found that faculty place a strong value on faculty governance. Departmental autonomy in hiring, for instance, is looked upon as a right. For years, Chicanos and other minorities have believed the myth that the majority of faculty members are liberal and fair-minded. However, we must ask the question: if faculty members are so liberal and believe so much in the equality of the races, why hasn't the ratio of minority hires increased during the growth periods?[24] Mainstream scholars are in control. Their decisions have a cumulative effect on society. They are able to ignore population shifts, even though these shifts impact the formation of public policy designed to bring about solutions. In judging Chicana/o and other ethnic studies to be less worthy than the "core" areas of knowledge, academe sends the message that the people are not as important.

A typical review of work by Chicana/o scholars or of the Chicana/o studies curriculum by mainstream scholars is guided by untested assumptions. When a course in science, business, or engineering is reviewed by the university-wide curriculum committee, there is scant discussion. The presentation is made and the vote is taken. There is more debate when a course is submitted by the humanities or by education. However, when the ethnic studies departments submit a course, everyone becomes an expert, even an engineer.

The USCB academic files show that the review of other Chicana/o scholars was often much more insidious than in my own case. Typically, the reviewers know nothing about the fund of knowledge in Chicana/o studies. The first line of attack is by scholars in related fields, on grounds of methodology. The rule is that not all social science theory is equal: mine is better. The second line of attack questions the adherence of the Chicana/o scholar to the eighth-grade level of assumptions of the American paradigm. If the scholar's research challenges this paradigm, the reviewers go on the offense. It is extremely difficult to prove ground-breaking ideas, and to collect sufficient evidence to challenge and reverse an accepted hypothesis. Proving a new paradigm often takes a lifetime of research. The review process thus works against any paradigm shift. The bottom line is that the review committee controls the definition of accepted truth and consequently is sovereign. It sets standards and practices in establishing "truth."

The university community defends its definitions, and it corrupts language. An example is compliance with affirmative action guidelines in hiring faculties. Categories such as "underrepresented" and "underutilized" are used to gauge whether the university discriminated in the hiring process. If Chicanos are 27 percent of the population in California, logically one would expect around 27 percent of the faculty in a given department to be Chicanos—if education and opportunity were historically equal. If a department did not meet that requirement, Chicanos would clearly be underrepresented. However, universities have decided to use another standard, calculating instead whether the university or department is underutilizing or overutilizing minorities, through a sort of invisible reverse quota system. The standard is based on the percentage of Chicanos in a given discipline nationally. If Chicanos make up 2 percent of the historians "nationally," and a department has more than 2 percent Chicanos, they are overutilized; if it has less, they are underutilized and the university is in noncompliance. A department with no Chicana/o professors might not be underutilizing them, if the percentage in the national field were insignificant, and a department that overutilized them, by the same measure, could use that "fact" as a reason not to hire another.[25] The hypocrisy of this illogical discourse is that the faculty come to believe they are not discriminating, because they are in compliance. This is yet another example of avoidance.

Most faculty communities are not open to free inquiry and free speech. They are not skeptical about their own meritocracy. The arrogance of the faculty communities makes it impossible for them to admit that they have violated basic principles of fairness. Fundamentally, reviewing others is not a matter of scholarship. It is the exercise of power over others. Meritocracy, objectivity, and rationality rest on control of the university; it is simply another form of political power and social coercion.

In Conclusion

My case against the University of California was about politics, from the first review through the appeal process. Judge Collins made this clear after the summary judgment, when she took all of the obviously political issues away from us, and said that she was more in tune with the defendants' reasoning than with ours. The judge's compatibility played into the defendants' strategy.

One lesson learned from this case is that academe will use every means possible to defend faculty governance as its bastion of fairness, and will defend it as essential to maintaining and preserving merit in the university even when it is racist to the core. Indeed, the invention of the myth that faculty peer group reviews at research institutions are rigorous, as well as objective, is part of the narrative that justified less teaching and higher and higher wages. It is a system that rewards faculty and administrators. It allows administrators to be paid salaries and pensions that are often in excess of private industry, where a more vigorous level of production is required. It pays faculty well and often keeps them in subsidized housing, enjoying a standard of living way beyond the means of persons with similar salaries. The University of California system justifies the fact that its professors do not pay toward their pension funds, unlike state university professors, based on so-called merit. It insulates itself from the marketplace.

My lawsuit is a suit that never should have happened. First, the UC could have aborted the case very easily because of its own procedural errors. If anyone had told me that I was incompatible with UC at the outset, I would have walked away from the position. Even afterwards, I would have walked away from the situation given an apology, a handshake, a gesture of reparation. But these things did not happen because of the arrogance of the reviewers and the system, which had to prove that the UC was right.

The lawsuit cost the taxpayers of the state of California heavily. It also exposed a pattern of conduct on the part of the UC. Instead of making an effort to settle cases, they dare the grievant to sue. The fact is that most suits never reach the trial level. Indeed, few suits are ever filed because the UC, like a good poker player, raises the stakes beyond the financial ability of the aggrieved party. Justice has a hefty price tag.

From the beginning, I said that the case went well beyond the cause of one individual. It was a community effort and the outcome had to be collectivized. So my wife, Lupita, and I took the money awarded to us for lost pay, and set up a foundation to fight employment discrimination cases, representing Chicana/o and Latina/o professors in higher education (largely in California, for the time being). To this end, the F.O.R. Acuña Committee has become the F.O.R. Chicana/o Studies Foundation. Another result of the case was that a core of politically conscious attorneys is now more conversant in employment discrimination. They have internalized the knowledge and know far more about the

University of California, faculty culture, and Chicana/o studies than they did before this case started. Moisés Vázquez, for example, is a national authority in the field. He and the other attorneys know what it is to win against the octopus. They have demythicized the power of the UC and proved that it can be beaten.

The Foundation recently committed itself to support the case of Dr. Yolanda Broyles-González against the University of California at Santa Barbara. The UC discriminated against her on the basis of gender, denying her promotions and compensation equal to that of male professors. The administration also retaliated against her because she supported me in my case against the university. Further, she was one of the only Chicana/o professors at UCSB to unconditionally support the student hunger strike. Unlike many of her Chicana/o colleagues, who have been compensated by the university with administrative internships, directorships of centers, research and release time, and other perks because they were "good citizens," she has championed the right of self-determination for Chicana/o scholars. Her case has been settled. The Foundation has at present approved funds for another suit against the University of California, if the candidate decides to seek legal redress. Thus, the fight for the truth goes on.

Appendix

The letters of the ad hoc committee and of the Committee on Academic Personnel in my case are typical of university reviews of minority scholars, not only at the University of California but at other institutions of higher learning. For this reason I include them here. Considered as the original documents of the historian, they display the prejudice and "philosophical" flaws with which I am concerned throughout this book. They expose the non-scholarly and biased nature of the review. In this, the University of California system is not an exception. It does not have a monopoly on inconsistency, ignorance, or bias.

The ad hoc committee in my case was central to the evaluation process, since other committees and administrators deferred to it. What follows is the final version of the ad hoc letter, which was written by Robert Kelley but toned down by the other members of the committee. It should be noted that the provost's evaluation and the ad hoc committee's letter were supposedly written separately and in parallel, in order to expedite the case. However the provost's report was written in late March, while the final ad hoc report was not written until June 3, 1991. Given the striking similarities in their reports, the gap in time was never accounted for. Close attention should be paid to the discourse within the ad hoc letter, to which I have added notes commenting on inaccuracies and contradictions.

[June 3, 1991 letter of the ad hoc review committee]

TO: CHANCELLOR BARBARA S. UEHLING
FROM: AD HOC REVIEW COMMITTEE
        (Yolanda Broyles, Departmental Representative)[26]
RE: RODOLFO ACUÑA, APPOINTMENT PROFESSOR VI
        CHICANO STUDIES DEPARTMENT

The ad hoc committee, after searching discussions and a close reading of Professor Acuña's file and scholarly publications, has grave reservations and mixed feelings about his proposed appointment. With regret we have arrived at the unanimous conclusion that it would be best for the Department of Chicano Studies if the appointment were not made. If it is concluded by the other reviewing authorities and by yourself that in fact it should be made, we believe unanimously that Professor IV offscale, so as to match his present salary, is all that could be justified. In our view, Professor VI is entirely out of the question.

Summary of Career. Professor Acuña was born in 1932,[27] took his Ph.D in History in 1968 from the University of Southern California, and has been a professor of Chicano Studies at California State University, Northridge since 1969. He founded that department at CSUN, and not only was the moving force in developing it into by far the largest such department in American higher education, he has since been a national force in the creation and shaping of Chicano Studies curricula in many colleges and universities by means of consultantships, lecturing, and membership on panels and conferences (his vita lists probably hundreds of such occasions). He has also had a busy career as a testifier before public bodies,[28] as an organizer of marches and other demonstrations, and as keynote speaker nationally and internationally.

This is, in short, an extraordinarily visible historian. Many awards within his field and from the Chicano community at large have come to him. In 1981 he won a Rockefeller Humanities Fellowship and in 1982 an ACLS research award. Earlier, in 1973 and 1975, he had garnered $500,000 in grants from the Ford Foundation to support "Operation Chicano Teacher" at CSUN, essentially, we are told by letters in his file, the only grant of such large size won at his institution.

In 1986 Professor Acuña opened a broad new sector in his work by becoming the author, since that date, of scores of op-ed columns on Chicano affairs in the *Los Angeles Times*. Whatever the issue affecting the Hispanic community—as in the currently debated national question of whether or not to establish free trade between Mexico and the United States—Rodolfo Acuña will be in the public dialogue with a strongly developed and vigorously argued op-ed piece in the *Times*.[29] As a voice in the public prints and in the broadcast media for his conception of the Chicano cause, he has been a tireless laborer.

His authoring of published scholarship is by no means so impressive, as to quantity[30]—leaving the question of quality until later. There is his powerful (in its impact and tone) textbook/scholarly synthesis *Occupied America: A History of Chicanos* (N.Y., Harper & Row), which first appeared in 1972 and in 1988 came out in its Third Edition (each chapter contains citations to sources). In addition, he has done a book on East Los Angeles, generally taken to be the core community of Chicano America: *Community Under Siege: A Chronicle of Chicanos East of the Los Angeles River, 1945–1975* (Chicano Studies Center, UCLA, 1984). It is not in the usual scholarly format, for it is not footnoted to sources. Rather, after its lengthy narrative it lists as bibliography many pages of articles drawn from two local newspapers.[31] Acuña's doctoral dissertation on a governor of Sonora appeared as a small book in 1974 as *Sonoran Strongman: The Times of Ignacio Pesqueira* (Tucson, University of Arizona Press). The rest of his work consists of a few articles or chapters, and two high-school level books on Mexican Americans.[32]

Discussion. We recognize fully that this is an unusual case, considerably beyond in its uniqueness the level of distinguishing marks which routinely attend any appointment to an advanced full professorial position. The Chair's letter of recommendation states that in spite of "the distinguished records of so many of the applicants one applicant clearly towered above the rest: Professor Rodolfo Acuña." Therefore, by unanimous departmental decision he constituted the full membership of a short list of one person, who was then brought to the Department for the giving of a seminar-presentation. In recognition of Acuña's rare standing in the field, UCLA full professor Juan Gómez-Quiñones[33] writes:

> Professor Rudy Acuna is among the top three senior professors in the field of Chicano Studies nationally. As a program catalyst and

contributor he is among the top two. As a proactive positive faculty influence his is unique.

One of the letters in support of Professor Acuña's appointment characterizes his principal work, *Occupied America*, as a "cult book"—and certainly, as we read in the comments of outside evaluators, it has had an immense impact on the conceptualizing and teaching of Chicano history. So too, we conclude, Acuña himself may with accuracy be termed a "cult professor."[34] *Occupied America*, which appeared just at the time Chicano Studies was emerging as a teaching field and therefore when it was in great need of a core book, lifted Acuña from relative obscurity to a position of almost solitary intellectual leadership in the Chicano movement and community. Accordingly, it must be clearly understood [that] this decision to turn down this nomination, if this is the final outcome, will have wide political repercussions in the Chicano community.

The name Rodolfo Acuña is to his supporters, then, one to conjure with in the Chicano world, in the sense that he is thought of as a master spirit[35] who can achieve remarkable things. This, we learn in the Chair's letter of recommendation, is explicitly what those in the Chicano Studies faculty who support his appointment (only three out of six voting—to this weighty fact we shall return) had in mind, indeed hoped fervently for, when they recommended that Acuña be brought here as a distinguished full professor to work another program-building marvel such as he achieved at California State University, Northridge.[36] Chicano Studies at UCSB has been a troubled, much-divided department since it lost its senior member, Mario García, to Yale, and thus is in need of strong new leadership.[37]

The Chair thinks of this remarkable person, too, as one who could instantly lift the Department's campus standing by becoming its distinguished ambassador to the UCSB faculty as a whole, and to the administration. We can fully sympathize with this sentiment. It is an honorable one, and at bottom line one which in general terms should be encouraged. We have here the spectacle of a department which is willing to bring in someone of an aura and prestige which far overshadows that of anyone else currently on its faculty, and this is extraordinary.[38]

This fact has, indeed, made us pause for a very close look at the proposal. It is not as though this is a long-established and nationally distinguished department of 40+ faculty members which is bringing in simply another senior person. There is no one in Chicano studies who even holds full professorial rank.[39] A person of Professor Acuña's stature and experience would stand so far above the rest of his colleagues that his position could verge on being dictatorial. Certainly he would be the most powerful single voice in all department affairs. His influence would probably be decisive in all future department hiring, and certainly in all internal decisions as to merit increases and promotions of those junior to him—which would be everyone. This would have a potentially dominating influence on the kind of research and writing that would be smiled upon, or rejected as wrong or unacceptable. More than ordinarily, then, the future character of the Department of Chicano Studies will be shaped for years into the future by this one hiring decision.[40]

We must, therefore, adopt the strictest kind of scrutiny, in a case like this.[41] The peer review process, as we understand it, is in a trustee relationship to all departments, seeking, by the exercise of its collective knowledge and wisdom and through the medium of its advice to the Chancellor, to insure that departments do not make serious errors in their faculty appointments, retentions, merit increases or promotions. With this is mind we have had to ask ourselves an inescapable question: would we be fulfilling our trustee responsibilities if we favored Chicano Studies putting itself in such an unusual position with this particular scholar?[42] We note, as an added factor, that he would be the first in that department not to have a joint appointment, involving periodic peer review in an established discipline and department, since he would be full-time in Chicano Studies.[43]

There is another crucial consideration to be borne in mind: Professor Acuña would arrive with only half of the department faculty having voted for him. The abstention of the other three professors voting is a most serious matter. Would a very senior person coming to a department with that precarious support be able, in a faculty so seriously divided against itself, to give it effective leadership, or would he inevitably create more divisiveness?[44]

Scholarship. These considerations forced us, therefore, to give very close attention to the central question: is the quality of Professor Acuña's rather thin scholarship such that he merits not only a senior full professorship, but in effect overwhelming priority of standing and influence in a small divided department? Does it in fact override, in its compelling quality, the reality that Professor Acuña has never trained doctoral students, would be arriving at UCSB at age 59,[45] and would necessarily have to spend much of his remaining time on the active faculty learning how to carry out this most difficult and demanding of all instructional tasks, the teaching of students at the Ph.D. level?[46] (Either through Chicano Studies, if that is possible, or, as others in that faculty have done, through other departments.)

All of us, in the ad hoc committee, finished reading the Chair's recommending letter feeling favorably disposed toward this appointment.

All of us, having read Professor Acuña's work, finished that task feeling strongly that he is an inveterate polemicist and pamphleteer who ignores the rules of evidence, fills his work with angry pronouncements on a wide array of subjects, and flagrantly, openly, and apparently on purpose shapes his analyses and narrative to serve a political purpose.[47]

From the opening pages of his book to its conclusion, Professor Acuña has many enemies to flog in *Occupied America*. Throughout, his scholarship is entirely overshadowed by his polemics. The book has a political agenda, and in service of that agenda it twists facts out of context, alleges other facts not so, preaches again and again a particular, and in the present scholarly scene seriously outdated, interpretive line. The Chair of the department herself, while present with the ad hoc committee, agreed that many younger scholars would think him obsolete in his emphases, arguments, and concerns.[48] The field he works in is now much more sophisticated, thoughtful, and scholarly, as may be seen, for example, in the splendid work of people like Mario García. The field concerns itself with subjects that *Occupied America* simply glosses over or ignores.

In the one book, then, upon which his whole case as scholar essentially rests, Professor Acuña has produced an angry special-pleading, moralizing work entirely lacking in a distanced, critical stance toward his subject.[49] As he specifically characterizes it, it is a "counter-hegemonic" book; its purpose, he writes, "is to dispel the myths that are manufactured by scholars who take refuge in patriotism."[50] The Chair, in her time with the ad hoc committee, said that what Professor Acuña writes is "solid, traditional" history, but though this "counter-hegemonic" book is entirely laudable in purpose within some of the major provinces of the published word, where requirements as to tone and approach and method are in operation, it hardly qualifies as solid, traditional history. We regret to say that he appears to be quite indifferent to what for generations have been taught as the core qualities requisite in all scholarly research and writing: judicious, thoughtful reflection on the evidence, and sincere efforts to ward off those impulses toward bias which can never, of course, be entirely expunged.[51]

We believe it would be most valuable for Chicano Studies to appoint a senior scholar of strong standing in the field, but the present candidate lacks the kind of reflective, theoretically sophisticated mind that every department needs in its older members to serve as models.[52] This is especially true in a field as yet so inchoate and lacking in firm intellectual identity as Chicano Studies. Throughout *Occupied America*, Professor Acuña is on a soapbox, ranting.[53] Questioning the value of the dominant majority culture is a most credible and venerable scholarly task, but to do it well calls for judicious scholarship, rather than simple name-calling. Questioning one's own certitudes is an essential part of this process.

We believe that placing a historian with Professor Acuña's definition of what constitutes scholarship in a predominant position, far beyond that of any of his colleagues, in such a department, would be an error. The example of his work for future graduate students in Chicano Studies disciplines, to take but one aspect of this situation, would be deplorable. This appointment to a full professorship in the University of California would be saying that doing his kind of scholarship is just fine. We cannot agree that this is so. Nothing in this record, therefore, inclines us to believe that Professor Acuña is scholarly equipped to give the kind of leadership to Chicano Studies at UCSB which his senior rank and cult status would automatically place in his hands.[54]

Wallace Chafe   Giles Gunn
Robert Kelley, Chair

* * *

The Committee on Academic Personnel, although it technically controls the case, does not make its determination until after it receives the provost's and ad hoc committee's report. The first draft of the CAP report was written by committee member Phillip Hammond, who was appointed to shepherd my file. The following is the final CAP letter of June 13. The influences of the ad hoc and provost reviews are evident; note too, the almost complete dismissal of the strong supporting letters of the Department of Chicano Studies and the many outside reviewers.

[June 13, 1991 letter of the Committee on Academic Personnel]

Academic Senate
Santa Barbara Division
June 13, 1991

Name: ACUÑA, RODOLFO   Department: CHICANO STUDIES
Proposed Rank and Step: PROFESSOR VI
Salary: $78,300   Effective Date: JULY 1, 1991

Department Recommendation: The Department of Chicano Studies recommends the appointment of Rodolfo Acuña as Professor VI, effective July 1, 1991.

Provost/Dean Recommendation: Provost Sprecher recommends that the appointment be denied.

Review Committee Recommendation: The ad hoc review committee (R. Kelley, Chair; G. Gunn; W. Chafe) recommends against the appointment; Y. Broyles served as Departmental Consultant to the Committee.

****

The Department of Chicano Studies recommends the appointment of Rodolfo Acuña to Professor VI. The vote was 3-0-3, with all ladder faculty in residence voting. (Two more were on leave.) The Chair, in a separate letter, explains the split vote in terms of a long tradition of dissension in the department and views the lack of any negative votes as significant.[55] She also states that the faculty voted unanimously to "single him out as a short list of one." Nonetheless, we observe that out of 8 potential voters, Acuña received only 3 positive votes. *The Provost, in a careful analysis, recommends denial, largely on the grounds that Acuña's scholarship is "marginal," "thin", and more political*[56] *and passionate than objective and substantive* [italics added]. The ad hoc committee (consisting of Robert Kelley, Chair, Wallace Chafe, and Giles Gunn) likewise recommends unanimously that the appointment be denied. Their analysis is a good deal more detailed than the Provost's, though similar in outline.

The ad hoc committee's report notes first that Acuña's undeniable national reputation arises from his entrepreneurship and polemical involvement, a statement confirmed by the outside letters, which dwell more on the candidate's dedication to Chicano Studies than to his scholarship. While conceding this point, the ad hoc committee then warns that Acuña's most noteworthy scholarly work (*Occupied America*, first published in 1972 and now in a third edition) is a "cult book" and Acuña a "cult professor." One major research project is mentioned as being "under way," but it has been so for 17 years.

Next is pointed out that Acuña, if appointed, would be much higher in rank (and therefore in power, visibility, etc.) than any of his Departmental colleagues. Moreover, he would be the only member who is not jointly appointed. Noting that one-half of the voting members abstained, the report suggests that a dictatorial, tyrannical situation might be created.

Yet another drawback is found in the fact that Acuña, at age 59, has never trained doctoral students.

Ad hoc committee members state that, though favorably disposed after reading the Department's letter, they switched their sentiments after reading Acuña's work, "feeling strongly that he is an inveterate polemicist and pamphleteer who ignores rules of evidence . . . to serve a political purpose." Believing that such a person might be insulated in a large, established Department, the ad hoc committee states that in a field "as yet so inchoate" as Chicano Studies, that kind of appointment would be an error, and one difficult if not impossible to correct. Better scholars might well be lost to the Department and the University. Further, Acuña's unsophisticated "activist" rather than scholarly, approach could well exercise a chilling effect on objective scholarship. This is a political appointment more than a scholarly one.[57] Acuña is a polemicist more than a seeker for truth, and his appointment is therefore inappropriate to the University of California.

CAP notes that the review process in this case has been conducted with great care; nonetheless this is an important case, and CAP wishes to add its independent review.

Research. Acuña's publications consist of the following: three K–12 textbooks published between 1969 and 1971, a journalistic book, *A Community Under Siege: A Chronicle of Chicanos East of the Los Angeles River*, published by the Center of Chicano Studies at UCLA in 1984, and two substantial books. The first of the substantial books is *Sonoran Strongman: Ignacio Pesqueira and His Times*, published by the University of Arizona Press (and at the same time in Spanish) in 1974. This is a scholarly monograph, which would merit appointment at a UC campus. The second substantial work; *Occupied America: A History of Chicanos*, first published in 1972 (and translated into Spanish), is now in its third edition (Harper and Row, 1988). This book is difficult to characterize. Previous editions were stridently polemical. The second edition (moderated from the shrillness of the first) still proclaims (p. vii) that it is a "reaction to the social scientists' utopian flirtation with 'pure research.'" The third edition is completely rewritten and more moderate. It is a well-written, footnoted, generally chronological (and also appropriately topical) history of Chicanos.[58] The author himself refers to it as a "text." It is a book appropriate for the general public or as a college textbook; indeed it is widely used as a college textbook throughout the Southwest. It has also served as a valuable background reference work for scholars (see the letter of Ramón Ruiz at UCSD). It is not however a scholarly monograph.[59] It would in our judgment be problematic as to whether such a book would move a scholar to tenure in the absence of other scholarly work. At most it would qualify the person for the Associate Professor level at UC.[60] And, the context of general research is weak indeed. As other published items, Acuña has one sole-authored chapter and two co-authored chapters in books. He has two articles, neither in major journals. Accepted for publication are two further chapters (not counting book reviews). The rest of his publications (aside from a few book reviews) is a vast quantity of op-ed and other journalistic articles. In summary, CAP does not consider this a record even remotely approaching that of a full professor in the University of California.[61]

Reviewers. Eleven extramural evaluations were solicited, eight by the department. Ten were received; one of the referees chosen by Acuña did not respond owing to travel plans. The ten letters are all favorable.[62] What must be noted is that with few exceptions they are solicited from people favoring politically "activist," over objective scholarly approaches.[63] For example, David Sweet (UCSC) writes in his laudatory letter that Acuña "has always displayed a nice balance between angry denunciation, scholarly reflection and political responsibility in his work. That is to say, I think of him as an exemplary scholar-activist, one whose influence extends far beyond the Chicano intellectual community to inspire real engagement in those of us who share his commitment to social justice for everybody in this country." Another letter is written by a Professor of Medicine at UCLA (Hays-Bautista), who believes that Acuña would have more opportunity in UC than at CSU to pursue scholarly work.[64] Mazón, an associate professor of history at Pomona,[65] calls attention to the polemical nature of *Occupied America,* while noting the extensive and voluminous revisions in subsequent editions; he also praises Acuña's administrative abilities. Arnoldo de León, Davidson Professor of History at Angelo State University, Texas, also praises his administrative abilities. Deena González, Associate Professor of History and Chicano Studios at Pomona, calls Acuña "a professor of the highest rank" and "one of the few Chicano scholar-activists still attempting to bridge the gaps between the academic world and the world of Latino/Chicano politics." She goes on to praise him for his mentoring of younger Chicanos and Chicanas; he is evidently regarded with wide affection in the community as a role model. Ruiz (UCSD) has relied upon *Occupied America* for background and comments that Acuña writes well. He would recommend him for Professor IV or V in the UC system. Carlos Vélez-Ibáñez, Director of the Bureau of Applied Research in Anthropology at the University of Arizona, recommends abovescale, calling *Occupied America* a "chilling account of the cultural, historical, economic, and political subordination of the Mexican population. It is not just a carefully crafted series of arguments of a single cohort of the Mexican population in the United States, but rather an impassioned treatment that shatters myths of interpretation and replaces them with a materialistic and cultural interpretation . . . Acuña clearly shows how the

Mexican community was gerrymandered, re-developed, freewayed, and policed." Two supporting letters come from CSUN: one from the Dean, Jorge García; the other from Bob Suzuki, Vice President for Academic Affairs. The most impressive letter is from Juan Gómez-Quiñones, Professor of History at UCLA, who places Acuña "among the top three senior professors in the field of Chicano Studies nationally" and comments that "as a proactive faculty influence he is unique."

Teaching. Suzuki comments particularly on the excellence of Acuña's teaching, and CAP has no doubt that he is an inspirational and energetic role model for his Chicano students. Gómez-Quiñones comments that he is "a tremendous resource" in graduate studies. At CSUN, of course, Acuña has had no opportunity to work with doctoral students.

Service. Acuña has been of great service at CSUN in organizing area studies and multidisciplinary studies, as well as bilingual teacher training. His service to the Chicano community is without any doubt extraordinary and devoted to the extreme.

Summary. CAP finds Acuña an admirable fighter for what he perceives as right and justice for the Chicano community. It hopes that he will continue to work for justice. But we do not judge his fiery brand of advocacy appropriate for a professorship in the University of California. CAP has doubts as to whether his teaching is unbiased; indeed it has every reason from the record to suppose that it would be strongly politically proactive.[66] As for his research, CAP finds it too meager for a full professorship. Further, CAP fears that Acuña's approach to both teaching and scholarship is less educational than indoctrination. This is not a man able or willing to stop back and analyze or question his own assumptions, for he is too committed to busily promoting them. CAP firmly agrees with and concurs in the unanimous judgment of the Provost and the ad hoc committee that Rodolfo Acuña not be appointed.

Jeffrey Russell, Chair

* * *

There are several themes in the above CAP letter. It makes the assumption that the provost made a "careful analysis" in recommending denial, quoting him as stating that my work was "more political and passionate than objective and substantive." It states that "Acuña's undeniable national reputation arises from his entrepreneurship and polemical involvement." Again, it suggests that if I were given the position that "a dictatorial, tyrannical situation might be created."

The influence of the ad hoc report is also evident in the use of the template, "at age 59." The committee also repeats unquestioningly the phrase, "in a field as yet so inchoate," exactly as it is used by the ad hoc committee.

The personal attacks abound: "Acuña's unsophisticated activism," work that is "stridently polemical," and abounds in "journalistic articles." Echoing Sprecher, the letters from the extramural reviewers are described as "solicited from people favoring politically 'activist,' over objective scholarly approaches." Sprecher recanted this evaluation during his deposition, which indicates that my politics indeed were the determining factor. In his deposition, Russell said that my work was Marxist because I used words such as "hegemony" and "struggle."

Perhaps the most astounding assumption involved CAP's evaluation of my teaching. In the file were two letters from immediate supervisors calling me a master teacher. There is nothing negative about my teaching. Even so, the reviewers make a leap in logic: "CAP has doubts as to whether his teaching is unbiased; indeed it has every reason from the record to suppose that it would be strongly politically proactive." No evidence is offered for this claim. The report concludes, "we do not judge his fiery brand of advocacy appropriate for a professorship in the University of California . . . CAP fears that Acuña's approach to both teaching and scholarship is less educational than indoctrination." The emotional tone of this letter betrays it. Evaluations in other files make similar leaps in logic, but they are not usually personal in the same manner as these reports.

As for the administrators who made the formal decisions, they are not required to submit written reports. They rely on faculty committees. Associate Vice Chancellor Julius Zelmanowitz concurred with the recommendations and defended them in public, although under oath he admitted that he never read any of my writings. Indeed, he had never read any of the writings of any of the Chicanas/os at UCSB, wrongly attributing Professor Zaragosa Vargas's book to Professor Mario García. Neither Vice Chancellor Gordon Hammes nor Chancellor Uehling read my works.

It was more than ironic to observe from the personnel files that some of the negative things that the review committee members said about me, were said about them. Indeed, I believe that many of them would be shocked if they could read what their colleagues had said about them in the past. It is difficult to read negative evaluations about oneself. In my case, the tone of the reports was one of very the reasons that I reacted so positively. It was clear that the attack was not a scholarly review, and that I had to stand by my reputation.

7

Truth and Objectivity:
Thomas Kuhn Applied

Part of the mythology of the American paradigm is the belief that the justice system is impartial, objective, and seeks the truth, and that judges and the law are color-blind. The reality differs. The courts, as we have seen, are driven by money, which buys the resources to certify one's version of what happened. More often than not, the end result has less to do with justice than with whether one had the money to properly litigate.

Because the justice system and academe are compatible, the evidence in discrimination cases has to go beyond the customary measure of the "preponderance of the evidence" even to withstand the initial demur. The standard of proof is almost converted to that in a criminal case: the evidence of racism is expected to be beyond reasonable doubt. Although a judge is not supposed to determine isses of fact, leaving them to the jury, often the judge does so according to his or her biases. In discrimination cases the scales remain tipped in favor of the defendants, whose set of values more closely fits that of the judge.

In my case against the University of California, as the plaintiff, I had the burden of proving that the University of California at Santa Barbara discriminated against me. The gathering of this proof is generally done in the discovery period, in which both sides have the opportunity to subpoena documents from the other side and to depose witnesses. Both sides question people under oath so that there will be no surprises during the trial. The case is fought based on the evidence introduced at this stage (assuming one's documentation is admitted as evidence).

Throughout the case, the University of California abused the discovery process. Its lawyers manueuvered and stalled, offering motion after motion, challenging the court's ruling and often muddying the waters to the point that the judge or the discovery referee seemed to forget what they had ruled in the first place. As mentioned in chapter 6, UC conducted depositions throughout the country and in Puerto Rico, knowing that we could not afford to send an attorney to sit in. The ability to sit down alone with witnesses, without us present, gave the defendants a tremendous edge, since they controlled the narrative the deponents heard. Money was very important in controlling and maintaining the momentum and setting the template for the truth. That it was done within the framework of the "justice" system gave it the aura of objectivity. Money gives one the opportunity to invent one's reality.

One frivolous charge by Corbett & Kane, the university's defense firm, was that I had lied when I listed an article on my vita as accepted for publication, when in fact it was never published. The UC spent tens of thousands of dollars attempting to prove that I lied, although it knew this was not the case. In 1986 David Montejano, then professor of sociology at the University of New Mexico, signed a contract with the University of New Mexico Press for an anthology on Chicanos. In 1987 I agreed to contribute a rough draft of an article on East Los Angeles politics, stipulating that when the anthology was ready for final editing, I would revise it and attach the footnotes. Because the book was very extensive, with many original articles, some delay occurred. In late 1991 or early 1992, Montejano contacted me with the news that the anthology was ready to go to the press, but because of the delay, he wanted me to update my article. I begged off at this point because I was involved in the lawsuit and also was in the process of writing the first draft of *Anything But Mexican: Chicanos in Contemporary Los Angeles* (Verso, 1996). So I withdrew my manuscript. (The article was later published in another venue.)

The UC attorney attempted to persuade Montejano to say that I had lied on my resume, calling him on the phone but never deposing him, which would have permanently put the matter to rest. The attorney finally hit on an angle—he would get the editor of the University of New Mexico Press, David Holtby, to say that he had never accepted the chapter. This was technically true, since the anthology was not submitted to the press until about 1993 and my piece was not among the articles submitted. He also wanted Holtby to say that he would not have accepted my piece if it were submitted. (In fact, the anthology was turned down by the press after a reader red-baited it.)

At first we decided not to send anyone to the deposition of David Holtby. My team argued that it was after-acquired evidence at best, and that the charge was so outrageous that the judge would throw it out of court. However, Eliot Grossman volunteered to go to Albuquerque, New Mexico, where the deposition was being held. Judge Audrey Collins seemed to be granting the defendants everything they wanted, and Grossman had a healthy respect for Corbett & Kane's ability to mythicize the truth. So in September 1994 he flew to New Mexico, where the deposition was conducted by Ian Fellerman, counsel for Corbett & Kane. Grossman originally believed that the deposition would take two hours at most. He was well prepared for the deposition since he is an expert in Chicana/o studies, having spent six years at the Seminario de Estudios Chicanos y Fronteras of the National Institute of Anthropology and History in Mexico City.

Fellerman went through what had become a ritual in our depositions. He asked David Holtby, an editor and associate director of the press, to define scholarship and objectivity. He then had Holtby testify that Holtby had read *Occupied America* (twenty-two years before, as a graduate student) and it was (that dirty word) "polemical." Grossman, who was naturally prepared to dislike Holtby, concluded that he was honest but was being blatantly led by Fellerman. The UC mystique surely played a part. Grossman, however, astutely ascertained that Holtby was not right-wing nor was he prejudiced against us; from that point, Grossman spun a web that lasted for the better part of the day. His questioning was based on Thomas Kuhn's notion of paradigms.

If the deposition had been conducted by an attorney less prepared than Grossman in the field of Chicana/o studies, Fellerman probably could have manipulated the situation. As it turned out, Holtby became our witness.

Occupied America

I have chosen to include large portions of the Holtby deposition in this chapter because it is a basic document. We rarely get the opportunity to look closely at this sort of testimony. Much of the case revolved around the question whether I was a scholar or not. This was a central question for the jury. If the stated reason against hiring me, because I was unqualified, were a pretext—thus, independent of scholarship—then it was a case of discrimination. In my case the real motive was tied to my politics, my race, and my age. The Holtby deposition exposed the pretext. His testimony, if allowed, established that the UC's evaluation of my work was pretextual. In order to achieve this end, it was also important to educate the attorneys; they had to understand how the UC was using the pretext that my work was not scholarly to cover up the real motive.

Occupied America eclipsed anything that I had ever written or done professionally. And, starting with its title, it gave the defendants a big target. In essence, the defendants claimed that I was not a seeker of truth and I was not objective; rather, I was emotional and biased. The defendants' narrative was tailored to the white middle-class professional who usually sat on juries in Santa Barbara. We knew that we were going to have a difficult time breaking down this narrative, since most people assumed that these gatekeepers were themselves objective and cared about the truth. We also realized that it would be easier for them to entice mainstream scholars and even judges to follow their line.

Grossman sought to establish that Chicano studies was an interdisciplinary field of study, which necessarily used a mix of methodologies. Part of the UC's narrative was that I did not employ the scientific method, and therefore, I ignored the rules of objective evidence. Grossman brilliantly distinguished methodology from objectivity, and emphasized the fact that a scholar can be "involved" but still apply the scientific method. Grossman then queried Holtby: "And I take it that as a scholar, you consider the role of a participant observer a legitimate scholarly role for someone to take in a field such as Chicano studies?" Holtby agreed, saying, "In general, yes. If you follow the methodology, it's better for sociology than—than, say, probably for psychology." Holtby conceded that Chicano studies is an interdisciplinary field, so it followed that its methodologies would differ. "In the interdisciplinary field, the scholar has more flexibility with regard to the methodology selected for a particular investigation than they might have in a more traditionally defined academic field; isn't that true?" Holtby agreed.

In academe, applied research is expected in the hard sciences, medicine, engineering, and the law. In the social sciences today, however, it is disdained. It is unsophisticated compared to theory. Indeed, applied research is often dismissed as popular or journalistic. The participant observer method was once popular among sociologists, but in recent years, sociologists prefer not to be applied researchers but "scientists," which they equate with developing theory. Throughout the case, the defendants had set up their own definition of objectivity. Grossman sought to show that "objectivity" in their sense, whether from the perspective of a theorist or a participant observer, was fraudulent. The following exchange was significant because even though Holtby understood their "objectivity" was an exaggeration, he tended to hedge.

Grossman: "All right. And working from that basic premise, don't those who do participant observer scholarship also contend that scholars who claim their work is objective are not being honest in their methodology, but rather are, in fact, concealing their own biases, prejudices, which are a necessary result of all the factors that you just explained when you were using this—this term?" Holtby replied: "That is the argument that is made, that bias is there, and to deny it is—is intellectually fraudulent."

Grossman established that very few people would claim to be "totally objective." According to Holtby, "Most researchers today—anybody trained probably since the sixties has an acute awareness of those variables, however subtle or however profound in your life." Holtby claimed that "a key part of what we do in graduate school is to train people to be able to—to deal with those issues." Grossman countered, "And you can find many scholars with very deep disagreements as to what the scientific objectivity is, and yet all these scholars are recognized as legitimate scholars in their field; isn't that correct?" Grossman continued, "And, . . . based upon what you have just told us, . . . you would also agree that there has been and continues to be a very strong debate in the entire field of social science as to whether or not, in fact, objectivity is a scientific term?" Grossman pointed out that some legitimate scholars in the field of social sciences believe it is impossible to be objective in social science. He asked Holtby, "And just because a particular scholar has the point of view that objectivity is impossible in science, and is not even a scientific term, and just because such a scholar pursues a methodology, based upon that basic assumption, you would not solely, because of that, consider that person not to be a legitimate scholar in the area of social science, would you?" Holtby agreed.

Grossman then asked a fundamental question: "Now, if someone presented to you a book on the history of Chicanos, who—among whose basic epistemological assumptions was that scientific objectivity, number one, is impossible, and number two, is a meaningless concept, without scientific value, you would not reject that book as unscholarly solely because the scholar had as one of [his] methodological assumptions that rejection of objectivity, would you?" Holtby vacillated but generally agreed. The not too subtle point was that this was precisely what the reviewers were having problems with in my case: they did not agree with my methodological assumptions and my criticism of their paradigm.

Grossman invoked the example of C. Wright Mills: "And, in fact, based upon your agreement with C. Wright Mills, would you not say that the proper role of a scholar, rather than hiding their biases by insisting that their own particular point of view is objective, rather should be to make clear to their audience precisely what their particular biases are, so that the audience can then evaluate it, the viewpoint of the scholar, in light of the specific biases that particular scholar has?" This question by Grossman hit at the heart of what many ethnic and women's studies scholars are about; one cannot privatize objectivity and confuse this claim with truth. Holtby agreed: "We are all imbedded in the world in which we live by our upbringing, by our education, by our religious, political beliefs, and one can go on and multiply these things . . . To what—the question is to what degree does any one or some combination of them inform what we do as researchers. The answer will vary case by case."

In his questioning, Grossman was careful to distinguish truth from objectivity. A scholar may be biased and still be a good scholar and still express the truth. This was also pertinent, since the narrative of the defendants claimed that they were objective and I was biased, consequently they were telling the truth and I was not.

Grossman posed the question: "[Do you agree that] what is considered to be historical truth at a given point in the history of the field of history, itself, at another point . . . may be rejected as not being historical truth, and a new truth may come to be accepted by the consensus of scientific opinion in the field of history?" Holtby replied, "Yes. We can quibble over truth. I would say interpretation, but, yes, that is true." Grossman then introduced the topic of Thomas Kuhn's book, *The Structure of Scientific Revolutions*, and Kuhn's principle that changes in the concept of consensus in scientific opinion are fundamental in all intellectual pursuits. Grossman and Holtby agreed that Kuhn's book, when it was published, created a sensation not only in the field of philosophy of science but in all the social sciences. Grossman: "A lot of reputable scholars were outraged by what Dr. Kuhn says in that book, weren't they?" Holtby pointed out that "There was, at that time, great dispute over his contention that our personal agenda can inform what we do, and that these are paradigms and . . . [that] paradigms shift. They didn't believe that paradigms shift." Grossman observed that one of the reasons "a lot of scholars were outraged by Dr. Kuhn's book is that Dr. Kuhn's book, if it is taken to be correct, substantially undermines not only the concept of objectivity in science, but undermines the very concept of scientific truth."

At this point, Holtby answered, "I have no trouble with paradox [presented by paradigms]. There are several different viewpoints. I'm collapsing everything down to what I call paradigm shift, which is for me, as a historian, a way of saying that the questions we ask and answer will change over time, that each person is going to bring to their questions what's uppermost in their mind at that time, and that's a product of the number of forces that I have talked about . . . Fifty years from now, . . . [the paradigm is] going to be different, and I regard that as inevitable, and probably for the better of the scholarly inquiry. Otherwise, . . . nothing would ever advance."

Grossman asked, "Dr. Kuhn's book was a rather polemical book in tone, was it not?" Holtby disagreed. Grossman: "Well, in terms of the way he expresses himself, doesn't Dr. Kuhn strongly express his own viewpoints?" Holtby: "Oh, absolutely." Grossman: ". . . and [it] reject[s] all competing viewpoints as totally incorrect?" "Yes." Grossman: "And doesn't Dr. Kuhn write in a polemical style in [*The Structure of*] *Scientific Revolutions*?"

Holtby attempted to separate Kuhn's work from polemics, the dirty word: "It's the process by which you go through, and so in that sense, no, . . . his is what—what I would regard as certainly a passionately argued piece, and very eloquent, to be sure, published by a university press, the University of Chicago Press, I believe, but I would not—no, I would not characterize that as polemical." Grossman probed: "But when Dr. Kuhn's book first came out, he was challenging the existing scholarly canon, wasn't he?" Holtby again hesitated, saying that the work would not have been dismissed because it was published by a respected university press. "University presses are . . . taken very seriously, . . . and that [the University of Chicago] press in particular has very high status, and deservedly so." Grossman: "Generally, academic presses, because of their definition of scholarship, and their concern with marketability, publish scholarly works that will be considered to be within the mainstream of scholarship; isn't that correct?" "No . . . not necessarily. It means—" Grossman: "Not necessarily, but generally?" "Generally, yes, but that's a very narrow 'generally.'"

Grossman then asked Holtby, "Well, in your experience as assistant editor, editor, and associate director, of the University of New Mexico Press, have you ever published a book similar to Dr. Kuhn's book with regard to its direct attack on the existing scientific consensus in its field?" "No." "And when is the last time, other than Dr. Kuhn's book, [*The Structure of*] *Scientific Revolutions*, that you ever heard of a university press publishing a book as controversial as Dr. Kuhn's book with regard to directly attacking the existing scientific consensus of opinion?" Holtby did not answer.

Grossman then, naturally, linked his discussion on Kuhn to *Occupied America*. "Dr. Acuña's book, the first edition of *Occupied America*, directly attacks the majority consensus in the area of American history with regard to the role of Mexicans and Mexican-Americans, doesn't it?" "Yes, it does." "Dr. Acuña's book . . . [also] directly attacks the majority consensus of scholars in the field of American history with regard to the interpretation of the Mexican-American War, does it not?" "Yes, it does." "In fact, the particular viewpoint that Dr. Acuña presents in the first edition of *Occupied America* is a viewpoint that is almost entirely absent from the field of scholarship in the area of American history, in the entirety of development of the field of American history, isn't it?" "Yes."

Grossman: "And when Dr. Acuña's book, *Occupied America*, first edition, was published, it created a tremendous controversy in the field, not only of Chicano studies, but of American history, as well, did it not?" "Yes." "And the controversy created by the first edition of *Occupied America* within the field of American history was certainly of equivalent dimensions to the controversy caused by Dr. Kuhn's book, *The Structure of Scientific Revolutions*, in the field of philosophy of science; isn't that true?" "In the sense that it was the book that a lot of people were talking about and reacting to. I can't say they were similar, but, yes, it certainly was widely talked about."

Grossman: "And a lot of people were outraged by Dr. Acuña's book, weren't they?" Holtby: "The reviews were often—boy, this goes a long ways back. Reviews were often very critical. If that means—I mean the attack methodology, the attack interpretation, question[s], you know, [of] sources, yes—all those things occurred, and that's—if your word was critical, yes, they were certainly very critical of it."[1] Grossman: "A lot of scholars, in the field of American history, were outraged by Dr. Acuña's book, . . . were they not?" "Yes."

Grossman: "And if the major thesis of . . . *Occupied America* was, in fact, correct, the effect of that would be to entirely invalidate numerous works of historical, supposed scholarship by white Anglo-Saxon American historians; isn't that true?" Holtby disagreed that it would invalidate the entire scholarship. "It shows that the hypotheses, the suppositions were—were not correct, but that doesn't invalidate them. It lends a greater complexity to it."

According to Holtby, I "put on the agenda a whole different set of assumptions, and . . . certainly provoked a lot . . . of thought." Grossman: "And by Dr. Acuña putting on the agenda a whole different set of hypotheses and assumptions, wouldn't you agree that he made a major contribution to the creation of the field of Chicano studies?" "Presented in that light, yes, light and heat. He generated a lot of heat, no doubt about that, a lot of comment, a lot of heat. Does heat lead to insight? In other words, does the kind of impassioned debate—does that then lead to insight? That's the real question, and . . . to the degree that that came out of his work, I can't really say. There was a lot going on in that time, in the late sixties, early seventies . . . You know, everybody wants the parentage of something that's—that then goes on to be very successful. He was there at the beginning, no doubt about it, and remains there, as do many of those other scholars, such as Juan Gómez-Quiñones at UCLA. . . ."

Grossman: "And wasn't one of the points Dr. Acuña was trying to make passionately in the first edition of *Occupied America* that the majority of scholars in the area of American history were blinded by their own hooks, by their own formation, by the fact that they were white Anglo-Saxon males, and that for that reason, they had ignored a whole realm of historical reality by the particular hypotheses and assumptions that they made, based on their own backgrounds, and that they needed to be more conscious and self-conscious of those kinds of biases which they concealed under the mask of so-called objectivity, if we were, in fact, to develop a true history of Mexicans and Mexican Americans in United States history?" "That is argued in his book. Yes." "And that particular point of view expressed by Dr. Acuña had never been expressed before in the field of American history, had it?" "Wow. Regarding Chicanos?" "Regarding the very last thing I said. . . ." Holtby: "It had not [been expressed] regarding Mexican Americans, yes."

Grossman: "And don't you think that by expressing that point of view . . . that Dr. Acuña had made an important contribution to scholarship in the field of American history?" "Phrased that way, that he got people's attention and [to the degee that they] began to think about [Mexican Americans], that is contribution. Its relative merit, I don't want to comment, but it is certainly a contribution." Grossman: "Well certainly, sir, in describing to us . . . the necessity that scientists be aware of their own biases and take them into account in their work, and also from the standpoint of sociology of knowledge, noting the historical fact that white historians in the field of American history previous to the first edition of *Occupied America* had apparently not been self-conscious about their biases and not taken them into account, . . . Dr. Acuña's work, first edition of *Occupied America*, made a significant and important contribution to scholarship in the field of American history, didn't it?" "Yes. I'll agree to that."

UC's Committee on Academic Personnel and especially its chair, Jeffrey Russell, made much of the fact that I had called *Occupied America* a counterhegemonic work. Grossman asked Holtby, "How would you define the term counterhegemonic?" Holtby: "What it would mean would be those activities and actions that I assume from the bottom up would oppose or tend to try to overturn whatever the form of hegemony is, and this could be individual, all the way up to societal actions, so that in this instance, the Mothers of East Los Angeles[2]—again, assuming my understanding of this is right—could be considered a counterhegemonic force, all right. . . ." "And if I were to tell you that Dr. Acuña has described his book, *Occupied America*, as a counterhegemonic work, would you feel that would be an accurate description?" "Yes. . . ." "And would you agree that a counterhegemonic work would be a work that consciously seeks to oppose a form of social control or hegemony exercised in society?" "Yes."

Grossman after some discussion continued, "Would you agree that it is legitimate in the social sciences for a scholar to write a consciously counterhegemonic work?" "Yes." "And why would you say that?" "The nature of how scholarship is advanced often deals not so much with the documents—we don't get that many new documents, but we get new interpretations that respond to different perspectives, different questions being asked, and so if you have got a kind of received opinion—I prefer to think of a thesis/antithesis. I mean if you have got all the movement in one direction, and suddenly somebody is able to frame questions and views from an opposing direction, yes, that—I mean we talked about Thomas Kuhn. Yes. That is certainly valid."

In the course of questioning, Holtby conceded that scholars whose work represents the very intellectual hegemony that the counterhegemonic work is directly attacking could be expected to react negatively to such a work. Scholars whose own hegemonic work was being "directly attacked by such a counterhegemonic work might well seek to deflect that attack by characterizing the counterhegemonic work as not scientific. . . ." This was an important discussion because it explains the violent reaction to not only my work but to that of Chicana/o studies in general. Criticisms of existing paradigms or methodologies become personal, preventing a paradigm shift from taking place.

Return to Objectivity

Grossman: "Now, in the field of history, there is even less agreement as to what is proper scientific methodology than in any of the other social sciences. Isn't that a fact?" Holtby's answer was idealistic, reflecting the vantage point of one working in an academic press and not in academe itself. It was also naive, given that he had already admitted that a reader had red-baited Montejano's anthology, and that it was one of the reasons why it was turned down for publication. Holtby thus responded, "No . . . we're using scientific here in a way that historians do. People agree on methodology. They don't agree at all on interpretation, or what it all means, but how you go about it, how you know what you know, because it's based on documents. The other fields are not really based on documents. The historians have less disagreement about that. They disagree violently—not violently. They disagree wholeheartedly over what it all means, but you have got to have documents. You have got to have some kind of evidence. You can't make this up . . . You get right up to the present, and you participate in it, and then you get the confounding issue of, well, how do you report on what you have been involved in, but that's . . . a very occult issue."

In this description of the role of the historian, I wholeheartedly agree with Holtby. Yet throughout my case, historian Robert Kelley, as well as Provost David Sprecher, tried to make the point that I did not use documents. When we showed them the footnotes, they ignored the evidence. They made assumptions without looking at the evidence. Intellectually, I could have accepted their questioning of the interpretation of the documents that I used, but not their denial that I used documents. Grossman's goal was to make the valid point that history, which is based on documents, can never be based on "absolute" truth because of subjectivity, both of the person reading the documents and of the authors of the documents. That is why debate is necessary.

Grossman asked: "So the basic evidence of history consists of documents which themselves are interpretations? What the historian is doing is interpreting interpretations that other people have made of documents, which in and of themselves are interpretations; isn't that true?" "Yes. Phrased that way, it sounds like all a house of cards. There can be some more certainty to it, but, yes, it is—the essence of history is interpretation." After more discussion Grossman queried, "So it's very difficult for any particular scholar in the field of history to prove to the satisfaction of other scholars that [his or her] position is right, and other scholars' position is wrong?" "That is most difficult." "And it's very common to have disagreement in the area of history on almost everything; isn't that true?" "Yes."

With this established, Grossman returned to *Occupied America*: "And there are a number of scholars who disagree with Dr. Acuña's interpretation of history; isn't that true?" "Yes." "And there are a number of scholars who agree with Dr. Acuña's interpretation of history?" "Yes." "That doesn't mean that any of these historians is any less a scholar, does it?" "Not in and of itself, no." "However, there are some people who purport to be scholars who consider Dr. Acuña not to be a legitimate scholar, because they don't like the point of view that Dr. Acuña expresses; isn't that true?" "From what I have learned today about this lawsuit, that's

apparently evident, yes." "And there are some people who purport to be scholars who consider Dr. Acuña not to be a legitimate
scholar, because they do not wish the particular point of view of
Dr. Acuña to be expressed in the field of scholarship at all, under
any circumstances; isn't that true?" Holtby begged off, saying that
"Motive in history is the difficult thing to access." He also found it
hard to accept that there could be racism in academe.

Grossman asked whether the historian's bias, his sources,
and the times would be taken into account in evaluating my
work. Holtby agreed: "By anyone reading that as a source, yes."
Grossman responded, "By any historian who wanted to evaluate
Dr. Acuña's work, they would want to take into account the political reasons he might . . . [have for writing] it at the present time,
even though he was dealing with a past period, such as 100 years
ago?" "Yes. Right." "But by the same token, someone evaluating
the work of historians who disagree with Dr. Acuña would want
to take into consideration the political reasons in the present that
those historians are writing the particular history that they are
writing in disagreement with Dr. Acuña's history; isn't that true?"
The answer was "Yes . . . Because each represents a point of view
and is a part of a dynamic, and to understand all of the interac-
tions, you need to understand all of the forces and the variables
and the people carrying those forth. . . ." Grossman: "So isn't it
true that one of the things that we have learned about the writing
of history in the last 15 or 20 years, partially because of the development of discourse analysis, partly because of the development
of the feminist movement, of the Chicano movement, and the
Black movement, in terms of motivating intellectual ferment—
isn't one of the things that we have learned is that the writings of
history at any point, and by anyone, is necessarily always already
a political act?" Holtby: "It—it can be a political act. You can have
other dimensions. I would agree that certainly for those who contend that—that it comes from human experience, and not from
the documents, yes. Whether it's solely political, I . . . would differ
with you." Grossman: "I'm not suggesting solely political . . . but
[do you agree] that the writing of history at any time, at any
moment, by anyone, is always already, in addition to other things
that it might possibly be, a political act?" "Yes. If we understand

by political that it will leave a record which will influence people in the future, then, yes, that is a political act."

* * *

Kuhn's thesis of a paradigm shift was essential to understanding the UCSB reviewers. In short, I was challenging their truths as well as their claim to objectivity. I was also challenging their scientific and time-tested process. My works mocked their pretensions of being scientists. The deposition of Holtby drove home the point that decisions of the UCSB reviewers were being made beyond the normal definition of racism. While race was a factor, interwoven with it was their rejection of the paradigm posited by *Occupied America*. Even Holtby initially reacted against the paradigm. If it had been put in acceptable Marxist meta-language, it would not have been as offensive. However, when Eliot Grossman took him through the process in familiar terms, Holtby began to recognize parallels between my case and that of a challenge to the dominant paradigm. (An interesting study would be to compare the reaction of Euro-American scholars to *Occupied America* with those of Chicana/o students and the Mexican community.) This simplification of terms would become the basis of our litigation strategy. We knew that as long as judges were allowed to adjudicate the facts, the positivist paradigm would prevail. We did not have the luxury of deposing the judge. We could win only if we stood before a jury, of any color. We just had to get them to listen to our narrative and to break out of the underlying premise of the American paradigm—that academe is objective and does not discriminate.

8

The Trustees of the Truth

Institutions of higher learning have long enjoyed privileges not available to private industry or even to the media. Years of special treatment have allowed them to commingle the definition of academic freedom with their right to conduct secret reviews. The courts are reluctant to encroach on review standards or to pierce the veils of secrecy. Judges have been educated by these institutions, and make the assumption that they are run by altruistic sages, who entered education for the sake of humanity, to mold young minds and to search for the truth.

Within academe's hallowed walls, however, political fights are often more vicious than in the private sector, especially when it comes to promotions and hiring. Academic life takes on shades of Sir William Golding's 1954 novel, *Lord of the Flies*. In Golding's book, the schoolboys cast on an uninhabited island at first try to establish a social order. Soon, however, there are dissensions, and the rationalist leader and his lieutenant find themselves alone against the breakaway "hunters." In academe the rationalists prevail; hidden from the public eye, the custodians of truth quietly implement their policies to conduct a sort of ethnic cleansing, while claiming that they are defending civilization against the hunters. Instinctively, academe adopts McCarthyite methods, which are disguised by the secret reviews of its members.

Golding's tale is metaphorical. It traces the defects of society back to the defects of human nature. It is a horror story of a rapid degeneration into a state of brutal savagery once the flimsy restraints of social order are removed. In academe, the rationalists are constantly worried about this savagery. Those who run academe come from relatively privileged classes dominated by the paradigm of a closed society and ordered by rules and rituals, which they fear could be perverted and overturned. Academe more resembles the aura of a British boarding school than that of its counterpart, the American military academy. The mission of the rationalists is to save civilization from the primitivism of a society in rapid decline. Ralph and Piggy's worst fear is that Jack will seize control of their island.

Breaking the Code of Silence

Any employer has the right to give you a job or reject you. Employers don't have the right to discriminate. At one level, however, faculties are like gangs, with a code of silence. It is very difficult to prove who did what. The culture is such that professors are reluctant to sue their colleagues. The members of the institution are rationalists, who believe that their rules are necessary to preserve their island. Peer group reviews are usually secret and, in good rationalist fashion, the tendency of a rejected candidate is to blame himself or herself but not the system.[1]

Until recently, university committees have enforced the rules, shielded by confidentiality. The whole culture of confidentiality produced an environment of mistrust, but there was little that anyone could do about it. The rejected candidate was never really certain whether the rules were followed. He or she merely had to assume good faith. Individual internal reviewers, if their names were known, could shield themselves by arguing that they had tried their best on behalf of the candidate, but that one of the confidential outside letters was the death knell. This kept the candidate busy trying to figure out who wrote the negative review. Until the 1980s, the courts diligently protected this secret society. Moreover, up to the 1980s the press treated academe like a sacred cow.

Without the ability to find out who had the "smoking gun," employment discrimination cases were impossible to win. It was like playing in a poker game when you have three aces and the other player tells you he has four kings, and the rules say that you have to assume that he is telling the truth. This situation partially changed under the *University of Pennsylvania v. EEOC* (1989), when the U.S. Supreme Court unanimously held that the EEOC had the right to obtain all personnel review documents in cases of alleged discrimination. The ruling was later expanded to include individual plaintiffs.

Unquestionably, without the Supreme Court ruling we would have lost our case against the University of California. We would have been denied access to letters and personnel files of similarly situated faculty, as well as the reports and notes of members of the ad hoc committee and the Committee on Academic Personnel (see chapter 6). Because we were able to pierce that corporate veil of secrecy that has historically surrounded the review process, and show how confidentiality (i.e., secrecy) has shielded the biases and often the meanspiritedness of reviewers, we met our burden of proof.

In 1985 the University of Pennsylvania had denied tenure to associate professor Rosalie Tung, and she filed charges of race, sex, and national origin discrimination against the university with the Equal Employment Opportunity Commission (EEOC), claiming that the university violated Title VII of the Civil Rights Act of 1964. Tung's department chair wrote a negative letter to the university's personnel committee after she allegedly refused to have sex with him. As a result, she was denied tenure. According to Tung, her qualifications were "equal to or better than" those of five named male faculty members receiving more favorable treatment. The EEOC requested, among other things, confidential letters written by Tung's evaluators; the department chairman's letter of evaluation; internal documents of internal deliberations of faculty committees; and comparable portions of the tenure-review files of the five males. The university, a private institution, refused to produce the documents, asking the court to exclude "confidential peer review information." EEOC successfully got an order from the district court enforcing the subpoena.

The university asked the Supreme Court to recognize a qualified common-law privilege against disclosure of confidential peer review materials, claiming a First Amendment right of "academic freedom" against wholesale disclosure of the contested documents. The defendants claimed that disclosure of peer evaluations would have a "chilling effect" on candid evaluations and discussions of candidates, that the quality of peer review evaluations would decline, and that tenure committees would no longer be able to rely on evaluations. The universities would end up with less qualified persons and the quality of instruction and scholarship would decline. The ending of secrecy would result in divisiveness and tension, according to the university, inhibiting the free interchange of ideas, the hallmark of academic freedom. A fact worth noting was that every teacher's union and professional organization opposed secret peer group reviews.

In 1972 Congress had extended Title VII to educational institutions, giving the EEOC broad subpoena powers with respect to peer review documents. Title VII in 1964 had exempted educational institutions. The Court, in a unanimous decision, recognized that access was essential, since any contentious employers could deny access for an alleged legitimate purpose. While admitting that universities and colleges played significant roles in American society, the Court also said that government had an interest in ferreting out this kind of invidious discrimination. The disclosure of peer review materials was necessary in order for the EEOC to determine whether illegal discrimination had taken place. The Court stated that if there is a "smoking gun" to be found that demonstrates discrimination in tenure decisions, it is likely to be hidden in peer review files. Employers should not be allowed to pick and choose the evidence.

Prior to this landmark decision, the courts had been reluctant to disturb the tenure decisions of educational institutions. After the Pennsylvania case, higher education's almost unchallenged right to confidentiality in tenure decisions gradually eroded. The Court recognized that in certain cases, the employer's claims of confidentiality were often pretextual. There was a public interest in seeing that educational institutions ensure that criteria are applied carefully and honestly. By no means did the Supreme Court ruling end the nightmare of secrecy. The law is one thing, but as Andrew Jackson once said of a Supreme Court decision, Justice John Marshall has made his decision, now let him enforce it. So getting the lower courts to enforce the decision is another story.

My case illustrates the gap between law and action. The documents in my case did not come without a price. The UC fought us tooth and nail, spending hundreds of thousands of dollars in attempting to prevent us from obtaining records used in the review process. The mountains of documents, the personnel files, and the depositions are a treasure trove without which we would not have won the case.

The Unbiased Reviewer

The role of the provost in my case was pivotal. He was the link between the Department of Chicano Studies and the administration. On April 25, 1991, Provost David A. Sprecher wrote Vice Chancellor Gordon G. Hammes, recommending that I be denied appointment to UCSB. He had been provost for over a decade and had amassed substantial power. His recommendation to the reviewing agencies generally carried substantial weight. Committee members made frequent references to his thoroughness and his meticulous care in reviewing files. After reading more than fifty letters of recommendation by Sprecher about other scholars, I reached quite the opposite impression.

As I am under a court order, I cannot specifically refer to particular files. However, there is a pattern in his evaluations that carries over from file to file: it includes a certain pseudointellectual quality of praising candidates whom he liked and employing a dismissive tone to those whom he did not like. I had the distinct impression that he never read the material about a candidate in the files, whether he disapproved or approved of the scholar. His reviews had a boilerplate quality. (This impression was confirmed by the depositions and cross-examination of the provost.)

Sprecher began his review of my proposed appointment with the words,

> The Department of Chicano Studies is recommending the appointment of Rudy Acuña at Professor VI, effective July 1, 1991. The chair presents strong rhetoric in support of this case. . . .

With the word "rhetoric," Sprecher had already established a template. From the beginning, he insinuated that the letter of support from the chair of the department was not substantive. He set the stage by saying that conversations with the chair revealed that there were "great tensions over this appointment, and rather weak support for it." In this statement the provost distorted his conversations with the chair, and he failed to reveal that the department had been in turmoil for some time. Also not mentioned is that he had *ex parte* communications with dissident members of the department, in violation of university policy.[2] As described in chapter 6, the Department of Chicano Studies consisted of joint appointments from various disciplines, who were always warring with each other, and it had a history of turmoil. It had failed to fill the appointment in the previous four years. Department members had recently elected a woman chair but soon turned on her, leading to a vicious internal battle. Furthermore, at this point, the provost had a clear responsibility to protect the candidate. Knowing the politics, he should have aborted the process if he was sincere in wanting an impartial review.

Sprecher's letter observed that I was "recognized as a major player in the Chicano Studies movement," and that during my years at California State University at Northridge I had championed the causes of the Southern California Chicano community. "These efforts won him a loyal following and the respect of his peers, and this is very evident in the letters received on his behalf. It is to his political activities rather than scholarly work that the letters are mostly addressed, and some of the support comes from writers without the expertise to assess the research." Sprecher described the letters on my behalf as, in general, not analytical. He did not give one example to support the generalization.

Sprecher cleverly cast doubt on the strong recommendations of the outside reviewers, who are leaders in the field of Chicana/o studies.[3] According to him, my work was political and the writers were my political admirers. It was apparent that the letter was never meant to be read under a microscope. According to the university's academic personnel manual, it was imperative that the internal reviewers, not being experts themselves, give weight to the outside reviewers who were experts in the field of the candidate. However, it is evident from the hundreds of other candidates' files that Sprecher and other reviewers paid attention to outside reviews only when it pleased them. This becomes more evident in the examination of Sprecher's testimony.

Sprecher's letter addressed *Occupied America*:

> Much of Acuña's support has its roots in his 1972 text *Occupied America* (Harper and Row), a book that went into its third edition with changes to keep it current with political dynamics. Of his several other books, one (*Sonoran Strongman*) was published by a university press, and the rest by what I interpret as minor publishers.[4]

Sprecher was critical of my newspaper writing, concluding that my career of twenty-three years in this arena had little worth. The "scholarly substance and significance of the materials accompanying this case are very meager." Sprecher continued,

> Much of the work does not fall into our usual basic research category, and more than some does not appear to be of major scholarly significance. My assessment of his writings is that the research is not archival, and in its nature differs from the quality of research expected of ladder faculty in the UC system. This is further underscored by what appears to be a lack of invitations to participate in scholarly meetings and to present papers, and the more general absence of participation in the profession.[5] As is observed by some of the extramural writers, Acuña's writings reflect the politics of the period, and they may have been guided by passion as much as objectivity.[6] The consistency of the published output and what is listed as in progress suggests more of the same rather than new directions or greater import or depth.

Sprecher's discourse is clear: my work is political, meager, irrelevant, not archival, unworthy of professional recognition, and more passionate than objective.

The Truth

The deposition of David Sprecher, like that of David Holtby described in the last chapter, was conducted by Eliot Grossman. Grossman, being well acquainted with academe, knew that academicians don't like to be challenged. They enjoy repartee, collegial sparring, but they don't like to be questioned. If you let them talk, they can make almost anything sound "rational." Most come from professional homes. The use of language is their distinguishing trademark. During the trial, I kept admonishing my attorneys for being too gentle with the defendants, who had been well rehearsed by defendants' counsel, Ian Fellerman.

From the beginning, Grossman went on the attack, noting Sprecher's resignation as provost in 1991 because of sexual harassment charges. Then he addressed Sprecher's evaluation: "Your evaluation that Dr. Acuña's research was not within the category of basic research was based solely upon Dr. Acuña's curriculum vitae, the departmental letter, and the extramural letters?" What followed was incoherent and often pathetic testimony by Sprecher, who kept saying that he could not remember. Sprecher claimed that he had reviewed the footnotes in *Sonoran Strongman* and the third edition of *Occupied America* and concluded that these were not works of research. Grossman: "You reviewed all the footnotes in *Sonoran Strongman*?" "No. I just looked for the presence." "I beg your pardon? You looked to see if there were footnotes?" (The *Sonoran Strongman* is based on my dissertation and it is heavily footnoted.) In disbelief Grossman asked: "There were no footnotes in *Sonoran Strongman*?" (The letter gave the clear impression that Sprecher had reviewed the books.) Sprecher replied, "I do not recall what was in the book."

Sonoran Strongman was almost exclusively based on archival material from the Bancroft Library, the Mexican State of Sonora state archives, consular records, and so on. Grossman kept pounding at Sprecher about the footnotes in *Sonoran Strongman*: "You looked at footnotes in *Sonoran Strongman* and reviewed them, your conclusion based upon that was that *Sonora Strongman* was not basic research?" "My recollection may be faulty. I thought that it was basic research. But again, I would have to review the material to try and reconstruct my thinking." "Well, I don't understand you, sir. Are you telling us that *Sonoran Strongman* was or was not basic research?" "If my recollection is correct, I did regard it as a research book." Sprecher's letter had implied otherwise and was taken as such by the other reviewers. "Did you regard *Sonoran Strongman* as falling within the category of, quote, basic research as you used that term in your letter which is identified as Exhibit 2?" "As far as I recall, yes."

It was evident that the former provost had not reviewed *Sonoran Strongman* and also that he was reversing his position. "All right. Did you consider that the third edition of *Occupied America* fell within the category of basic research?" "As far as I recall, no. I regarded it as in the category of teaching." When pressed, Sprecher said, "I no longer remember the details of the case. I cannot answer that." He admitted that he relied in his "determinations . . . only upon the departmental letter, the extramural letters, and the curriculum vitae of Dr. Acuña." He also alleged that he based his opinion that Acuña's work was not basic research on the lack of footnotes in *Sonoran Strongman* and in the third edition of *Occupied America*. Grossman later handed copies of both books to Sprecher, who admitted that there were extensive footnotes.

Grossman then turned to the extramural letters. According to Sprecher, "The extramural letters are expected to provide assessment of the person's career in terms of the research significance and any other information that they know about teaching and other information relevant to the four criteria. But I would say that a very important role they play is in the evaluation of the research . . . because they are solicited from experts in the field." After some discussion, Grossman asked: "And in the case of Dr. Acuña, did you take into account the extramural letters in reaching your determination?" "Yes." "[Y]ou believe the extramural letters are mostly addressed to Dr. Acuña's, quote, political activities, unquote, rather than his scholarly work; . . . you believe that some of the extramural writers are without the expertise to assess Dr. Acuna's research; and . . . you believe the letters are not, quote, analytical, unquote. Would that be a fair summary of your conclusions in your letter of recommendation with regard to the extramural letters?" "Yes." The logical next question was, ". . . can you tell me which extramural letters in particular you believed were mostly addressed to Dr. Acuña's political activities instead of his scholarly work?" Although Sprecher had been rehearsed, he could not remember any. He could remember nothing without reviewing them.[7]

Of the letter dated March 21, 1991, from David E. Hayes-Bautista, director of the Chicano Studies Research Center at the

University of California at Los Angeles, Specher denied that this was one of the letters by reviewers without expertise. He admitted that it was in "part analytical." Grossman: "What part is not analytical?" "He refers to one book. It is not clear from the letter how much of Dr. Acuña's work he is familiar with." "And in your opinion, that makes that part of the letter not analytical?" "If I may have a moment, please. There are no substantive comments referring specifically to the work itself." "Which work?" "*Occupied America.*" Grossman: "So you are saying that when Dr. Bautista refers to *Occupied America* as a classic work and says that in his experience, it is the most often utilized title in Chicano Studies course work, that this is not a substantive comment?" "He talks about the book. He doesn't analyze it." Grossman: "He does not analyze the book . . . when Dr. Hayes-Bautista said that the book is the most utilized title in Chicano Studies course work, what did you conclude from that?" "That it is a very respected and often used book." Grossman then asked: "All right. Now, he also says that, 'It should not be considered a mere textbook. It was and continues to be a book on the cutting edge of Chicano Studies research.' Doesn't that to your mind reflect upon the substantive merit of the book?" It was clear that Sprecher did not have a definition for analytical. The examination left Sprecher intellectually defenseless.

Grossman then queried Sprecher on the weight given to political commentary in the evaluation process. According to Sprecher, the university culture did not give weight to this kind of productivity even under the category of creative works. Yet in the personnel files I reviewed, I found frequent evidence that others had received credit for this kind of production. Indeed, one scholar listed them as "political essays."[8] Sprecher had participated in some of these evaluations.

Grossman: "Now, sir, in Dr. Bautista's letter, besides pointing out that writing in the newspapers is part of the Latin American intellectual tradition, he also says that in writing these articles, Dr. Acuña 'brings to the various issues in Latino policy a keen sense of historical dimensions.' And he also says, 'In research terms, Dr. Acuña offers a meta-analysis of the issues, which is a necessary step before the more fine-grained quantitative analysis can begin.' Now, given what . . . Dr. Hayes-Bautista says about the newspaper articles, don't you think that these articles should have been taken into consideration under the research category?" "I no longer can reconstruct my thinking at the time."

In another vein Grossman asked, "Given that you determined in your evaluation of Dr. Acuña that he was highly qualified under the teaching criterion, why didn't you say that in your letter of recommendation to the university?" "That I do not recall. I do not recall how I constructed the letter after reading the file." Sprecher also testified that he had determined that I was highly qualified in university and public service, although he did not put this in his letter. In the letter, Sprecher wrote that I was not qualified on the basis of professional activity. Having pressed Sprecher in vain for the criteria he used, Grossman moved "to strike the answer as nonresponsive."

Plaintiff's counsel then showed Sprecher the extramural letter dated February 22, 1991, from Dr. Mauricio Mazón.[9] He had Sprecher read the part that referred to my political activities, asking whether this letter "is not one of the letters that you were referring to in your letter of recommendation from the extramural examiners which are mostly addressed to the political activities of Dr. Acuña rather than his scholarly work?" The former provost agreed. Grossman then reviewed Mazón's letter, which was extremely positive. Grossman: "Dr. Mazón also says that Dr. Acuña's research was prodigious and the process of reducing the manuscripts to press specifications was painful. Now, sir, with regard to your determinations in your letter of recommendation that Dr. Acuña's work does not fit into the basic research category and is not archival, did you take into account . . . Dr. Mazón's information that he provided in his letter with regard to his part of the process in editing Dr. Acuña's book with regard to the amount of research that went into producing that book?" "As far as I recall, I did." "And on what basis did you decide, despite what Dr. Mazón says, that Dr. Acuña's work is not basic research and not archival?" "I can no longer reconstruct my thinking without reviewing the case." Even when Grossman showed Sprecher the pages in which primary sources were quoted, Sprecher offered no other response.

Grossman's cross-examination was scathing, as he proceeded methodically through Mazón's letter. Grossman: "Dr. Mazón notes that at the time Dr. Acuña was writing the second edition of *Occupied America*, there was a flurry of research on Chicano history and there were many unpublished manuscripts being presented at conferences of scholars, and that Dr. Acuña tried to have all of these unpublished manuscripts, theses, and dissertations cited in *Occupied America*." He then asked, "Did you take this into account, sir, in your determination that Dr. Acuña's scholarly work does not represent the basic research and is not archival?" "Yes, I did as far as I recall." Grossman: "All right. In the introduction to the second edition of *Occupied America*, Dr. Acuña indicates that in writing the second edition, he filled approximately 10,000 index cards with bibliographical citations. Did you take that into account, sir?" Asked if these facts should be considered, Sprecher answered, "I don't know."

After reviewing Mazón's comments on *Sonoran Strongman*, Sprecher conceded merit; according to Grossman, "This is a book that would do credit to any scholar employed by the University of California; isn't that true?" "Correct." Grossman then introduced *A Community Under Siege*. "But you were aware when you evaluated Dr. Acuña that that was another of the books that he had written." "Yes." "And Dr. Mazón in describing *A Community Under Siege* says among other things that, 'Among the available studies of Los Angeles in general and Chicanos in particular, none of them offers the depth of *A Community Under Siege*. A large number of dissertations are indebted to this work,' and that it is his sense that this is the work of Dr. Acuña's which is most frequently cited. Do you have any reason to disagree with any of those opinions?" "No, I do not."[10]

Grossman then questioned Sprecher as to what went into the creation of a field of study. "But, sir, isn't part of scholarship or other creative achievement the development of a field and particularly a new interdisciplinary field? Wouldn't that be included?" "No. We did look at administration as part of service only."

We questioned this definition since in the case of a new field of study, the creation of a core curriculum goes well beyond the normal community service. I had written more than sixty course proposals over the years, which included extensive syllabi and bibliography. I formed the bachelor of arts and the master of arts curricula in addition to taking them through committees and defending them. This, to my knowledge was the first such endeavor of this magnitude.

In Sprecher's recommendation letter he wrote: "This [weakness in scholarship] is further underscored by what appears to be a lack of invitations to participate in scholarly meetings and to present papers and the more general absence of participation in the profession." Grossman: "So it was your conclusion after reviewing Dr. Acuña's curriculum vitae and letters of extramural examiners that Dr. Acuña had a general absence of participation in his profession as a Chicano Studies specialist?" "As a faculty member." "What was Dr. Acuña's profession, sir, at the time he was applying for appointment to the University of California at Santa Barbara?" "He was a faculty member with expertise in Chicano Studies." After some wrangling, Grossman asked: "He was applying for a position of professor of Chicano Studies; is that correct?" "Correct." "So his profession was professor of Chicano Studies; is that correct?" "Yes." "You concluded that he had a general absence of participation in his profession?" "Correct." Grossman then ticked off a litany of conferences at which I keynoted, spoke at the plenary session, or presented papers. Among them were the National Association for Chicano Studies, the Southwest Council on Labor Studies, and several international conferences. "Sir, in regard to your conclusion that Dr. Acuña had a general absence of participation in his profession as a professor of Chicano Studies, did you take into account that in 1989, he received the National Association of Chicano Studies Distinguished Scholar Award?" "As far as I recall, yes." "At the time that you were provost, did any of the members of the Chicano Studies faculty at the University of California, Santa Barbara—had any of them ever received the Distinguished Scholar Award of the National Association of [for] Chicano Studies?" "To the best of my knowledge, no."

Grossman then showed a letter of March 13, 1991, from Dr. Juan Gómez-Quiñones of the University of California at Los Angeles and proceeded in much the same fashion as he had with

Mazón and Hayes-Bautista, with much the same results. He introduced a letter of March 5, 1991, from Professor Deena J. González of the department of history at Pomona College, and again methodically went through the letter. Sprecher admitted that the letter was analytical in nature.[11]

Grossman continued in this vein through the remainder of the extramural letters from the leading scholars in the field. Quoting from a letter by Dr. Arnoldo DeLeon, the foremost Texas Mexican historian, Grossman asked, what "makes you feel that it is not analytical?" "Again, I see positive assessments of the work, but no analysis." Grossman: "Where Dr. DeLeon says that Dr. Acuña succeeded in establishing a model Chicano Studies program, [which] would seem to imply that other universities may look at it as a model to emulate, that would be analytical, wouldn't it?" "That is a positive statement." "But it's not an analytical statement?" "It is not an analytical statement."

Key in the case was the defense argument that I was turned down because I had never supervised doctoral students. The Chicano studies department at UCSB did not have a graduate program, and to this day one has not been instituted. At CSUN I helped establish one of the first, if not the first, M.A. program in Chicano studies. Grossman asked: "When you were provost at the University of California, Santa Barbara, did they have a master of arts program in Chicano Studies?" "No." "Did they have a Ph.D. program in Chicano Studies?" "No."

Dr. Ruiz's letter of recommendation in my case stood out. He is unquestionably a respected scholar and is the senior scholar of Mexican ancestry in the United States. He was a founding chair of the Department of History at the University of California at San Diego. Grossman asked Sprecher whether Ruiz was without expertise to assess Dr. Acuña's research. "I would say [he had] marginal expertise." Sprecher later added, "Because he clearly has some knowledge and interest in the field, but he himself acknowledges that that is not his main area of scholarship." This statement was remarkable. Ruiz did overlapping research on the Mexican border while Sprecher was a mathematician, and yet Sprecher could label Ruiz "marginal." "Now, sir, if I were to tell you that Dr. Ruiz's field of specialization is, in fact, Mexican history, would that cause you to reach the conclusion that he has more than just marginal expertise to evaluate Dr. Acuña's research in the area of Chicano Studies?" "No." "Why not?" Sprecher based his response on a narrow definition of specialized areas of inquiry within history. He put Ruiz in the same category as a historian who specialized in medieval history of Europe and knew nothing about Chicano studies, as indeed was the case with Jeffrey Russell and even Robert Kelley.

Sprecher did not consider Ruiz's letter to be analytical because, according to him, "He talks about Dr. Acuña's work. He does not really give specifics. . . ." Grossman: "Dr. Ruiz says that Dr. Acuña is a fine scholar. Now, do you disagree with that?" "That is an opinion." "Yes, I know it's an opinion. He thinks he [Acuña] is a fine scholar. Do you think Dr. Acuña is a fine scholar?" Sprecher replied, "Yes, I do."

Grossman: "All right. Now, Dr. Ruiz says that when he wrote his own book on Sonora, he relied on Dr. Acuna's book *Sonoran Strongman* for some of the background material. Now, do you consider that to be an important factor to take into consideration in evaluating the scholarly worth of Dr. Acuña's book *Sonoran Strongman*?" "I regard it as a factor. I don't know how strong a factor." Further on, Grossman said, "Dr. Ruiz points out that the first edition of . . . *Occupied America* was published by ERA Publishing in Mexico, and that that was a feather in Acuña's cap. Now, sir, do you consider ERA Publishers in Mexico City to be a minor publisher?" "I have no reason to believe that."

Grossman cited the letter of the CSUN dean of humanities, Jorge García, going through the same litany as he did with the other extramural reviewers. The next letter was that of Carlos Vélez-Ibáñez, who subsequently became the dean of humanities and behavioral sciences at the University of California at Riverside. Vélez-Ibáñez had been a tenured associate professor at the University of California at Los Angeles and was hired as a Professor VII by Riverside. His testimony at the trial was also key. Grossman: "[I]s the letter from Dr. Vélez-Ibáñez [dated February 21, 1991] one of the extramural letters that you feel is mostly addressed to Acuña's political activities rather than his scholarly work?" "No, I do not." After laying the groundwork, Grossman

asked: "Dr. Vélez-Ibáñez states in his letter that as a former tenured faculty member at UCLA, it is his unequivocal opinion that
Dr. Acuña belongs in an off-step category beyond the eight steps
used by the system to denote full professorial status because he regards Dr. Acuña to be a public scholar whom he would compare
to such intellectual giants—he uses the word 'notables.' I would
use the word giants—as Ernesto Galarza, Julian Zamora, George I.
Sánchez, Arthur Campa, and Carlos Castañeda; and furthermore,
that of second-generation scholars, he ranks Dr. Acuña as one
cut above Mario García . . . Now, sir, do you agree with that or disagree with that?" "Okay. I no longer remember the assessment,
but I do regard this as a very—as a comparative, very useful and
very good paragraph. I no longer recall the context with the letter,
but this . . . was and is a very useful, comparative analysis of
Dr. Acuña's standing." "Why did you find it to be very useful?"
"Because he has here some landmarks in which he places Dr.
Acuña relative to the Chicano scholars. In that sense, if I recall
correctly, it was one of the more useful letters because of that."
"Nonetheless, sir, although Dr. Vélez-Ibáñez considers that Dr.
Acuña is beyond all eight steps of your evaluation system, you
reached the conclusion that he was unqualified to be hired by the
University of California even at Step I; isn't that true?" "Correct."
"Well, sir, on what did you base your rejection of Dr. Vélez-
Ibáñez's opinion and arrive at your opinion that Dr. Acuña was
unqualified to be hired even at Step I by the University of California?" "On balancing the evidence in the file as I saw it. This was
one additional piece of information among several." "Well, what
was it in the file, sir, that you balanced against Vélez-Ibáñez's
opinion in order to arrive at your conclusion?" "I would have to
review in detail the entire file, including departmental letters. I do
not recall the detail and cannot reconstruct my thinking."

The examination continued the next day, with Andrés Bustamante taking over from Grossman. (We used a team of a dozen
solo practitioners.) Much to our surprise, Sprecher changed a key
element of his review: "You also stated that some of those letters
were political, correct?" "Yes." "Did the aspect of being a political
letter play a role in your evaluation of recommending Dr. Acuña
to the position?" "None at all. I would like actually to make one

correction, if I may. Upon rereading the letter, I concluded that the characterization—and I want to use my exact language—'It is to his political activities rather than scholarly work' is an incorrect characterization, and it should have read, 'it is to his professional and scholarly activities that the letters are mostly addressed.'" Incredulously, Bustamante asked, "Are you referring to the April 25, 1991 letter, memorandum that you wrote?" "Yes. The second paragraph, fourth line from the bottom of the second paragraph, the middle paragraph." Bustamante read: "It is to his political activities rather than his scholarly work that the letters are mostly addressed." Sprecher: "The correct characterization should have been 'to his professional activities, professional and scholarly activities.'" Bustamante: "Are you now changing your testimony, sir, with regard to this recommendation?" "I guess so."

This was incredible, since the CAP report and other reviewers relied heavily on Sprecher's evaluation and made frequent reference to the judgment that the outside reviewers spoke to my political activities rather than my scholarly ones. In this instance, as in many others, Sprecher had infected the entire process with his bias. We could not use Sprecher's deposition during the trial because Judge Collins had ruled that only references to age could be used, thus depriving us of this important piece of evidence.

* * *

A close look at testimony like the above is important because the process of academic review is repeated thousands of times over. Rarely do candidates have the opportunity to expose such sloppiness in what is supposed to be a scholarly review of a candidate's credentials. Over and over, the reviewers at UCSB testified that it was not their job to write a scholarly review or know anything about the candidate's publications, and in most cases their comments were based on the comments of others or on assumptions about what they said. It was perfectly all right to sound as if they had read the work. This level of intellectual dishonesty surprised me, since these same professors would fail their students if they based their book reviews, for example, solely on someone else's book review.

The UCSB administration wrote off such inconsistencies, arguing that a system of checks and balances operated to make the process fair. This rationale, however, is against existing case law, which says that bias at any level infects the entire process. One instance of this is found in *Maivan Lam v. University of Hawaii*, United States Court of Appeals for the Ninth Circuit, 1994. In this case, "Professor Maivan Clech Lam, a woman of Vietnamese descent, alleged that the University of Hawaii's Richardson School of Law discriminated against her on the basis of her race, sex, and national origin on two occasions when she applied for the position of director of the law school's Pacific Asian Legal Studies Program."

The law school's first search in 1987–1988 was aborted after improprieties took place. A professor who had serious disagreements with Lam requested that he be placed on the search committee, although the administration knew of his bias. Lam was one of four finalists, but the committee leaned in favor of a white male professor. Lam complained about the professor's bias, and a vigorous dialogue took place in which the professor claimed that Lam was unqualified and lacked collegiality. Soon afterwards he resigned from the committee. The search ended, and Lam filed a discrimination grievance. The university rejected her grievance after investigation, but did issue a report detailing breaches in confidentiality and procedural violations. The university vice president promised Lam that the next search for the PALS directorship would be conducted according to the highest standards.

The second search took place in 1989–1990. The process had become polarized, and all of the members of the previous search committee refused to serve on the current one. The committee, when finally constituted, had members who were not favorable to Lam; she was not even a finalist in the second search.

The lower court granted a summary judgment for the university but was overturned by the Ninth Circuit, which is, incidentally, the federal circuit that also controls California. The Ninth Circuit found that "significantly, . . . [a senior faculty member] who headed the appointment committee for a month and disparaged Lam's abilities before the committee and the faculty as a whole, had a biased attitude toward women and Asians." The district court specifically found that the evidence suggests that this professor harbored "prejudicial feelings towards Asians and women." The university had argued that "any faculty prejudice that existed could not, in its view, be attributed to the named defendants in the action." The Court of Appeals held that the principal defendant in this case was the university, which had delegated to the faculty nearly total control over hiring. "The faculty, first in committee, then as a whole, reviews applications, chooses the final candidates, and votes on whether to extend any candidate an offer of employment. The hiring process is therefore not insulated from the illegitimate biases of faculty members. Indeed, since the law school faculty is small—only fifteen members— and great emphasis is placed on collegiality and consensus decisionmaking, even a single person's biases may be relatively influential." The *Lam* decision emphasized that "discrimination at any stage of the academic hiring or promotion process may infect the ultimate employment decision." A "university discrimination case need not prove intentional discrimination at every stage of the decisionmaking process; impermissible bias at any point may be sufficient to sustain liability."

While it is obvious that my case is parallel to the *Lam* case in the infectious results of bias, it is difficult to make the point before the courts, which are naturally inclined toward academe. They enjoy not only the same rationality but the same paradigm. And with the demise of affirmative action, the employment discrimination laws are all that minorities, women, and gays have left to protect their constitutional rights. It is not a matter of intellectual rednecks beating up on them, but rather of the the preservation of what many white scholars consider a credo, the American paradigm. To them, Jack is at the doorstep of academe.

9

El Rodeo:
Truth and Consequences

What I sought to do in this book is to draw the link between the American paradigm and two institutions—the judicial system and higher education—and to show how the New Right has reasserted its hegemony over these institutions. A culture that favors a neoliberal interpretation of society conditions the resulting logic of its institutions. The *Bakke* case, for example, represents this logic, not only as applied by the courts but also as applied in higher education to control and limit the knowledge that doesn't fit the accepted concept of truth and objectivity.

The writing of the book has raised more questions than I originally was prepared to deal with. I am the product of a Jesuit education—Jesuits being the rebels within their own fold—and I have never been prepared to deal with disciplinary objectivity "tied up with the dynamics of the modern academic enterprise, which is sharply divided by discipline and field and rent by competing claims to authority."[1] When the anomalies produced by the "scientific" knowledge contradict my understanding of the facts, my impatience with the superficial "collegiality" of the academy creates tensions.

The culture of the courts and of research universities resembles the moving-picture images of British colonials that I saw in the movie theater as a child. The British all appeared to belong to the same eating club, and they all seemed so much in control. I often sat in awe of the majesty of this culture romanticized on the big screen. I now realize that this fascination with a society's so-

cially constructed version of beauty, civility, and power was natural. Indeed, throughout my trial I had to keep a similar image of
the academic community in balance. We are all conditioned to respect authority and to model ourselves after what we are taught
to consider the best. My parents respected education and vener-
ated teachers. The educated people were the gentlemen, the big
leagues. Thus, when it came to dealing with the so-called scholars, I kept reminding myself and my attorneys that we had to
destroy the myth that these were necessarily the "good people."
The distinction had to be made between schooled people and
educated people.

This image of fairness is very powerful. The tradition of the
Supreme Court hides the truth: its image is that it is not political.
Its non-partisanship allows it to keep the other two branches of
government in check. The American vision of the Court is itself a
romantic construct of the American paradigm. It was invented to
link all social groups in the United States, bringing minorities into
the traditions of governance. The Court plays a part not unlike the
mythical role of the monarch during the Spanish Colonial Period:
the monarch looks after the interests of the indigenous peoples,
the Court looks after minorities. In the United States the courts
perpetuate the illusion that everyone is equal before the law,
when in reality, the courts have served special interests while re-
specting the presence of the middle class. The courts are painfully
aware that the white middle class holds the power to disrupt, and
that this class sets the parameters of what is socially and politically accepted.

Many of the discussions in this book have revolved around
the term "objectivity." Yet the philosophical discussion of objectivity can be seductive. During depositions, my attorneys often
wasted time asking the deponents about their definitions of truth
and objectivity, to the point that I had to quarrel with them to
move on. Objectivity is a construct of academe, which scholars
will admit is relative. At the same time, within academe there are
competing disciplinary claims to objectivity. Each discipline believes that it is more rigorous than the next and that its methods
are more scientific. However, in a crunch they consider each other
as part of one elite body. Through an analysis of my case, I hoped

to expose these elements of the culture of academe that embody and reinforce domination, by exploring the academic culture and the discourse of the defendants. The key was the discourse found in the mountain of personnel files.

We found that the defendants systematically distorted communication. We linked this process to the social theory that suggests that distortion of language is a source of strengthening power relations; its purpose is to privilege one social reality over others and favor some interest groups at the expense of others. For instance, during the case, defendant attorneys persistently distorted case law and the facts. Their ability to do so without being sanctioned by the court was a source of privilege. The university is enveloped by a similar aura. The power to distort, to make decisions, as well as the prestige of the university, converts the members of its reviewing agencies into a privileged caste which is accustomed to being obeyed.

By looking at culture, language, and symbols used by the UCSB reviewers, I hoped to provide an insight into a pattern of these power agendas, and show their meanings in the overall struggle for inclusion of other knowledge. Thomas Kuhn's work on paradigms proved extremely useful in this regard. My purpose was to prove that the defendants had crossed over that thin line that separates social theory and ideology, and that most of their conclusions were based on their political biases. Admittedly, I had assumptions of my own about the process. The normal secrecy that surrounds academic reviews appears to be a model of fairness, tests, checks, and impartiality. Until the decision in the *University of Pennsylvania v. EEOC*, we had to take on good faith that this was true. I assumed that there was another truth, and I had the burden of proof.

Although the documents obtained in discovery overwhelmingly confirmed my assumptions, the courts prevented me from making my findings public. Based on the so-called breach of other professors' rights to confidentiality, these records are for all intents and purposes sealed from the view of the public. The discovery, however, is not lost. It is locked into my historical memory. I proved both to myself and to my attorneys that the system was fraught with cases of discrimination, that my case was not an anomaly, and that the real anomaly was the romanticized portrait of the review process.

Language was exceedingly important in connecting my micro-level experience to the macro-level reality of the super-structure that controls people of color. A link exists between the actions of individual reviewing agencies and society's margin-alization of the "other." There are similarities in the types of questions at the micro and macro levels that reflect the common culture or, better still, the ideology of the movers and shakers at both levels. Society operates in a similar manner at the macro level, where an epistemological tension exists between the judges' and the public's "common-sense knowledge" and the alien facts introduced by people such as myself.

It would be wrongheaded to impute conspiratorial motive to all of the reviewers in my case, or even to all of the supporters of 209, for that matter. My contention is that there are deep structural meanings that determine issues and questions of legitimacy. It is fundamental to understand the distortion of communication that took place in my case, since academic reviews in general are an arbitrary exercise, meant to reward persons who agree with the reviewers and the administration. Similarly, the courts reward those who complement their thinking.

It is also an understatement that I have concerns about the review process and especially its positivist bent. The reader should not, however, conclude that I am against any kind of merit review of faculty members. The opposite is true. I oppose the kind of process that gives faculties and administrators the ability to reward their friends and manipulate the system. This leaves many faculty, including faculty of color, at the caprice of administrators and the majority of their own "colleagues," and it also encourages unequal performance among faculty. In regard to the review process, I feel much like the protagonist in Jack London's *The Iron Heel*. In response to workers' demands that they break the machines, he replied that it wasn't the machines that were bad, the problem was with those who controlled the trusts who in turn controlled the machines. Moreover, while I am a critic of posi-tivism, I concede the strength of the scientific method and its im-portance in the accumulation and interpretation of knowledge.

My quarrel is with those who manipulate and distort knowledge to dominate others, especially the working class.

Bakke *Revisited*

Bakke gave the right wing a weapon. *Bakke* revived and invigorated a language which gave meaning and strength to the culture war. Incredibly, the reputed legal scholars on the Supreme Court failed to test the crucial hypothesis that white males as a class were being discriminated against by affirmative action. Besides failing to carry out quantitative testing, the Court failed to place Bakke's case into a social or historical context. Words of legislators were taken out of context. The justices did not test their own assumptions. The dicta in *Bakke* were more the ideological consensus of the justices than reasoned decisions. Nevertheless, it was the use of the language of the decision that confuses an understanding of affirmative action. The justices gave the opponents of affirmative action culture-bound assumptions, and thereby gave them a source of power. The authority of *Bakke* is based not on logic but on the court's constitutional power to interpret the law. It has nothing to do with fairness. It has everything to do with power.

The nexus of *Bakke* and the assault on the concept of racial equality is the notion that Californians are creating a "color-blind" society. It gives those in the vital center, as Clinton calls it, the pretext for abolishing the only real remedy that exists for a pattern of racial discrimination in this country. With 209, Californians wash their hands of responsibility. They cloak the issue with the legitimacy of law. It is the will of the people. A critical analysis of the discourse not only raises questions about the motives of the 209 leaders but also reveals why and how even some minority-group members and women are drawn into this web of deception.

Part of this deception is the invocation of a lofty commitment to civil rights in the form of "color blindness." The logic says that through presumably value-free merit examinations, fairness is achieved. In the case of academe and the courts, for example, the legitimation processes are put in the hands of those who, because of their training, are fit to administer the rules of fairness, color blindness, and merit selection. I have sought to explode this myth by showing that these processes are administered by a privileged caste whose biases impede efforts to diversify, change, or remedy racist practices, especially when this caste traditionally has been privileged in the workplace. These biases override established tests, which more often than not become ways to evade the written law.

A device of those in power is to prevent critics from showing that events and actions are part of a general pattern. If an injustice is portrayed as an individual case, it becomes an aberration. Police supporters attempted to portray the case of Rodney King as an isolated exception. The vicious discussion of whether the Germans killed six million Jews serves to distract from the inhumanity of the deed, as does the discussion of whether Spaniards were guilty of the genocide of the indigenous peoples of the New World. An understanding of pattern and practice is vital to an understanding of the American paradigm and how it is maintained. In this context, the *Bakke* decision of the late 1970s was no aberration. It is central to the death of the idea that there should be a remedy for discrimination. It opened the floodgates.

Proposition 209 Revisited

The passage of Proposition 209 should have been a wake-up call for progressives in the United States. It represented a tremendous victory for the New Right. Many people who voted for 209 believed in their souls that they were not racist, and that the only thing they wanted was fairness. What I posited in my argument is that their belief is part of an American paradigm that distorts the meaning of fairness and the meaning of affirmative action; their assumptions were based more on their ideology than on fact.

Proposition 209 symbolizes the culmination of a power struggle that began three decades ago to refocus the "common sense" of the courts and higher education. Just as the body naturally rejects a "foreign" heart implant, the American common sense naturally rejects concepts not firmly embedded in the paradigm. In the case of 209, the rejection was induced by its proponents' harping that anyone who works hard enough can make it in

America. Proposition 209 is a testament to the ability of the New Right to exploit the fundamental set of beliefs of Americans. It is carefully crafted by culture warriors such as William Simon. Through its organization, the right regained ideological hegemony. The New Right masterfully packaged the neoliberal tradition of this country as the wave of a new world order that supposedly demonstrated the superiority of capitalism. Fairness and equality were hindrances to the natural development of this new order.

As a late boss of the California Democratic party, Jesse Unruh, once quipped, "Money is the mother's milk of politics." The New Right foundations followed the example of the private sector in molding public opinion through the use of ads and misinformation. When the spin doctors got through with the expensive ad campaigns, voters repeated the same pattern that they followed in response to efforts of citizens' groups to tax or regulate tobacco and alcohol. In the case of the tobacco and liquor lobbies, voters believed that they were voting for freedom of choice. With 209, in some cases voters even believed they were voting for part of Martin Luther King's dream.

Proposition 209 cannot be separated from other right-wing movements, such as Proposition 187, English Only, and the *Bell Curve* proposition that minorities don't make it because of their genes. All of these measures are framed in terms of a crisis, the loss of American values. Subjectivity is framed by claims to objectivity. Most important, the right has a coherent narrative: the discourse suggests that the crisis and failure in education are produced by policies promoting equality for people of color, which results in inequality for whites. The logical conclusion is to make sectors of a society unequal once more, in order to ensure the quality of American institutions. It is a return to an absurd theory of the survival of the fittest, a theory that justifies inequality and unfairness yet appears to satisfy the American obsession with being ethical, objective, and truthful.

In the early legal challenges to Proposition 209, Chief U.S. District Judge Thelton Henderson, an African American, pointed out that the measure, though neutrally worded, would abolish only programs benefiting minorities and women, while leaving other groups, such as veterans and children of college alumni, free to ask government agencies for preferential treatment. The court said the measure discriminated against minorities by preventing them from seeking local remedies. The 9th U.S. Circuit Court of Appeals overturned Henderson. If a court agrees that Californians were seeking a "color-blind" society, are they therefore absolved? The "legitimacy" of positivist law does not make it right; it does not make it the truth; and it does not prove that the justices were unbiased. It does say that the neoliberal rationality has the power of socially constructing truth in order to promote the status quo and perpetuate the social outcomes which exploit people of color. It is the prism through which accepted language, policies, and practices, as African American historian Manning Marable has said, "always served a larger class objective." It creates a political culture around which the right organizes.

A Pattern of Resistance

Americans have an obsession with isolating arguments to individual cases instead of looking for patterns of behavior, although patterns abound. The University of California, for instance, has spent millions in public funds to settle sex bias cases during the past few years, involving female professors who claimed sexist biases stood in the way of their tenure. As a condition of settlement, UC has insisted on a gag rule barring women plaintiffs from discussing the agreements or testifying in other disputes. Secrecy is very important in preserving the mystique of fairness in academe. To protect this image, the UC has gotten protective orders that sanction women for deviating from the terms of settlements. It has also historically denied that any suits have been filed against it, even when the record shows otherwise. It was not until recently that the legislature has forced the UC to give annual reports on the payment of outside counsel.

I am in no way insinuating that individual employment discrimination cases, including my own, are as important as Proposition 209. California's 209 is one of those major battles that have occurred in this century. Even so, at the micro level there are hundreds, thousands of skirmishes that are fought by local communities and individuals. Cases such as my own will become increasingly important as the idea of affirmative action goes the way of the nation's commitment to desegregation. The passage of 209 has sent us back to the pre–Civil Rights era. It's back to the old equal protection clause of the Fourteenth Amendment.

My case, *Acuña v. The Regents of the University of California, et al.*, is important because it represents a victory: a jury found that the UC discriminated against me, using the pretext that my work was not scholarly. It is unique because of the volume of documents produced in discovery, which have proved invaluable in testing my analyses. It also happens to be the most expensive case of employment discrimination involving the UC system in at least the past ten years, and probably the most expensive in its history. The costs alone raise the questions of abuse, and of the rationale of the defendants. As I mentioned earlier, an apology, some reparation, such as a scholarship fund, would have resolved the issue. The reality is that the arrogance of the "scientists" does not allow them to be wrong. Their process has to be objective and truthful, and they will defend it even at the cost of millions of dollars.

One of the highest-profile employment discrimination cases involving UC was settled in December 1995. Berkeley architect Marcy Wang won a million-dollar settlement including attorney fees. (Her lawyers, incidentally, called my attorneys to thank them for going to trial, thus opening the way for Wang, who up to this point had been stonewalled.) After fighting the university for ten years, Wang found letters in her tenure file from two professors who said she had been "railroaded" out of the department. Wang refused to agree to secrecy in her settlement agreement. She never returned to UC and instead ran her own architecture firm in Berkeley.[2]

Another settlement was made in the case of a UC Berkeley mathematician, Jenny Harrison, in a tenure dispute. Harrison had gained worldwide attention in the mid-1980s for solving a problem that had baffled mathematicians for nearly a half century. Instead of making Harrison the second tenured woman in a 75-member faculty, her male colleagues denied her the ultimate status in 1986. She appealed. She alleged that math professor Calvin Moore, who was serving as UC's system-wide affirmative action officer, said, "Women's brains are biologically inferior to men's" and that another professor, Robion Kirby, said: "Women belong at home in the kitchen caring for their families." Professor John Neu allegedly made sexist jokes in class; Neu stated that his jokes didn't influence his opinion of Harrison. Another professor allegedly said Harrison "didn't smell like a mathematician." Harrison, in what has become standard UC practice in discrimination cases, was harassed and intimidated by the UC. After a seven-year legal fight, Harrison won a full professor's job with tenure and a $200,000 confidential settlement. Harrison and Wang are both members of WAGE (We Advocate Gender Equity), a group formed by women employees at the UC aimed at ending the secrecy and breaking what they see as a pattern of bias. One of their main concerns is that the UC frustrates meritorious suits by spending excessive amounts on outside legal fees which are designed to suffocate the other side.

Investigative reporters, through the California Public Information Act, have learned that the UC faced sixty-nine sex-discrimination lawsuits in the six years ending in 1994. Six of those suits were filed by female professors who claimed they lost tenure because of sexual stereotypes. Other suits alleged women were denied even a chance at being reviewed for tenured positions. UC has paid more than $4 million in damages and attorneys' fees in those cases, according to UC reports to the state legislature—all of this in the name of defending abuses in the faculty governance processes.

The review process in my case revealed a great deal about the distortion of language, domination, and power agendas on university campuses, the arrogance of positivism and academe, and the exclusion of unwanted elements of society from institutions of higher learning. The very language of the ad hoc report, in stating that it has a "trustee relationship" to Chicana/o studies, excludes that department from parity in the university. Chicana/o studies, to the reviewers, was an "inchoate" field that had to be guided by the wisdom of those holding keys to the truth. If left to their own devices, members of the field would be too emotional, lack objectivity, and fail to reach a level of excellence.

The testimony of David Holtby highlighted the fact that my own paradigm of history is incompatible with that of most American historians. Patriotism and/or the adherence to an eighth-grade vision of American history should not be the litmus test of methodological objectivity or of historical truth. Reviewer and historian Robert Kelley was demanding an ideological purity matching his idea of patriotism. Since he was deemed the expert, and the reviewers considered me a historian, he became the authority to whom even UCSB Chancellor Barbara Uehling deferred. Like marionettes, others repeated his ridiculous charge that because I said that the United States was to blame for the Mexican-American War, I had lied.

The deposition of David Sprecher, the former provost, showed that although he claimed to make an unbiased evaluation of my file, he had not even read the material. Either he could not remember what he wrote in his review letter and why, or he simply distorted the truth. Almost exactly worded letters of outside experts on behalf of other candidates whom Sprecher liked were praised, while in my case the outside letters were called "not analytical" and criticized for addressing my "political" rather than scholarly merit. From the personnel files I found that in general, the letters of outside experts on behalf of other candidates were not as strong as mine. I did not have a single negative letter in the file. This was not the case in the majority of the files that I read. Indeed, there were highly negative letters in the files of the defendants, which Sprecher and other administrators ignored.

The role of the Committee on Academic Personnel in nominating members to the secret ad hoc committee was suspect. Every effort seems to have been made to evade the appointment of a minority scholar to the ad hoc committee.[3] The outcome was an emotional, unscholarly, and highly biased, value-laden report, which violated procedures by not basing the review on the documents. Depositions of other members, Giles Gunn and Wallace Chafe, showed that they did not carefully read my materials nor did they respect the Chicana/o experts in the field.

CAP itself was headed by Jeffrey Russell, a historian, who had deeply negative feelings about affirmative action. CAP's final report was in great part based on the ad hoc committee's report. From the depositions it was clear that the other CAP members did not read the evidence.

The final administration review was just as negligent. The administrative analyst called to the attention of Associate Vice Chancellor Julius Zelmanowitz the fact that the reports were highly emotional. Zelmanowitz dismissed this advice. There was *ex parte* communication about my candidacy between administrators, dissident members of the department, and even off-campus parties. It was established during depositions that no one in the administration read my works. They relied on the reports.

Throughout the process, ideology framed and limited discourse. It fed the bias of the members who had assumptions about Chicana/o studies research and the role of a scholar. Communication was systematically distorted so as to maintain and enhance the privilege of faculty governance to define abstractions such as truth and objectivity and to judge what is meritorious. One of the generalizations that I make from reviewing documents in my case is that university professors routinely perpetuate conditions that make it possible for them to ignore the views of working people and of others "unlike" them. They popularize the notion that criticism is generated by those who aren't winners within the system and that "established interests" work for the common good. In my case, my links to the activist community added to their suspicions. I was therefore portrayed as a "popular" historian, which amounted, in their code, to damning criticism.

The discourse in their reports and the depositions show clearly that while questioning authority is usually considered democratic, in my case it was vilifed as demagogic. I became a "cult professor." They rationalized that they were searching for the truth and I was trying to distort it. With few exceptions, the reviewers portrayed me as a malcontent, not a seeker of truth. They perpetuated the notion that it was I who was portraying Chicanos as victims of exploitation. I could not be believed because my career depended on finding discrimination wherever I looked. I was a threat to the American paradigm that defines Americans as inherently democratic and just.

My case illustrated the power of the faculty governance process, which functions to suppress unpopular knowledge and to silence those professors who do not adhere to the American paradigm. Professions are inherently monopolistic, controlling the production of new practitioners. The academic disciplines control the graduate programs that confer the privilege of teaching in the university. Elitism is inherent in the system. Professors have lifetime tenure, which gratifies their egos and reinforces the positivist culture. They operate in a closed market where conformity is greatly rewarded, and they defend their elitist system from change. The academy has specializations within specializations. Every discipline supposedly is run as an autonomous enterprise that sets its own standards for employment and advancement. It would seem logical that one such specialization within these disciplines would include Chicanos and Chicanas, who comprise some 18 million residents of this country, and that specialists would be hired within the discipline to teach its classes. But this is not the case.

One of the important outcomes of my lawsuit is that it has demythicized the cult of the "expert." My court experience also taught me considerably about the system. Many if not most plaintiffs are forced to carry the case *pro per*, which means that they represent themselves. Equity would warrant that the courts take this into account. They do not. The case taught me that the judges have vast networks. In California it is more probable than not that they are UC graduates, mainly UCLA graduates with ties to alumni and professors, reinforced through law school interns. They understand a common language which is based on the same positivist model as that of the university professors with whom they have ties. In other words, they enjoy a similar culture. They are from the same class background and in most cases the same racial ancestry. The experience taught me that if there is any hope of including variables such as fairness and justice, the jury system has to be preserved and expanded to include working people of all races.

My case also taught me a lot about Chicana/o studies scholars. They are part of the culture of the university, and subject to its reward system. They crave acceptance by the academy, to the point that much of their research is tailored to fit what the institution wants. Much less is said about the need for paradigm shifts in Chicano literature than in its African American, Native American, or women's studies counterparts. There is also a certain immaturity about many Chicana/o scholars, a lack of confidence, even an inferiority complex, which leads them to go to extremes, rationalizing their biases through the use of pretexts. They charge others with bias (of gender, race, politics, and so forth) to conceal their own. The main reason for this, I believe, is that an essential part of positivist logic is to evade responsibility for one's actions and recognition of one's true motives—in this case, opportunism and a lack of political commitment.

Cultural Resistance: Change It or Lose It

If Proposition 209 is taken to its logical conclusion and excludes from higher education minorities—who in many states are becoming the majority—one of the questions must be, Should leaders in these communities seek alternatives? In the 1960s, many activists embraced the dream of creating alternative institutions. Today, minorities suggest that we should to look at televised courses in higher education, which also bring the classroom to the public. Such courses already provide more interesting and innovative material than do most professors. The microcomputer also brings the world to the classroom, as does multimedia computing, still in its infancy. Presently, students in Mexico City can take courses via TV, and the practice is becoming more widespread.

The questions, however, really should be, Why should the public pay for professors who don't teach Latinos and other people of color? Why should the excluded continue to be taxed for the maintenance of these universities? On whom should the burden fall of proving that present research in academe is worthy of public support? Even the solutions to poor teaching suggested above have been vigorously resisted by faculty culture. In virtually all research institutions and large universities, faculty do not feel they have time to devote to serious innovation in the classroom. For one thing, they have been doing quite well financially

and professionally without these innovations. Faculty culture resists innovations because, as in the case of solar energy, there is no
running meter. Why fix something that is serving you so well?
Faculty fear that reforms would affect faculty perks, such as
tenure and promotion based on research activities.

Arguments about what to teach, to whom, and by whom,
are standard in the history of higher education. This discourse is
not new; it has been taking place at least since the latter half of the
nineteenth century, when the shift from emphasis on religious
learning to scientific knowledge occurred in higher education.
The research universities, however, redesigned their research mission in response to the priorities of funders and the government.
Poor folk do not presently have that sort of *palanca*.

These core issues of the university's teaching and research
mission intertwine with a number of less central, though still serious, problems: athletic scandals, sexual harassment, scientific
misconduct, fiscal mismanagement, administrative inefficiencies,
and litigation of tenure cases, to name those most in public view.
In my opinion, the universities are vulnerable. The public is skeptical and the universities are losing credibility. Recent scandals
at the UC and other institutions of higher learning don't help,
for example, the hefty bonuses and large pensions given to UC
president David Gardner and other UC administrators when they
resigned, and the more recent scandal surrounding "preferential
treatment" given to wealthy alumni and influential parents of applicants to the UC. Although research universities have enjoyed
an extraordinarily high level of public trust throughout American history, this is changing, and Chicanas/os should exploit the
growing skepticism. It is during these periods of the erosion of
public confidence that changes in the culture of the institution can
be made—witness the gains made by the New Right in the present culture war.

The strategy to change academe and reverse the right's success can be implemented in part by just telling the truth. The vast
majority of the so-called research turned out in the modern university is worthless. It does not result in any measurable benefit
to society. Many academics have disdain for their students and for
their teaching; very few are of the caliber of Nobel prize recipi-

ents. As one conservative critic said: "They are the corrupt priests of America's colleges and universities and, while small in number, their influence is large and pervasive. They are the great pretenders of academe. They pretend to teach, they pretend to do original, important work. They do neither."[4]

We cannot live with the consequences of the present "truth." The question must be asked: Why should minorities follow ethnically charged law made at the ballot box? The human consequences could be devastating. Proposition 209 will mean fewer lawyers and doctors of color, fewer minority college students, fewer women firefighters, police, and highway workers. While the full impact of 209 has not yet been measured, a federal court-imposed ban on affirmative action in *Hopwood v. University of Texas* at the University of Texas Law School has resulted in a 92 percent decline in African American admissions and 74 percent decline in Latino admissions. In 1997 the number of black students admitted dropped to 11, from the 65 admitted in 1996 under affirmative action. In May 1997, Texas officials announced that not a single black student would attend their law school in 1997–1998, in part because those few blacks UT had accepted decided to enroll at schools they found more "hospitable to minorities." Similarly, as a result of the 1995 decision by the University of California's Regents to do away with racial preferences, black admissions at Berkeley's law school dropped from 75 in 1996 to 14 in 1997, while at UCLA's law school, black admissions fell from 104 to 21. Changes in undergraduate admissions are not quite so dramatic nor is the fall-off quite so steep for Hispanic students. But the pattern is striking nonetheless. The University of California's Boalt Hall School of Law is unlikely to have many more Mexican American or Central American first-year law students.

Discrimination crosses class lines. Although Latinos are stereotyped by most Euro-Americans as poor, Latinos made up a quarter of the southern California middle class in 1990. American-born Latinos there were four times more likely to belong to middle-class households than to poverty-stricken ones. Even foreign-born Latinos are moving up, with a third of households headed by foreign-born Latinos classified as middle class in 1990. The reaction of this sector to the glass ceiling presently being riveted into place by 209 and 187 will and should have consequences. The proportion of Latinos in southern California has increased from 14 percent in 1970 to 38 percent in 1996. This group, as well as other minorities, is becoming increasingly sensitive to the growing discrimination against them.

Disparity is evident in the arena of education. California taxpayers, for example, subsidize University of California undergraduates from families with college-educated parents to a much larger extent than they do minorities and poor working-class students of all races. These families earn median incomes as high as $66,000 a year, whereas the average taxpayer makes about $16,000 a year and is not college-educated. According to an article in the *Nation* of September 18, 1995, a rich/poor gap exists in Los Angeles which ranks third behind those of Calcutta and Rio de Janeiro. The average black taxpayer makes $12,000 a year; the average Latino taxpayer in Los Angeles earned about $10,000 a year in 1990. Neither has a college degree. Black and Latino taxpayers work to subsidize the educations of children from relatively wealthy families, a fact that will certainly come to grate on them in the future.

The decision of the Regents of the University of California to abolish affirmative action seemed to raise troubling questions about university governance. Ostensibly, the Regents opposed the wishes of the university president, all nine chancellors, and the faculty senates. The Regents were criticized by these entities, who thus gave the appearance of opposing discrimination. However, in reality, the professors were engaging in doublespeak. The academic culture reflected institutionalized barriers to equality even before the Regents acted at California Governor Pete Wilson's behest. In fifteen years the percentage of black faculty in the UC system increased from just 1.8 percent to 2.5 percent. The number of Native American faculty fell in this period from 21 to 19. Latinos are 4.2 percent of faculty, a figure that includes wealthy Latin Americans from countries such as Argentina and even Spain, who do not necessarily identify with Chicanos or Latinos. The number of Mexican American professors is under 3 percent. In 1996 blacks made up about 10 percent of the total state population and Latinos approached 30 percent.

The new color-blind policy in California and the *Hopwood* ruling in Texas have created an air of uncertainty about the future representation of minority students within research institutions. They have substantially lowered the glass ceiling. Proposition 209 bars minorities and women from winning affirmative action programs from local governments in cases of discrimination. It marks an era when the courts have turned a blind eye to history. The judges act as if the effects of discrimination are behind us. Regardless of whether or not Proposition 209 is ultimately found to be unconstitutional, it is creating a divided society.

I have argued that affirmative action should not just be about diversity. It should be about remedies. I do not believe, for example, that upper-class South Americans are entitled to remedies. In contrast, first- and even second-generation university students of working-class parents should be assisted to make the leap. The evidence is incontrovertible that the quality of life for minorities improves as they increase their political representation and produce more lawyers and other professionals. Discrimination laws should be strictly enforced. Remedies should be defended.

Political struggle and resistance at the ballot box do have positive consequences, even for the losing side. The campaign against 209 at least averted the potential disaster of minority communities voting for the measure. Initial polling in 1995 suggested heavy minority support for it: 55 percent of African Americans, 70 percent of Latinos, and 78 percent of Asian Americans. On the day of judgment, 74 percent of African American voters, 76 percent of Latinos, and 61 percent of Asian-Pacific-Americans said no. Also, 58 percent of the Jewish community statewide voted against the initiative, as did 59 percent of those with incomes less than $20,000. Latino voter turnout increased 40 percent more than in 1994 and the African American turnout doubled, while the City of Los Angeles rejected 209 with 60 percent of the vote. And voters must remain vigilant: with affirmative action still warm in the grave, individual districts in California, including Orange County Unified south of Los Angeles, have moved to eliminate bilingual instruction. The culture warriors are already pushing the English Language Education for Immigrant Children Initiative, which proponents say is based on the ideas that schools have a "moral obligation" to teach students English. At the same time, the language of 209 has been extended. An unintended consequence is that outreach programs focused on predominantly minority schools are in jeopardy.

The Chicana/o Scholar

It is now more important than ever for a dialogue on why Chicana/o scholars have failed to come up with new questions that challenge the American paradigm. The problem is not whether Chicana/o scholars have produced new knowledge. It is about the narrative. Chicana/o scholars spend too much time trying to be scientists rather than gaining experiential knowledge. The gap between knowledge and the qualitative experiences of Chicana/o scholars is widening, and it is exacerbated by their relative isolation and lack of parity in the university. The lack of identification with either a university or outside community has dissociated Chicana/o scholars from the outcome of the culture war, in which they should be at least politically and intellectually interested. As scholars and as residents, we should be involved in the debate over truth and objectivity in history. The acceptance of myths and distorted truths is a threat to real democracy.

If the present direction of Chicana/o studies continues, the field will be mainstreamed in a few years. I personally have a preference for advocacy research in the tradition of W. E. B. Du Bois, since it has a moral and societal purpose. I recognize that the scope and content of these studies have to be broadened to include many areas that have been excluded because of the lack of scholars to do the research. The inclusions of diverse methodologies are important—but not at the exclusion of empirical evidence. Octavio Romano used to criticize the anthropologist who studied people as if they were laboratory animals. I fear that much of our research, as we remove ourselves from our own people, will make the same error.

Advocacy, as a guiding principle of research and discourse, is not simple. Revisionists are only tolerated within prescribed parameters. We remain the unwanted children of the academy, which instinctively moves to reject alien ideas and viciously attacks the credibility of dissidents. Myths are rampant, for example, that historians make herculean efforts to curb and control subjective tendencies and that the training of American historians and other social scientists include at almost every level lessons on "methodology," on the proper use of sources, and on the need for substantiating the countervailing evidence. These myths must be exploded. "Everything is political" is more than just a cliché—and everyone consciously or unconsciously is an advocate for his or her interests. Chicana/o scholars should be taking the lead in promoting discourse on these issues. This debate would invigorate discourse.

Instead, the present establishment is demanding and getting conformity from Chicana/o scholars, whose perspective and source of knowledge are becoming like those of the mainstream scholar. The result is that many Chicana/o scholars are not bringing new knowledge to the table. They are recycling knowledge based on limited survey sampling and quantitative data, without contact with the culture of working-class Chicanos and Latinos. The situation is critical since the research is conducted by professionalized young Chicana/o scholars whose historical memory does not include any sense of a struggle.

Advocacy challenges neoliberal ideas such as those above. Without advocacy, conformity results. In the process, knowledge is homogenized to the point that new ideas are purged. To conceal their purposes and their resistance to change, many scholars devise sophisticated theories and methods. Theory and methods become weapons to hide their lack of facts. Advocacy is necessary for the competition of ideas; it is the driving force behind scholarship.

Neutrality, in contrast to advocacy, implies coexistence with, and thus approval of, those who control the superstructure. It implies tacit acceptance of the operating paradigm. I reject the proposition that objectivity requires neutrality, and is the process of justifying both sides. Another point of view can be described but not justified. There are a right and a wrong.

The meaning of truth and objectivity has been debated in philosophy for centuries and it is a proper concern for scholars. In the sciences it goes beyond the level of discourse, becoming dogma.

In the 1960s, truth and objectivity were flatly denied by a larger network of historians, sociologists, and literary critics, who evolved into feminists, multiculturalists, and antagonists of cultural hierarchies. In recent years, however, skepticism about American society has fallen into disrepute. Nativist scholars have once more become credible and, instead of arguing the facts, have fallen back on pretensions to "truth" and "objectivity." In this context, criticism of American society becomes the opposite of truth and objectivity.

Is objective truth obtainable? It depends on whom you are talking to. The scholar can strive to find the evidence and learn what really happened, within the limitations of a multiplicity of facts. In any type of humanist or social science research, the scholar must make assumptions and generalizations about patterns of social interaction, and then put them into a historical context. These syntheses greatly rely on the craft of the scholar, who uses the raw material and then refines it through interpretive methods. How the scholar handles the evidence is an art. It is much the same as pathology. Not all pathologists are equal, and they differ in making judgment calls, such as whether to diagnose a cancer at the borderline stage or at stage four. The lower the level, the harder it is to distinguish the type of cancer.

It is here that qualitative knowledge is so imperative. Anyone can interpret the obvious facts. It becomes difficult, however, when the facts are complex and when more than empirical knowledge is of the essence. The scholar must penetrate the culture. And even then, understanding is difficult, varying with the scholar's range of knowledge, gender, and class background.

In almost every case, the establishment of Chicana/o studies has been accompanied by intense institutional resistance. Success in even gaining a foothold has been directly related to population growth and not to the willingness of the institutions to make needed reform or to include knowledge about Chicanas/os and Latinas/os. With this growth, just as in the historical past, there are pressures to make the curricula more relevant, not only to students of Latin background but to students of the general population. The escalation of societal problems is also making research more solution-oriented. The growing attitude is that we expect answers from medicine, the law, and engineering; why not from the universities? Thus far, higher learning has evaded accountability. However, it is just a matter of time before the public will demand results from all institutions in the assimilation of the "unmelted minorities." Latinos, at least, despite poverty and victimization, are fighting back.

Latino and Chicano scholars cannot afford to be used to check the rising tide of anger among Latinos. It is a natural reaction to the hatreds in this country. The present

> economy of scarcity has made traditional European-American populations fearful for their jobs, resentful about their fallen or never-realized fortunes, and angry at immigrant and indigenous non-European populations whom they blame for their eroding fortunes. Working-class whites have become the striking point for neoconservative middle-class intellectuals, for politicians, for the religious right, and for others who have interests in staving off cultural change in America.[5]

It is not people of color who have incited racial divisions in this country. The culture warriors have made the expression of angry rhetoric a necessity.

The Outcome

The infamous Hollywood madam, Polly Adler, once said that a house is not a home. In the same manner, the United States is not a color-blind society, and it will never be one as long as there are gaping class differences among various peoples in society. Today's upholders of "European ethics"—or their parents and grandparents—made it because of the availability of jobs that, after unionization, paid double and triple the minimum wage. Good schools, the availability of low-cost housing, and low interest rates gave them an equity in society. Today, in contrast, the nation is getting rid of union jobs and is spending less on schools and other social programs.

The evidence is incontrovertible that income gaps in the U.S. narrowed in the first decade after the Civil Rights Act. It is also incontrovertible that as the *Bakke* mind-set became more popular, income gaps widened and social tensions increased. The percentage of young Latinos living in poverty in the United States has increased from 27 percent in 1970 to 40 percent today. Latino males in 1997 earned just 66 percent as much as white men, down from 74 percent in 1980. The widening wage gap has been driven by discrimination against people of color and cannot be reasonably explained by a merit system. While there is a statistically significant disparity between Latinos and whites, the courts allow higher education, for example, to evade culpability. It can easily be proven that Latinos are underrepresented in higher education; however, the courts have accepted another test which makes it nearly impossible to prove a discriminatory motive based on race. For Chicanas/os to prove that they are underrepresented, they must prove that they are underutilized, which means that their institution employs less than the overall percentage of Ph.D.s in the fields of study to which they belong. These percentages are not based on a region, such as the Southwest, where Mexican Americans are concentrated, but on national figures, further diluting the pool. In good positivist fashion, cases live and die on numbers. It all centers on statistical probability.

Education is important in explaining the gap in income. But it is not the sole element. Latin American males over the age of 16 participate in the Southern California work force at a higher rate than members of any other ethnic group. Despite language and cultural barriers, Mexican and Central American immigrants in general go to college, and they succeed. But systematically, these efforts are being undermined by hysterical voter initiatives and the courts. Only recently has President Bill Clinton acknowledged that "white racism remains the nation's chief destructive edge." Only in 1995 did he recognize unemployment rates of African Americans and Latinos; the wage gap between women and men; and the fact that white men with high school degrees make more than Latina women with college degrees. According to Clinton, white men make up 43 percent of our work force but hold 95 percent of top corporate jobs. A Chicago Federal Reserve Bank report affirmed that African American and Latino applicants are denied home loans up to twice as often as white applicants with the same qualifications. Out of 90,000 complaints to the federal government of employment discrimination based on race, ethnicity or gender, fewer than 3 percent were for so-called reverse discrimination.

The present telecommunications revolution is expanding the gap between the haves and have-nots, as well as between different races. During the nine years before 1993, computers increased dramatically in white in contrast to black and Latino homes. Historically, the public library softened this gap. But because of antitax initiatives, many libraries that were accessible to poor people and minorities have closed. As the eminent sociologist Manuel Castells, a professor at the University of California at Berkeley, has pointed out, "the information technology development is creating an increasingly productive global economy, but, at the same time, social inequality and social exclusion are increasing . . . individuals could become handicapped, and then they become unable to leave their condition of unemployment, or unable to be valued by society."[6]

Some recent studies suggest that income gaps are beginning to narrow again. But this is not true for all, especially Latinos.

In 1995, the poverty rate declined, the median income rose, and the economic growth of the nation was not only strong but broad-based, reaching the bottom end of the population and the middle class. Wonderful news, right? Not for Hispanic-Americans. Among Latinos, 8.4 million, nearly one in three, were still living in poverty.

The new census data, based on a survey of 50,000 households, showed that the widening gap between the haves and have-nots has slowed. While income increased for wealthy families during the last two decades, it declined for the poor and middle class. But for the second year in a row, that polarization of incomes has diminished for most Americans, except for Latinos.

While the median household income increased by 2.2 percent for non-Hispanic whites, and by 3.6 percent for African-Americans, from 1994 to 1995, for Latinos it fell by 5.1 percent, and by 14.6 percent since 1989.

And the gap of income inequality between Latinos and the rest of the population is likely to grow over the coming years, potentially reaching all-time highs in Hispanic poverty. While the poverty rate for African-Americans reached record lows last year, the Hispanic poverty rate, which decreased only from 30.7 to 30.3 percent, 'failed to show any statistically significant improvements in 1995, remained near its all-time high, and surpassed the African-American poverty rate for the first time,' according to an analysis of the Census data by the Center on Budget and Policy Priorities, a Washington-based, anti-poverty research institute. The non-partisan organization noted that this is one of the elements of 'disturbing news' that tempered the otherwise good news from the Census Bureau.[7]

The American paradigm dictates that scholars should not be concerned with solutions to problems outside its bounds. Naturally, class should not be mentioned or considered as a factor in social analysis. Moreover, one is branded as a liberal by the statement that less government hurts the working poor. According to Stanford University economist Martin Carnoy, the invisible hand "that shapes the ugly job market for African-Americans is neither IQ nor laziness. It is government or, to be precise, the decreasing use of it."[8] Government in this equation must oppose job bias, not promote it by measures such as 209. I, for one, am still looking for those color-blind employers. We must drive home the message that while the labor market in 2005 will still be overwhelmingly Anglo, about 73 percent of all workers, the number is down from 78 percent in the early 1990s. Moreover, the Anglo population is aging, and their numbers will shrink. Nationally, Latinos, who accounted for just 7.7 percent of all workers in 1993, by 2005 will be 11.2 percent, almost equal to the African American percentage. In California, Latinos made up 25 percent of the work force in 1993. In Los Angeles County, Latinos make up 55 percent of the population under the age of 20. By 2005 they will dominate the workplace.[9]

According to James P. Smith, a senior economist at RAND, a Santa Monica think tank, "There will be a two-tier system. The top tier will be Anglo and the bottom will be Hispanic."[10] He predicted "a period of 'chaos' as companies search for ways to upgrade skills through training programs and other means." The outcome is that many jobs will be mechanized or shipped out of the United States—to Latino nations such as Mexico. The outcome is a caste society based on race, which the color blindness of the courts and other institutions is creating. This reality has been ideologically framed by the discourse of the time, which produces a structure that embodies and reinforces domination. Proposition 209's consequences include the systematic exclusion of Chicanas/os and Latinas/os from higher education either as students or professors. The discourse supports a social reality "in which the white, male-dominated, working-class culture perceives itself as being robbed of its rightful place."[11] Our ability to understand, and to teach our students to understand, the distortion of communication to impose power, and to respond to its seemingly arbitrary exercise, gives us a particular responsibility in the defense of affirmative action and the struggle for a just society.

In considering whether this fight is necessary, observe that Dr. Allan Bakke ended up in a part-time anesthesiology practice in Rochester, Minnesota. Dr. Patrick Chavis, the African American whom they said "took Bakke's place" in medical school, runs a huge OB/GYN practice in Compton, dispensing primary care to poor women of color. The obvious questions are: Bakke's scores were higher than Chavis's, but from whom did the taxpayers benefit more? Can we live with the outcome of fewer professionals? Can we live with a caste system?

Notes

1. *The Children of* Bakke

1. Percentages would be even lower for students of Mexican extraction.

2. In 1997, upon the retirement of Los Angeles Unified School Superintendent Sid Thompson, an African American, the Board of Education balked at appointing Dr. Rubén Zacarias, a thirty-year veteran who had served as second in command, to replace Thompson. Only the pressure and unity of the Latino community kept his candidacy alive and persuaded the Board to do the right thing and appoint the popular and very capable Zacarias.

3. Californians passed Proposition 209 by a 54 to 46 percent margin. During the campaign many apologists argued that voters really weren't voting to end affirmative action—because they really supported affirmative action—but that they were confused by the language of the initiative. The fact is that they did vote for dismantling the idea that minorities and women had the same rights as white males to go to school or to bid for a contract. More important, this act set a precedent. It is provoking similar efforts and divisive debates across the United States. As in the case of Proposition 187, the anti-immigrant initiative passed in 1994, the debate over 209 is a mirror of Americans' sentiments on a host of social and economic issues.

4. One may quarrel whether the Reverend King would have supported Proposition 209, that is, if that person wants to mythicize reality. As the result of the anti–affirmative action crusade, not a single black student will enroll in the University of Texas Law School or the University of California at Berkeley in the school year 1997–1998. The number of Mexican Americans has also been drastically reduced. It is mendacious to suggest that this was part of King's dream.

5. John H. Bunzel, "The Nation: Post-Proposition 209. The Question Remains: What Role for Race?" *Los Angeles Times*, December 8, 1996.

6. The rich are able to afford private schools, which are not under the same scrutiny as public institutions. What one tends to forget is that private institutions receive public grants and tax exemptions which are subsidized by taxpayers.

7. The UC system moved against affirmative action more than a year before Proposition 209 passed, when the Board of Regents did away with so-called preference programs.

8. As a result of 187, voting became more polarized. In the *Los Angeles Times*, November 28, 1994, Orange County edition, the article "O.C. Precinct Typifies Latino Voter Apathy" by Gebe Martinez showed that the voter turnout was low in this immigrant community. It took a profile of precinct 68302, just south of the Civic Center. While the turnout was low, the results in precinct 68302 showed definite tendencies among those who did vote. All of the Democrats solidly beat their Republican rivals. Rep. Robert K. Dornan of Garden Grove was the top vote-getter for his party in aggregate votes, followed by state Assemblyman-elect Jim Morrissey, who heavily courted the Latino vote, and Gov. Pete Wilson. A candidate with a Spanish surname was likely to pick up votes even if he or she was not from a major party. In the race for lieutenant governor, Peace and Freedom candidate J. Luis Gomez finished only four votes behind Republican Cathie Wright. The Green Party's candidate in the race for secretary of state, Margaret Garcia, finished three votes behind Republican Bill Jones. In both those races, the Democrats beat the Republicans by about 2-to-1 ratios. In three Santa Ana City Council races, Ana Y. Vasquez beat Robert L. Richardson; Tony Espinoza got more votes than Alberta Christy; and Noemi C. Romero received more votes than her four Anglo-surnamed opponents. And of the twelve Supreme Court and appellate court justices who were running unopposed, five received more "no" than "yes" votes. The seven who got positive ratings scored between 52 percent and 58 percent of the vote, except for one—Appellate Court Justice Manuel A. Ramirez, who garnered 81 percent of the vote.

9. In Arizona, Latinos voted Democratic by a 10-1 margin, according to a *Los Angeles Times* exit poll. In Florida the solidly conservative Cuban-American bloc vote split between Clinton and Dole. Nationally, the same poll found that 71 percent of Latinos voted for Clinton, a 16-point increase over the 1992 percentage.

10. A recent example of race voting is the case of Nick Pacheco, a young assistant deputy district attorney who was relatively unknown, never having run for elected office. Pacheco ran for Charter Reform commissioner in Los Angeles City in the fourteenth city council district. His run-off opponent was David Tofosky, a member of the Los Angeles Uni-

fied School District Board of Education. Tofosky had the support of organized labor. Mayor Richard Riordan poured $16,500 into Tofosky's
campaign. The school board member had mailers, paid volunteers, and
the endorsement of major newspapers. Pacheco had practically no funds
and only the endorsement of a handful of Latino elected officials. The results, reported in the *Los Angeles Times*, June 5, 1997: Pacheco received
5,748 votes (63.2 percent) and Tofosky received 3,340 (36.8 percent).

11. Mark Z. Barabak, "GOP Seeks New Image among Latinos:
Politics after Setbacks in November. Party Attempts to Put Lid on Any
Wedge Issues in the Next Election," *Los Angeles Times,* March 30, 1997.

12. Harold Myerson, "A New Latin Beat. Election Day Turnout Sets
Tone For L.A. Politics," *LA Weekly*, April 18, 1997.

13. See Glenn W. Price, *Origins of the War with Mexico: The Polk-
Stockton Intrigue* (Austin: University of Texas Press, 1967). Price discusses
a similar tension between the "war-making habit of Western societies . . .
and the accepted ethical system on the other," and the difficulty U.S. historians and Euro-Americans have in dealing with the U.S. invasion of
Mexico.

14. See Eric Hobsbawm and Terence Ranger, eds., *The Invention of
Tradition* (Cambridge: Cambridge University Press, 1983).

15. Shelby Steele, *The Content of Our Character: A New Vision in
America* (New York: St. Martin's Press, 1990).

16. Michael Marriot, "Educators See Need for Diversity on Campus, but Debate How to Achieve It," *New York Times*, December 19,
1990.

17. When I attended Los Angeles State College (1955–1957), tuition
was $6.50 a semester. Education was affordable. Today, capital refuses to
pay for the cost of social production and tuition and student fees are
about $1200 a semester.

18. Glenn Loury, "Absolute California," *New Republic*, November 18, 1996.

19. Indeed, Clinton allegedly used Wilson's work as a justification
for signing the bill.

20. Derrick Bell, "Hooked; Divisions over Diversity," interview by
Charlayne Hunter-Gault, *MacNeil/Lehrer NewsHour*, May 10, 1990, transcript no. 3729.

21. Linda Chávez, "GOP Need to Mend Hispanic Fences," *Dallas
Morning News,* November 20, 1996.

22. When I first read the *Bakke* decision, I could not believe what I
was reading. In my foggiest moments I never would have so liberally interpreted documents. However, after my own court case, I know that this

is common practice in law. Lawyers dig up cases that agree with their position and cite them. They are under no obligation to cite cases which contradict their point of view; that is the job of opposing counsel. The job of the judge is to agree or disagree with the cases cited by the attorneys.

23. On March 18, 1996, the 5th U.S. Circuit Court of Appeals in *Hopwood v. Texas*, 1996 U.S. App. Lexis 4719 (1996), issued a decision that jeopardizes virtually every affirmative action admission program used in colleges and universities. It held that almost all forms of affirmative action are unlawful. It is inconsistent with *Regents of the University of California v. Bakke*, 438 U.S. 265 (1978), and is not supported by any other affirmative action decisions. The Court disregarded applicable Supreme Court precedent. *Hopwood* had challenged admission policies of The University of Texas School of Law. Cheryl Hopwood, a white female, and two white males claimed that by taking race into account, the law school's admissions policy violated the equal protection clause of the Fourteenth Amendment.

24. Logically, equal protection implies equal educational opportunity and the elimination of funding disparities among school systems. The Court has consistently refused to consider education a fundamental right or to regard wealth as a classification. Indeed, in *San Antonio Independent School Dist. v. Rodriguez* (1973), the Court stated that wealth as a classification has none of the traditional indications of being suspect. The Court illogically concluded that residence in a district with less taxable income than other districts does not mean that this was the result of officially imposed disabilities, a history of discrimination, or political powerlessness.

25. The argument that remediation stigmatizes the recipient is mendacious. Poor whites who managed to enter universities at the turn of the century were still discriminated against by their classmates. They were excluded from fraternities and sororities; they were excluded from prestigious dorms by those with money. Few would dare suggest that remedying this social and class discrimination would be wrong because it would "stigmatize" the poor whites.

2. It's the Law

1. One of the most enlightening works on the topic is *No Mercy: How Conservative Think Tanks and Foundations Changed America's Social Agenda* (1996) by Jean Stefancic and Richard Delgado, both of the University of Colorado Law School.

2. The new ideologues, such as John Tanton, a retired ophthalmologist, founded the Federation for American Immigration Reform (FAIR) and U.S. English. Tanton wrote a paper in 1986 for a private study group know as WITAN which dealt with the consequences of immigration to California:

> To govern is to populate. Will the present majority peacefully hand over its political power to a group that is simply more fertile? . . . As Whites see their power and control over their lives declining, will they simply go quietly into the night? Or will there be an explosion? (quoted in Stefancic and Delgado, *No Mercy*, p. 11)

3. Kuhn himself never gave a clear-cut definition of a paradigm. See Steve Fuller, "Being There With Thomas Kuhn: A Parable For Postmodern Times," *History and Theory* 31, no. 3 (October 1992). Fuller makes the point that "Since 1962, when the book was first published, over a million copies have been sold worldwide, including translations into sixteen languages. Yet, from the first opportunity he was given (up to his most recent interview), Kuhn had disavowed all of the more exciting and radical theses imputed to him by friends and foes alike." With this in mind, I interpret his written word and not what Kuhn said he meant. My own interpretation aligns itself with the reading of the text which appears to make anti-positivist arguments. See also M. A. Notturno, "Thomas Kuhn and The Legacy of Logical Positivism," *History of The Human Sciences* 10, no. 1 (February 1997). According to Fuller, Kuhn openly capitulated to the positivists and "openly solicited that doyen of positivists, Rudolf Carnap, to have *structure* published as part of the International Encyclopedia of Unified Science."

4. Thomas S. Kuhn, *The Structure of Scientific Revolutions*, 2nd edition (Chicago: University of Chicago Press, 1970).

5. UC Ethnic Studies Professor Alfredo Mirandé, *The Chicano Experience: An Alternative Perspective* (Notre Dame, Ind.: University of Notre Dame Press, 1985), for example, has called for a Chicano sociology paradigm (as distinguished from the sociology of Chicanos), because of the inadequacies of the prevailing paradigm to explain the Chicano experience. See also Octavio Romano, "Social Science, Objectivity, and Chicanos," *El Grito: A Journal of Contemporary Mexican-American Thought* 4 (Fall 1970): 4–16.

6. Fuller, "Being There With Thomas Kuhn."

7. No one really knows what the framers intended. Learned Hand admitted that *Marbury v. Madison* was probably contrary to the intent of the framers of the Constitution. He added, however, that "without some

arbiter whose decision should be final, the whole system would have collapsed" (so it was all right to perpetuate a myth). It is important to add that the Marshall Court did not challenge the constitutionality of any other acts of Congress during the remaining thirty-two years Marshall acted as Chief Justice. No further federal legislation was declared unconstitutional until the *Dred Scott* case (1856). James Madison, the principal author of the Constitution, disapproved of letting judges "set aside the law" because it made "the Judiciary Department paramount in fact to the Legislature, which was never intended and can never be proper."

8. Tribe's main concern was *Roe v. Wade* and other liberal issues, and the fear that Thomas would use natural law theory to dictate his brand of morality.

9. Interestingly, legislators were less tolerant of Professor Lani Guinier than of Clarence Thomas. Guinier was a Clinton nominee to head the Civil Rights Division of the U.S. Justice Department. She was not allowed to defend her scholarly writings. Apparently, Guinier's academic work also did not reflect positivism, but she was not allowed to confess her sins before the Inquisition.

10. Of course, there are ample reasons other than morality and theory to disobey the law. Corporate America, with the rationale that it must remain competitive in the leaner and meaner global market, flagrantly disobeys the ceilings set by positivist law. For example, U.S. corporations escape U.S. positive law by establishing *maquilas* just inside Mexico in order to avoid environmental monitoring.

However, theory does determine what questions are asked about laws and their consequences. In the spring of 1997 it was announced that as a result of the *Hopwood* decision (see chapter 1, note 23), only one black applicant would enroll to the University of Texas Law School. To ask the questions, Should blacks and Latinos support an institution that excludes them? Should it matter if it burns? requires stepping outside the positivist theoretical framework. Depending on the theory, the questions and the answers are different.

11. The views of the legal realists paralleled that of revisionist historians Charles Beard and Carl Becker.

12. Peter Novick, *That Noble Dream: The 'Objectivity Question' and the American Historical Profession* (Cambridge: Cambridge University Press, 1988), p. 149.

13. Although it is not the purpose of this work to describe all existing theories of law or social science, it is important to point out that for every legal theory, there is a corresponding social science method. For example, critical legal studies is similar to critical social science. Versions of

the latter involve dialectical materialism, class analysis, and structuralism. Critical social science is a process of inquiry that looks at structures in the material world in order to understand changes in society. According to its adherents, social reality is rooted in tensions, conflicts, or contradictions of social relations or institutions. Unlike positivism, it does not assume that facts are incontestable or neutral, or that all rational people will agree on the facts. Moreover, it is not detached. It holds that all science must begin with a value position. Like critical legal studies, the method of critical social science is heavily influenced by Marxism.

14. See Richard Delgado, "The Imperial Scholar: Reflections on a Review of Civil Rights Literature," *University of Pennsylvania Law Review* 132, no. 561 (1984); see also Delgado, "The Imperial Scholar Revisited: How to Marginalize Outsider Writing, Ten Years Later," *University of Pennsylvania Law Review* 1349 (1992).

15. Novick, *That Noble Dream.*

3. Ideological Combat: The War over Who Controls History

1. D'Antonio, Michael. "Science Fights Back: Is It Winning? The Answer Is Not In the Stars." *Los Angeles Times Magazine,* February 11, 1996.

2. Ibid.

3. Corporations use their academic contacts to buy credibility at a low price, legitimizing their research. Lawrence Soley's *The Leasing of the Ivory Tower* (Boston: South End Press, 1995) is critical of the growing college-corporation partnerships. This type of research is tied to immediate expectations of profits. As corporate money becomes more of a factor at universities, some fear that research projects, and even the results, will be skewed toward corporate, rather than scientific goals—which is already the case. Who pays for the research is important to students and the public. It affects the mission of the university.

4. Jim Phillips, "Are Research Universities Selling Out?" *Austin American-Statesman,* January 14, 1996. Also see Soley, *The Leasing of the Ivory Tower.*

5. Note that Adela de la Torre, discussed in the first chapter, makes accusations against Chicana/o studies professors with roots in the 1960s.

6. Eugene D. Genovese, "Voices Must Unite for Victory in the Cultural War," *Chicago Tribune,* December 22, 1993.

7. Cheney, quoted in "Oh, the Humanities!" by Thomas Goetz, *Village Voice,* April 18, 1995.

8. Ibid.

9. For much of the information contained in this section, I am greatly indebted to Stefancic's and Delgado's book, *No Mercy: How Conservative Think Tanks and Foundations Changed America's Social Agenda*.

10. For a more recent view on the resources of the culture war, see Nurith C. Aizenman, "The Man behind the Curtain: Richard Mellon Scaife—and $200 Million of His Money—Is the Man behind the Conservative Revolution; Heir to the Mellon Family Millions Funds Three Right-wing Foundations," *Washington Monthly* 7, no. 29 (July 17, 1997).

According to Aizenman's study, Scaife, an oil and banking heir, is the biggest financier of right-wing causes in the U.S. Over the past thiry years, Scaife has disbursed over $200 million through his three foundations, the Carthage Foundation, the Allegheny Foundation, and the Sarah Scaife Foundation. In 1995 alone, Scaife gave $20 million to conservative think tanks such as the Heritage Foundation, the American Enterprise Institute, the CATO Institute, the Manhattan Institute, and the Center for Strategic and International Studies, among others. Just a sampling of his causes: Scaife promotes conservative thought on college campuses through organizations like the Intercollegiate Studies Institute, Inc. ($325,000 in 1996 alone), which funds conservative student newspapers. The Landmark Legal Foundation ($275,000 in 1995) files ethics complaints against Democrats in Congress and helps defend Republicans. Scaife gave over $1 million to Pepperdine University toward the establishment of a "School of Social Policy," intended to be another right-wing answer to Harvard's Kennedy School.

Along with the Adolph Coors Foundation, the John M. Olin Foundation, the Smith Richardson Foundation, and the Lynde and Harry Bradley Foundation, Scaife has provided the money to build a conservative establishment much more sophisticated and effective than the Ralph Nader organization and the Brookings Institution. Thomas Ferguson, a political science professor at the University of Massachusetts, says that Scaife helped create the new political and intellectual establishment which has shifted American politics toward a repudiation of the New Deal and the Great Society.

11. Title VII and the California employment provisions include "religion" or "religious creed." Proposition 209 has no such provision.

12. In 1997, the Chicano graduation ceremonies had to be held off-campus as a result of Connerly's abuse of power.

13. The *Legislative Analyst* has said that it will affect programs such as counseling, tutoring, outreach, student financial aid, and financial aid to selected school districts.

4. The Culture of the Academy

1. William Massy of Stanford University has observed that the faculty governance system has shifted vast university resources from teaching to research, resulting in teaching loads falling from about twelve contact hours per semester in the 1960s to about six hours at most research universities today. Salaries have also ballooned, with off-scale professors earning around $100,000.

2. The UC system has a review process which over-indulges the biases of a small clique of professors. At the other extreme is the sham process of the California State University sytem, where the president of the individual campus has dictatorial powers. At the Northridge campus, for example, President Brenda Wilson refuses to give criteria for her decisions, which include denying merit raises to professors with proven publication records, yet in one case rewarding another professor for accumulating 350 bookmarks on the Internet, even though the professor was a notoriously bad teacher. However, the justification is the same as that in the UC and other institutions of higher learning: in each case the system claims that the purpose of review is to reward merit.

3. In one case I reviewed, the candidate for promotion received a negative vote by the department because of the candidate's numerous sexual harassment incidents. The reviewing committees and the administration, however, determined that the increase was merited because the candidate was an excellent researcher.

4. For an example of this view, one should look at the depositions of UCSB historian Jeffrey Russell in my court case and his handwritten notes on the margins of the report sent for faculty review. In his words, the CAP committee he chaired turned back higher administration attempts to water down "quality" vs. "Pister."

5. David Glidden, "Why not Reward a Political Scientist Who Helps a Neighborhood? UC: Research Should Be More Than Specialized Investigation. It Should Include Applying Scholarship to the Classroom and to the World," *Los Angeles Times*, November 17, 1991.

6. Although UC guidelines require teaching excellence for employment at advanced ranks, personnel files I have reviewed show that it is not uncommon for scientists with little or no teaching experience to be appointed at the highest ranks of full professor.

7. The deposition of Karl Pister during the discovery phase of my court case was one of the most disappointing experiences of my life. I genuinely respected the man, who has a progressive history. However,

during the deposition he denied almost everything he stood for, even praising the peer group process at the UC. During one of the breaks I turned to him and said: "What hope is there for the academy if good men such as yourself will not fight for the change recommended by their own reports?"

8. John Leo, "The espresso uprising," *U.S. News & World Report* 120, no. 18 (May 6, 1996): 23.

9. California State University at Northridge has a department with 22 faculty positions and 680 FTES (one FTES equals 15 semester units). The curriculum is interdisciplinary and integrated into the university as a whole. If identity politics were the central focus, enrollment would dramatically decline; secondly, if we maintained the current enrollment in the face of strong identity politics, we would have a cadre that would have taken over the San Fernando Valley. The truth is that the program meets curricular needs, teaches skills, and helps integrate students coming from a highly segregated K–12 experience into the university. Neither Mr. Schlesinger nor any other critic has ever bothered to visit the campus and to compare the facts with their generalizations.

10. James A. Banks, "Multicultural education: development, dimensions, and challenges," *Phi Delta Kappan* 75, no. 1 (September 1993).

11. Ibid.

12. Ibid.

13. California State University at Northridge provides an example. Tensions have lately surfaced because of the academic vice president, who is a multiculturalist. She allegedly sees the existence of a large Chicana/o Studies Department and a Pan African Department as a barrier to multiculturalism and the hiring of more faculty of color in other departments. The faculty of color responds that this is not true, and that the vice president does not give sufficient focus to the faculty governance process in excluding faculty of color. The reality is that any critique of these movements must keep in mind that there are differences, and the movements within themselves have differences.

14. Evelyn Hu-DeHart, "The history, development, and future of ethnic studies; Multicultural Education," *Phi Delta Kappan* 75, no. 1 (September 1993).

5. Chicana/o Studies and the American Paradigm

1. The attitude of society toward Latin America is mirrored in its attitude toward Chicanos. Latin America has about 600 million people, is

near the U.S., yet it receives only 7 percent of the U.S. foreign aid budget. (Military assistance is another matter—here the 7 percent it receives is far too much.) Few universities in the United States offer degrees in Latin American studies.

2. A newly created position within the CSUN department is for a Central American specialist, with a view to expanding course offerings for this growing sector.

3. In the spring of 1977 I heard a presentation by an Argentine-American graduate student in Chicana/o studies. This student was from a middle-class family, with almost no involvement with Mexicans. Her paper was based entirely on library sources. When I questioned her on how she could make intelligent assumptions on the topic, her response was that she was a scientist. My criticism is not that she was a Euro-Latina or even from the middle class. However, one should expect a certain level of involvement with the community one is studying—in her case, for example, the Casa Blanca Colonia near UC Riverside, where she was studying for her Ph.D. Being a scientist involves more than making deductions.

4. In David R. Maciel and Isidro D. Ortiz, eds. *Chicanas/Chicanos at the Crossroads: Social, Economic, and Political Change* (Tucson: University of Arizona, 1996).

5. *Los Angeles Times*, December 12, 1996. See also chapter 1.

6. García makes some errors, for instance, his statement that the program at California State at Los Angeles was the first department. It was the first program, but it received departmental status after San Fernando Valley State College (later, California State University at Northridge).

7. Edward Hallett Carr, *What Is History?* (New York: Vintage Books, 1961).

8. Oscar Handlin, *Truth in History* (Cambridge, Mass.: Harvard University Press, 1979).

6. *A Case Study:* Acuña v. The Regents of the University of California

1. Dr. Yolanda Broyles-González was the first Chicana chair of a department at UCSB, and probably the only within the system. Males had run the department for two decades, and administration documents show clearly that they had been incompetent in the management of Chicano Studies, using it largely for career opportunities. Broyles-González wanted to lay down a vision for the department, moving it from dual

appointments to sole appointments in Chicano Studies. There is little doubt that much of the reaction to her was sexist.

2. According to a mutual friend and the note she wrote to my attorneys, Cody-Váldez testified against me because she believe that UCSB discriminated for political reasons, but not on the basis of age discrimination, the single charge left standing at trial.

3. By June 1993 the Center for Constitutional Rights dropped out of the case for all intents and purposes. It did not have the resources to press litigation, and it alienated my team of lawyers through actions which they termed malpractice. In order to prevent losing the case, we restructured.

4. The discovery referee was expensive. It would have been completely beyond my means to pay the costs. The California Faculty Association and the California Teachers' Association gave us about $15,000. The F.O.R. (Friends of Rudy) Acuña Committee raised over $50,000 for expenses.

5. In employment discrimination cases it has become almost routine for the courts to order psychiatric examinations. The defendants are given a wide latitude. The examiners do not test for stress, which was what we claimed, but for psychosis. The psychiatrist also asks questions which are far beyond the scope of the issue.

6. In all fairness, Corbett & Kane informed us of this fact. The judge herself never notified us of this conflict of interest.

7. WAGE, a women's advocacy group comprised of UC employees, has recently charged that there is a pattern of IRS audits against plaintiffs against the UC. Soon after I filed my suit, by an odd coincidence, I was audited by the Internal Revenue Service, a practice that was repeated in each of the next three years.

8. Beth Minsky worked without salary for the National Coalition for Universities in the Public Interest. We only paid her flight and expenses during this period.

9. In effect, Collins threw out our disparate impact claim, ruling that the defendants' statistics report was more credible than the plaintiff's. This is a matter of fact which should have been decided during trial. It is also relevant that our report had been written by UCLA demographer Dr. Leo Estrada, who is a highly respected expert, nominated by Clinton in 1993 to head the U.S. Census Bureau. At the very least, Collins was not qualified to make such a determination.

10. The federal court had agreed to accept discovery which took place in that venue.

11. The judge also would not allow as evidence Kelley's evaluation of another historian, written about the time he reviewed me, which cast further doubt on his "objectivity."

12. Collins abused her discretion by holding a mini-trial because defendant counsel complained that I was intimidating witnesses Ray Huerta and Denise Segura. After Ms. Yvonne Flores, president of the Mexican American Bar Association, contradicted these allegations, the judge almost apologetically dropped the matter. Collins sealed the record but then arbitrarily, during the instatement motions, unsealed the record without notice to plaintiff's counsel to use the unverified charges against me to deny me instatement. When plaintiff protested this clear violation of due process, she threatened to sanction plaintiff counsel for filing a frivolous motion, inviting the defendants to file for sanctions. Collins did not hold hearings and allowed libelous statements to stand.

13. Lomeli's testimony was on videotape.

14. The abstaining votes were never the issue in our minds. We knew from the beginning that this was a political case, and that their votes were merely pretextual. Two of the abstentions were from assistant professors; the reviewers were all full professors. What later became the issue was that the abstaining professors backed the administration. We still consciously refrained from attacking them, and in fact sent the message that if they stayed out of the fray we would not even depose them—the defendants took this initiative. The fact was that if any of the abstainers at the time of the Santa Barbara interview in February, 1991, had expressed any reservations about my candidacy, I would have withdrawn my application. Even at the time of trial, I did not want to criticize the Chicana/o abstentions; however, my attorneys pointed out that, counting their time, we had over $2 million invested in the case, that it was a war, and that I had no choice. They also pointed to the contradiction of the defense team and the Chicano defense witnesses staying at the Otani Hotel, which was being picketed by Local 11, Hotel Employees and Restaurant Employees Union. María Elena Durazo, president of H.E.R.E., was one of our committed backers. We strongly felt that the community needed a victory.

15. All too prevalent among Chicana/o scholars is the practice of raising the R(acism) word or the S(exism) word. When we raise these terms for personal reasons, they detract from our moral authority. For example, during my lawsuit, Segura raised the question whether *Occupied America* was sexist because it did not deal with the women's question in the 1972 edition (she hadn't read the 1988 edition). In history we call this

kind of analysis presentism, for example, judging 1972 public discourse in terms of 1991 public discourse. This kind of accusation is frivolous, since in no instance did the 1972 edition use sexist examples. It just did not have enough original research on women, a gap which has been corrected in the light of twenty years of experience. This also raises the question of whether historians are expected to be prophets. Is every book that does not mention women, sexist? Is every book which doesn't deal with Chicanas/os, racist?

Segura gave no other examples. She also made the accusation that I was anticommunist because I said that workers in the 1933 San Joaquin Cotton Strike did not need communism to take them to a higher level of consciousness and revolt. Many were the product of the Mexican Revolution; many were miners, anarchists, and veterans of other strikes. She testified that this was contrary to what she had read. On this slender basis I was anticommunist to her, and therefore a non-authority. Ironically, most Marxist scholars would agree with me, since it is basic to historical materialism to look at the circumstances of the workers themselves.

16. On several occasions, Collins informed defendants of her ruling on a motion without informing us. We would learn how she ruled from reporters.

17. UC paid another $500,000 to Corbett & Kane in 1996 and 1997 for answering our appeals. In total, it spent close to $5 million.

18. Some of it involved peculiar predispositions For example, Jeffrey Russell, whose specialty is the devil in the Middle Ages, testified at length during his deposition about the role of the scholar, which, according to him, is to search for truth; however, he observed, "absolute truth is whatever would exist in the mind of God, to which we have no access . . . we cannot even hope to get close to it [absolute truth]." In a 1991 lecture Russell stated, "The purpose of the University is to proclaim the intricate mystery and glory of God." In reviewing my work he claimed that it was a Marxist because I used terms such as "hegemony" and "subjugated people." Despite these biases, I would have expected Russell to be moral and less ruthless than the neoliberals. However, Russell was one of the linchpins of the defense case.

19. The Mexican and Central American immigrant student and their families to me are heroic. They are accomplishing what it took many European ethnics three generations to accomplish. A sizeable portion of these students are attending college despite inferior schools and the racist backlash in our society, which has seen a so-called taxpayer revolt, Proposition 187, and Proposition 209, as well as a host of other exclusionary measures. The European ethnics did not make it in significant

numbers until the third or fourth generation, after World War II, and after a host of entitlement programs and federal aid to education.

20. My networks within the community gave me the sufficient moral and financial support to sustain a fight against the University of California. Labor, community organizations, students, and individual activists were always there. Juana Gutierrez of Mothers of East Los Angeles, Saint Isabel Parish, for example, made over a hundred dozen tamales and contributed the proceeds of their sale to the case.

21. While I accept the right of the individual to make choices, I also ask, should he or she be permitted to fall back on the gains made by the group? Is he or she entitled to respect from the group? Is it wrong to expect a personal moral commiment? In answering these questions, I always rely on an answer given by Stanley Sheinbaum, an important Los Angeles philanthropist, who once served on the Los Angeles Police Commission. As a human rights activist, he was often at odds with the Jewish community on the question of the Middle East. When asked about these differences, he replied that although he differed with the Jewish community, he acted within the parameters of that community because it was important for him to be accepted by it. He didn't go too far out. I respect this sincere statement because I feel the same way about my community. I care what it thinks of me. This invisible bond is formed by a historical consciousness. I also realize that if I am going to change my community for the better, it must first respect me.

22. In my experience, political ideology has little to do with making the review process equitable. Universities are not liberal institutions, although there are wide variations within each campus. Few professors have defined constituents. Conservatives range from neoliberals to the religious right—with many of the neoliberals being even more intolerant of the religious right than they are of modern-day liberals. On the left, they range from ethnics to gays and lesbians, to warmed-over multiculturalists and postmodernists, wanna-be hippies, and the Marxists, with each of these groups having different agendas. Many continue to live in the glory days of the 1960s, repeating and embellishing their war stories. In my experience with Santa Barbara, I met an old SDS (Students for a Democratic Society) activist, who prided himself on being a communist but had no history of involvement with Mexican or minority student struggles in or out of his institution, although Mexicans and other Latinos were clearly the largest exploited class in that community.

Administrators are also far from liberal, although they are more pragmatic than faculties. I have found most intelligent administrators more prone to accept changes. They are often placed in the position of defending the university from intransigencies of the right, whose members still function in the Middle Ages. Administrators are politicians who have to deal with the real world. On paper at least, administrators are committed to diversity. This is probably because they sense the changes that are taking place in the larger society, whereas the faculty members literally live in an ivory tower. One of the problems at UCSB was that it had weak chancellors, and thus faculty governance became more of a force. Matters were not helped by the fact that the administrators involved were hacks.

23. In the case of minority scholars, traditional departments often tell the ethnic studies programs which scholars will make it through their review process. Thus, they screen the applicant before any paperwork takes place, making it even more difficult to sue on grounds of discrimination.

24. The percentage of Chicano and Latino faculty at the University of California is dismal. Less than 1 percent of its doctoral students are females of Mexican extraction. Presented with choices, liberal and conservative faculty are all alike; faculty consensus on issues such as eliminating a department does not favor Chicana/o studies or other ethnic studies departments.

25. On occasion at Santa Barbara, for example, this would be taken to ridiculous ends. Affirmative action officer Ray Huerta warned the School of Education that it should not use a target of opportunity to hire a Chicano educator, because Chicanos were overutilized in Education—they already had three Mexicans.

26. Yolanda Broyles-González, the department chair, was present for only one hour at a committee meeting to answer questions. The departmental representative could be interviewed by the committee but was not part of any deliberations.

27. This, and the references to "at the age of 59," was the guts of our age discrimination case. The fact that the members of the committee went out and dug up my age, based on the personnel application that no one reads, showed that they were thinking of age. There was no reason for them to have alluded to age. It revealed the state of mind that infected the process. *Lam v. the University of Hawaii* held that if any part of the process was infected, and this infection affected the ultimate decision, the whole process was infected.

28. In reviewing another candidate, committee chairman Kelley stated that being designated as an expert witness was the highest form of scholarly recognition, and proved the scholar's mettle. In my case, Kelley apparently forgot this evaluation.

29. The reference to NAFTA raised questions among the attorneys, who believed that they smelled (another) smoking gun. Through Mexus-Nexus, a UC institute on Mexican-U.S. studies, the University of California received considerable financial assistance through the Mexican government. This relationship was especially close during the administration of Mexican President Carlos Salinas de Gortari, who in the midst of my case gave UCSB $130,000 for an endowed chair in Chicano Studies. Some of the Chicana/o professors who had opposed my appointment, although considering themselves pro-labor, turned and supported NAFTA. Rumor had it that three professors tightly associated with Mexus-Nexus had contacted the UCSB administration, complaining about the possibility of my becoming a tenured professor in the Chicano Studies Department. Juan Palerm, then director of the Chicano Studies Research Center, eventually became director of Mexus-Nexus. Palerm is well connected in Mexico and was appointed in the early 1980s as an associate professor, which automatically carries tenure, to the anthropology department without a Ph.D. in hand.

30. Again, the question is, what is scholarship and what is quality? Disparate treatment is when a minority candidate is treated differently than a white scholar. My study of the UC personnel files found that if the committees are favorable to the candidates, op-ed pieces are touted as "political essays," as in the case of Mario García. Book reviews are mixed in with articles and in the case of scientists, are counted as articles. Some scientists will count as many as two hundred pieces as articles, although they are often merely 1–2 page reports on their research, coauthored with their graduate students. During the trial, the UC presented them as items published, not differentiating between "articles" and books or anthologies. Only in my case were these technicalities raised. The experts in the field of Chicana/o studies said that I was well published. Even the three abstaining votes in the department did not contest this point, whereas white scholars with no expertise stated otherwise.

31. See the deposition of Sprecher discussed in chapter 8, on this book.

32. Most first books are based on one's dissertation. Most dissertations are not published at all. Mario García, for instance, whom Kelley later holds up as a model, published his dissertation as a book after he had been promoted to full professor, and was promoted to Professor, Step V, on the basis of seven chapters in a new book. The reference to two high school books requires correction: I had written two elementary-level texts, one of which was used to train teachers, and a high school text used in community colleges, which was reviewed by scholarly

presses. They were published before *Occupied America*, during a period when I was pioneering the training of Chicana/o teachers.

33. Juan Gómez-Quiñones is one of the premier Chicana/o studies scholars, who has contributed immensely to the definition of the field.

34. The letter was written by Bob Suzuki, academic vice president at California State University at Northridge, who later became president at California Poly Pomona. He is a fine scholar and leading force in the Asian-American community. The ad hoc committee made a quantum leap in characterizing me as a "cult professor"—and it was a clever ploy in portraying me as a cult leader such as Jim Jones.

35. The use of the words "master spirit" added to "cult professor" is telling.

36. The CSUN Chicana/o Studies Department had fifteen tenured positions, half of them female, at the time. It had B.A. and M.A. programs. It was one of the few M.A. programs in the country. None of the UC campuses had an M.A. program.

37. The department was already a split department when Mario García was at its helm. Here the ad hoc committee totally distorted the facts. Significantly, the only one on the ad hoc committee that had any knowledge of Chicano studies was Kelley—and it can only be surmised that the other members of the committee went along with him. The year before my candidacy, García's reign had come to an end by a coup that included some of the abstainers. This led to the appointment of Dr. Yolanda Broyles-González, the first female chair of the department.

38. The contradiction is blatant: I stood so far above everyone else in the department, and I was still not qualified.

39. This is in error. García, who was on leave, was a full professor and Francisco Lomeli was a full professor. Broyles-González was soon to be promoted to a full professor.

40. In this paragraph, the political motivation of the committee members was obvious. They felt threatened by the political influence that I might exert.

41. Analysis of the discourse here would lead to the conclusion that they had to employ special "scrutiny" only because Chicano studies was involved. This is again a case of disparate treatment: "You can't trust those Mexicans to make their own decisions."

42. The idea of a trusteeship has the strong flavor of colonialism. It is the white man's burden not to allow the "little brown people" to make mistakes. They are incapable of governing themselves. The use of the words "this particular scholar" does not reflect a scholarly review but refers to my ideas—my politics—with which they did not agree.

43. This point was especially galling to members of the ad hoc committee. I would have been the first appointment in Chicano studies that would not have involve a joint appointment. In other words, I would not have been subject to the peer review of a mainstream department that was by majority white, male, and Eurocentric.

44. I was not applying for the chairship, but they treated the matter as if I were. They assumed that Mexicans had to have a "dictator" and that I would add to the division. The chair's letter pointed out that there had been four previous searches and that this was the closest that the department had been to reaching some kind of unanimity. To this day the department is in disarray. The administration retaliated against Broyles-González for her support of my candidacy and removed her, although a majority of the department rated her outstanding.

45. The use of my age, 59, along with the earlier mention of my birthdate and persistent references to younger and older scholars, wove the web that demonstrated age discrimination. A pattern existed, just as if I started an evaluation with a reference to the fact that a candidate was pregnant and then brought up the fact repeatedly, either by innuendo or direct reference.

46. Here, as we inferred in court, they were saying that you couldn't teach an old dog new tricks. As noted earlier, Ramón Ruiz totally annihilated this argument by pointing out that when he arrived in the late 1960s to UCSD from Smith, he had little experience at training graduate students, and since that time had mentored hundreds of Ph.D.s. At the time of my candidacy, Mario García, who had a joint appointment in history, had never signed off on a doctoral student. Vélez-Ibáñez, Mazón, and the other outside reviewers corroborated this. There was also the fact that I had supervised M.A. students. The hypocrisy is blatant: UC typically assigns recently arrived Ph.D.s to teach classes with 350 students and four teaching assistants, none of whom have previous teaching experience, and then claims that a person with thirty-five years of teaching and writing cannot learn how to supervise Ph.D students.

47. The only so-called evidence of this that the ad hoc reviewers gave at the time of their depositions was that I said that the United States had invaded Mexico and then occupied the territory that was the bounty of this war. Professor Kelley wrote (over a year later) his analysis, which boiled down to this point. He misquoted Ramón Ruiz's works on the topic. His criticisms were verbiage repeated by Giles Gunn and Wallace Chafe, who knew even less about the subject of the Mexican-American War.

48. Broyles-González during her depositions and at trial denied that she had ever made this statement. Note again the use of the word "younger." Kelley lists as a younger scholar Mario García, who is about ten years my junior. Broyles-González did state that during the interview, Kelley asked questions about my political orientation, about how well I could work with middle-class students, and why I looked so angry (presumably in a photo). Admittedly, there has been some criticism of my work (and considerable criticism of Professor García's work) among scholars; criticism is a matter of course. However, here Kelley was fabricating reality for his political purposes. At this point, it had become a political critique (using the word "critique" liberally).

49. Kelley totally ignored the different editions of *Occupied America*, which are different in content and which define the status of Chicano history at that particular time in history and its impact on Chicano research. He ignores *Sonoran Strongman* and dismisses *Community Under Siege*. I was extremely disappointed, since I would have expected more intellectually from a man who called himself the "Father of Public History." As such, I would have expected him to take into consideration what the building of a field took: the course proposals, the conceptualization of the major, the bachelors and the masters, a teaching credential, the op-ed articles, and the children's book and community college text. These all involved knowledge of the subject.

50. Many American scholars would agree with my statement. This opinion does not disqualify a work from being scholarly unless the requisite for scholarship is a loyalty oath.

51. Here again, is the old argument of truth and objectivity.

52. The report does what it accuses me of doing. Moreover, it displays a paternalist attitude (at best) in wanting to control who the role models of the minority community should be and how they should act. The further use of the word "inchoate" is also telling.

53. The tone of the language is telling. It was considerably toned down from Kelley's first draft. The other two reviewers admitted that the emotional tone of the report was unfortunate; however, they agreed with it. The fact is that they never expected the report to see the light of day. They could say what they wanted. The report was designed to convince the administration to turn down the appointment, by evoking the Willie Horton metaphor of a scholar who was out of control.

54. "Nothing in the record"—despite the department chair's letter, the outside letters, and the vita? The building of the largest ethnic studies program in the U.S. did not indicate, suggest, or prove leadership?

55. CAP, like the ad hoc committee, made a point of the split votes, which we saw as pretextual given its unimportance in other cases. As-

sociate Vice Chancellor Julius Zelmanowitz early on had told Broyles-González that the split votes played no factor in the rejection. In another case, an entire department had voted against the candidate for promotion because of alleged charges of sexual harassment, and the administration advanced the candidate on the basis of good research.

56. Note, as shown in chapter 8, that Sprecher changed his testimony as to the "political" nature of the work.

57. Again, the link to Sprecher's evaluation is obvious.

58. Here the report contradicts Sprecher's report.

59. Even if it had been a textbook, the UC academic personnel manual provides that in a new field of endeavor, texts that have a major impact on the field should be considered under this category. Of the three editions, only the second was intended to be a textbook, and that only half-heartedly since it had a hypothesis. This argument was completely torn apart by expert witnesses.

60. This is insulting, especially in light of the personnel files we obtained. Many professors were moved up without even having one book.

61. Russell ignores *Community Under Siege,* which he did not understand, and whose form was influenced by the French Annales School.

62. In most of the files that I read, there were one or two dissenting letters. This was especially true in the case of some of the inside reviewers. In my case they questioned the fact that the letters were all positive—they must have come from my friends.

63. How could Russell have known this? How did he know which reviewers had a history of political activism? Moreover, the words echoed Provost Sprecher's report.

64. These remarks were taken out of context.

65. Mazón was at USC. He was also the head of the department and a psychoanalyst. He had not been passed on to full professorship because of his involvement in a budding practice. An excellent scholar, his letter was much more extensive than this review suggests. On his letter, see chapter 8.

66. What record? For more than thirty years I had been a master teacher and a trainer of teachers. The report contradicted everything in the file on the subject of my teaching.

7. Truth and Objectivity: Thomas Kuhn Applied

1. Actually, the reviews were generally positive when the book first came out, the most positive appearing in the *American Historical Review.* The unfortunate part is that there has never been an attempt by

mainstream scholars to discuss the issues, the facts, or the sources. They dismiss the arguments of scholars such as myself out of hand, without attempting to understand them.

2. The Mothers of East Los Angeles was a group in Boyle Heights centered around Resurrection and St. Isabel Catholic Churches, that demonstrated against attempts by the state to build a prison on the doorsteps of their community. The group was headed by women and also lobbied, petitioned, and marched against attempts to build a toxic waste incinerator in their community as well as a gas pipeline under it. The height of their activity was from 1986 to 1991.

8. The Trustees of the Truth

1. The cult of secrecy is everywhere in academe. A recent graduate does not see the letters of recommendations sent by his or her professors, many of whom are jealous of their students, or simply don't like the newly consecrated scholarly priests, or are hypercritical of their own students. Not having the right to review these letters, the young scholar often continues to list the negative reviewer as a reference. In other cases, submitted articles and books are sent out to review to so-called experts in the field, who take a dislike to the work of the candidate; the same process starts over when another press sends the article or book to the same expert.

2. Sprecher tried unsuccessfully to interfere in 1990 with the appointment of Dr. Yolanda Broyles-González to chair the Department of Chicano Studies. At university expense he flew in Dr. Francisco Lomeli from his sabbatical leave to speak against and vote against her candidacy. Lomeli generally had access to Sprecher and other administrators, toeing the administration line.

It was established during the trial that there were *ex parte* conversations among the defendants. The administrators stated flatly that, although the academic personnel manual forbade communication of any sort after the file left the department, administrators were privileged and could have *ex parte* communication. Faculty members at UCSB argued that this was not true; you could not have one set of regulations for faculty and another for administrators. It would be a violation of faculty governance.

3. Because this was a Mexican appointment, the administration required that each of the ten outside reviewers send resumes. I was later told by two of the reviewers that they were insulted and almost refused

to send their letters (but did so because they knew that not sending a letter would be perceived as nonsupportive). I was allowed to recommend only two of the ten outside reviewers.

4. The "minor publishers" to which Sprecher refers include the University of California Los Angeles Chicano Studies Research Center (UCLA Press), which at the time was the premier scholarly Chicano studies publisher in the country. It also published *Aztlan*, a respectable journal in the field.

5. The former provost changed his testimony in his deposition, and admitted that I had ample proof of participation in professional activities. Indeed, in 1989 I received the distinguished scholar award from the National Association for Chicano Studies and gave a major speech in Guadalajara, Mexico, where I was named the outstanding border scholar in the United States of Mexican ancestry by La Feria de Libros. I had keynoted numerous professional conferences and spoke at two plenaries of the Southwest Labor Studies Council. In addition, in 1992 I spoke at a plenary session of the American Historical Association.

6. Sprecher changed this testimony during the second day of depositions. In his study, Novick makes the point that passionate writing is generally associated with nonobjectivity.

7. Yet Sprecher had been an Israeli Military Intelligence officer, trained to remember detail.

8. I had written close to a hundred "political essays" in newspapers and magazines from 1986 to 1991, and close to fifty book reviews. The articles were very valuable in establishing the presence of Chicana/o studies in the Los Angeles area, and the research on these articles, including extensive oral interviews, served as research for *Anything But Mexican: Chicanos in Contemporary Los Angeles,* published by Verso Press in 1996. During the trial, Judge Collins said that I could not enter this manuscript into evidence because it was not the same title I had listed on my resume. The UC maintained that it had to have the same title. This is ridiculous, considering the different turns a book takes in its formation. It may start as a collection of essays and end up as a monograph, and it may be retitled by the author or the publishing house.

9. Mazón had been the chair of the Department of History at USC, and is currently the director of American Studies at the same institution. Mazón also holds a doctorate in psychoanalysis.

10. *Community Under Siege* was the most difficult for the evaluators. They did not read the book, so consequently were thrown by its unorthodox format. What I did there was to follow the dictates of the French Annales School. Instead of the standard footnote, I microfilmed a

community throwaway weekly and listed the majority of articles on Chicanas/os in chronological order. I took a second local newspaper and did the same. Based on these two sources, my personal observations, the Edward R. Roybal Collection, and countless secondary sources, I put together a chronological history of East Los Angeles from 1945 to 1975, establishing its patterns. For instance, in my first edition of *Occupied America* I had characterized the Chicana/o communities as almost dormant during this period. The laying out of the history allowed me to see another picture, i.e., the interaction between Mexicans and Jews and the land question. The reviewers labeled the work a journalistic work because it was based on newspapers.

11. During the trial the defense attempted to label the letter again as "not analytical." They distorted its meaning, taking words out of context. This tactic backfired; we exposed the defense distortion by reading the letter word for word.

9. El Rodeo: Truth and Consequences

1. Alan Megill, "Introduction: Four Senses of Objectivity," in Megill, ed., *Rethinking Objectivity* (Durham, N.C.: Duke University Press, 1994).

2. University officials still insist Wang was a poor teacher, with insufficient research to her credit. If this were true, why did they pay $1 million in settlement? Vice Chancellor Christ of UC Berkeley has admitted that some members of the review committees were biased. (In my case UCSB claimed that it never had a case of bias.) Wang got the university to appoint an advocate to root out possible bias, and indeed, a male professor "with a history of hostility to women" serving on a committee considering a woman for tenure was taken off the panel. But how often, in other cases, was there bias? We must assume, often.

3. I have previously noted the failed attempt to appoint Otis Graham Jr., an anti-Mexican immigrant activist, as head of the committee.

4. Kenneth Prewitt, "America's Research Universities Under Public Scrutiny," *Daedalus* 122, no. 4 (September 22, 1993): 85ff.

5. Michele Zak, "The deep structure of the field," *Journal of Business Communication* 33, no. 4 (October 1996): 503–511.

6. Castells, quoted in Hiroko Kono, "Working to keep hitchhikers off information highway," *Daily Yomiuri*, August 4, 1997.

7. Miguel Perez, "Positive Economic Trend Leaves Hispanics Behind," *Record*, December 22, 1996.

8. Carnoy, quoted in Derrick Jackson, "Less government hurts working blacks," *Dallas Morning News*, November 30, 1994.

9. Robert A. Rosenblatt, "A Shortage of Skills? Analysts Fear Minorities' Education Won't Keep Pace," *Los Angeles Times*, June 1, 1993.

10. Smith, quoted in Rosenblatt, "A Shortage of Skills?"

11. Zak, "The deep structure of the field."

Selected Bibliography

"About 'The Peculiar Institution,'" *Washington Times*, February 27, 1993.

Acuña, Armando. "Coalition Flunks UC on Efforts for Latinos." *Los Angeles Times*, May 27, 1988.

Acuña, Rodolfo F. *Anything But Mexican: Chicanos in Contemporary Los Angeles*. London: Verso, 1996.

———. "Chicano Studies: A Public Trust." In *Chicano Studies: Critical Connection between Research and Community*. The National Association for Chicano Studies, March 1992, pp. 2–13.

———. *A Community Under Siege: A Chronicle of Chicanos East of the Los Angeles River, 1945–1975*. Los Angeles: UCLA Chicano Studies Research Center, 1984.

———. "Forming The Debate: The Present Interprets the Past." In *Renato Rosaldo Lecture Series Monograph*, pp. 55–82. Tucson: Mexican American Studies & Research Center, University of Arizona, 1992.

———. *Occupied America: The Chicano Struggle for Liberation*. San Francisco: Canfield Press, 1972.

———. *Occupied America: The History of the Chicano*. 2nd ed. New York: Harper & Row, 1981.

———. *Occupied America: The History of the Chicano*. 3rd ed. New York: Harper & Row, 1988.

Acuña v. The Regents of the University of California, et al., Superior Court for the County of Santa Barbara, Case No. SB196297. United States District Court Central District of California, Case No. CV 93-1548 HLH.

Adams, Guy B. "Culture, Technical Rationality, and Organizational Culture." *American Review of Public Administration* 20, no. 4 (December 1990): 285 ff.

Adams, Noah. "Author Charles Murray Defends His Theories." *All Things Considered* (NPR), October 28, 1994, transcript no. 1649-6.

Akerman, Robert. "Academic Freedom Isn't Necessarily a Federal Case." *Atlanta Journal and Constitution*, September 9, 1991.

Alden, Bill. "Peer Review Records Opened in Tenure Denial Challenge." *New York Law Journal* (November 15, 1996): 1.

Alexander, Edward. "Multiculturalists and Anti-Semitism; African American-Jewish Relations." *Society* 31, no. 6 (September 1994): 58 ff.

Ali, Derek. "Confidence, Blacks Told; Speakers Stress Self Worth." *Dayton Daily News,* February 27, 1994.

Allen, Henry. "The Epistemology, Philosophy, History, Psychology, Anthropology, Aesthetics, and General Absolute Necessity of Making Lists." *Washington Post,* June 12, 1977.

Allen, Walter R., and Joseph O. Jewell. "African American Education since 'An American Dilemma.' An American Dilemma Revisited." *Daedalus* 124, no. 1 (January 1995): 77 ff.

Alter, Jonathan. Review of *The Twilight of Common Dreams: Why America Is Wracked by Culture Wars,* by Todd Gitlin. *Washington Monthly* 28, nos. 1–2 (January 1996): 55.

American University Law Review and Law and Government Program of Washington College. "The Supreme Court, Racial Politics, and the Right to Vote. Shaw v. Reno and the Future of the Voting Rights Act," a conference. *American University Law Review* 44, no. 1 (Fall 1994).

Amin, Samir. "1492: Columbus and the New World Order 1492–1992." *Monthly Review* 44, no. 3 (July 1992): 10 ff.

———. "The Real Stakes in the Gulf War; Analysis of the Real Motives behind the Persian Gulf War." *Monthly Review* 43, no. 3 (July 1991): 14 ff.

Anderson, Charles H. *White Protestant Americans.* Englewood Cliffs, N.J.: Prentice-Hall, 1970.

Anderson, Lee. "Student Mob vs. Equal Rights." *Chattanooga Free Press,* December 22, 1996.

"Anthropologists Challenged to Be More Responsible in Comparing Folk Medicine with Scientific Medicine." National Council Against Health Fraud (NCAHF) Newsletter 13, no. 5 (September 1990).

Appleby, Joyce, Lynn Hunt, and Margaret Jacob. *Telling the Truth About History.* New York: W. W. Norton, 1994.

Arnold, Gary. "Haunting Images on Film: Museum Casts Light on Pain and Endurance." *Washington Times,* April 18, 1993.

Arriola, Christopher J. "For Latinos in U.S., Mendez Case Fired Up Hopes of Equal Treatment." *Sacramento Bee,* April 16, 1997.

Asante, Molefi Kete. "Point of View: Afrocentric Education." *Washington Post,* April 7, 1991.

Asgar, Jack. "Give Me Relevance or Give Me Nothing: Corporate Training." *Training: The Magazine of Human Resources Development* 27, no. 7 (July 1990): 49.

"Assure faculty review." *Austin American-Statesman*, September 18, 1996.

Astin, Alexander W. "How Are Students Affected by Multiculturalism?" *Change* 25, no. 2 (March 1993): 44 ff.

Atkinson, Dorothy. "Understanding the Soviets: The Development of U. S. Expertise on the USSR." *Washington Quarterly* 10, no. 3 (Summer 1987): 183 ff.

Ayres, Edward L. Review of *The Southern Tradition: The Achievement and Limitations of an American Conservatism*, by Eugene D. Genovese. *New Republic*, 211, no. 26 (December 26, 1994): 35 ff.

Balter, Joni. "Dolphins, Rain Forests and Clear-Cuts—Eco-Education Flourishes in Schools—Environmentalists and Corporations Target Eager Young Hearts and Minds." *Seattle Times*, January 31, 1993.

Banks, James A. "Multicultural Education: Development, Dimensions, and Challenges." *Phi Delta Kappan* 75, no. 1 (September 1993): 22 ff.

Barinaga, Marcia. "A Bold New Program at Berkeley Runs into Trouble: College of Natural Resources, University of California at Berkeley." *Science* 263, no. 5152 (March 11, 1994): 1367 ff.

Barry, Bruce, and Thomas S. Bateman. "A Social Trap Analysis of the Management of Diversity." *Academy of Management Review* 21, no. 3 (July 1996): 757 ff.

Barzun, Jacques. "Scholarship versus culture." *Atlantic* 254 (November 1984): 93 ff.

Basri, Carole, and Benjamin Nahoum. "Update on How In-House Counsel Can Use and Expand the Privileges." *Metropolitan Corporate Counsel* (June 1996): 48 ff.

Bennett, David H. *From Nativist Movements to the New Right in American History*. Chapel Hill: University of North Carolina Press, 1988.

Bennett, Stephen Earl, Eric W. Rademacher, Andrew E. Smith, and Alfred J. Tuchfarber. "Polity Watch: Backdrop to '96; Affirmative Action: Why Do Whites Oppose It, And Will It Play A Role In November?" *Public Perspective* 7, no. 3 (April/May 1996): 42 ff.

Berg, Steve B. "Affirmative Action and Higher Education: California's Universities, Nation Rethink Race, Fairness. The University of California Board of Regents Has Prohibited Its Campuses from Using Race, Ethnicity or Gender as Factors in Admissions. Will the Trend Spread through the United States?" *Star Tribune*, April 2, 1996.

"Black Culture Study Grows in Europe." *Charleston Daily Mail,* May 26, 1995.

Bolvin, Jean. "The Status of Academic Relations as an Academic Discipline within Canadian Universities." *Industrial Relations* (Canadian) 47, no. 2 (March 22, 1992): 220 ff.

Bozeman, Adda B. "Culture Clash and Liberal Democracy: Toward a New World Order." *Current* 367 (November 1994): 24 ff.

"British Scholar Files Multimillion-Dollar Job Loss Suit." Reuters North European Service, May 10, 1986.

Brodsky, Joseph. "Profile of Clio: What Is History? An Argument for Nomadism." *New Republic* 208, no. 5 (February 1, 1993): 60.

Brodsky, Richard E. "Confidentiality a Primary Feature of Peer Review; Legal Briefs." *Accounting Today* 5, no. 22 (November 25, 1991): 8.

Brody, David. Review of *Class Conflict and Cultural Consensus: The Making of a Mass Consumer Society in Flint, Michigan,* by Ronald William Edsforth. *Business History Review* 62, no. 3 (September 22, 1988): 533.

———. "Labor History, Industrial Relations, and the Crisis of American Labor; Labor History and Industrial Relations: A Symposium." *Industrial and Labor Relations Review* 43, no. 1 (October 1989): 7 ff.

Brown, Eleanor Marie. "The Tower of Babel: Bridging the Divide Between Critical Race Theory and 'Mainstream' Civil Rights Scholarship." *Yale Law Journal* 105 (November, 1995): 513.

Brown, Raymond E. "The Narratives of Jesus' Passion and Anti-Judaism." *America* 172, no. 11 (April 1, 1995): 8 ff.

Bunzel, John H. "The Nation: Post-Proposition 209. The Question Remains: What Role for Race?" *Los Angeles Times,* December 8, 1996.

Burke, Peter. *The French Historical Revolution: The Annales School, 1929–89.* Stanford: Stanford University Press, 1991.

"Campaign Ads Often Disguise Prejudice: Buzzwords Used To Court Racists." *Record,* November 9, 1994.

"Campus Life, U.C.L.A.: Upgraded Status Urged For Chicano Studies." *New York Times,* February 10, 1991.

Cannon, Ellen. "Why It's Up to Business to Save American Schools." *Washington Times,* October 6, 1995.

Carpenter, Dale. "Bumping the Status Quo." *University of Chicago Law Review* 58 (Spring 1991): 703.

Carr, Edward Hallett. *What Is History?* New York: Vintage Books, 1961.

Carter, Stephen L. *Integrity.* Boston: Basic Books, 1995.

Castro, R., and R. Chabran. "Discourse and Discord: Voices from an Academic Library." *Reference Librarian* 45 / 46 (1994).

Cattan, Peter. "The Diversity of Hispanics in the U.S. Work Force." *Monthly Labor Review* 116, no. 8 (August 1993): 3 ff.

Chabram, Angie. "Chicana/o Studies As Oppositional Ethnography." *Cultural Studies* 4, no. 3 (October 1990): 228–247

Chabran, Richard. "The Emergence Of Neoconservatism In Chicano/Latino Discourses." *Cultural Studies* 4, no. 3 (October 1990): 217–227.

Chacon, Richard. "Conference Urges Harvard to Focus on Ethnic Studies." *Boston Globe,* November 12, 1995.

Chambon, Adrienne, and Donald F. Bellamy. "Ethnic Identity, Intergroup Relations and Welfare Police in the Canadian Context: A Comparative Discourse Analysis." *Journal of Sociology and Social Welfare* 22, no. 1 (1995): 121–147.

Chávez, Linda. "GOP Needs to Mend Hispanic Fences." *Dallas Morning News,* November 20, 1996.

Cheney, Lynne. "Humanities Controlled by Fringe." *St. Louis Post-Dispatch,* March 17, 1995.

———. "Mocking America; Reality of Arts and Humanities." *Phoenix Gazette,* March 15, 1995.

———. "Testimony January 24, 1995. Lynne V. Cheney, Member American Enterprise Institute, House Appropriations Interior Reducing Federal Spending." Federal Document Clearing House Congressional Testimony, January 24, 1995.

Citrin, Jack. "Affirmative Action in the People's Court." *Public Interest* 122 (Winter 1996): 39–48.

Clark, Thomas. "Culture and Objectivity." *Humanist* 54, no. 5 (September 1994): 38 ff.

"The Cole Example: William Cole Resigns from Dartmouth College Faculty." *National Review* 42, no. 18 (September 17, 1990): 18.

Cole, Jonathan R. "Balancing Acts: Dilemmas of Choice Facing Research Universities." *Daedalus* 122, no. 4 (September 22, 1993): 1 ff.

Coleman, Dana. "New Jersey Ahead of U.S. in Sexual Harassment." *New Jersey Lawyer,* November 15, 1993.

Collins, Denis, and Steven L. Wartick. "Business and Society/Business Ethics Courses: Twenty Years at the Crossroads." *Business and Society* 34, no. 1 (April 1995): 51 ff.

Comstock, Gary. "Ethics and Scientific Research." *SRA Journal* 26, no. 2 (September 22, 1994): 33 ff.

Constable, Pamela. "Nye, of Harvard, Named to Head Council at CIA." *Boston Globe,* March 2, 1993.

Cooper, Marc. "Prop. 187's True Colors: After the Vote, Will Californians Ever Get Along?" *Village Voice,* December 6, 1994.

Cordova, Teresa. "Power and Knowledge: Colonialism in the Academy." *Taboo: A Journal of Culture and Education* (Spring 1996).

"Court Upholds Stanford U." *Jerusalem Post,* September 17, 1991.

Cox, Gail Diane. "Voters Tough on Criminals." *National Law Journal,* November 21, 1994.

Cruickshank, Alexander M. "Gordon Research Conferences." *Science* 223 (March 2, 1984): 941 ff.

Curtis, Diane. "Crises May Reunite SF State: President, Faculty Have Been at Odds over Ethnic Studies Decisions." *San Francisco Chronicle,* February 11, 1991.

———. "SF State President Meets with Critics: Faculty, Students Charge Unfair Cuts to Some Programs." *San Francisco Chronicle,* October 4, 1990.

Cutlip, S. M., A. H. Center, and G. M. Broom. *Effective Public Relations.* 7th ed. Englewood Cliffs, N.J.: Prentice-Hall, 1994.

D'Antonio, Michael. "Science Fights Back: Is It Winning? The Answer Is Not in the Stars." *Los Angeles Times Magazine,* February 11, 1996.

Davidson, Jean. "Union Cites Pattern of Discrimination in UCI Pay, Promotion." *Los Angeles Times,* May 16, 1989, Orange County edition.

Davies, Norman. "A Communist Party Congress Meets in Complete Agreement." *Los Angeles Times,* February 23, 1986.

———. "No Stalinists, Simply All the President's Men: They Come Not To Bury but to Save Perestroika, the Creation and Now the Last Hope of the Party's Continued Dictatorship, Argues Norman Davies." *Independent,* August 20, 1991.

Deibel, Mary. "High Court Has Tall Order: U.S. Supreme Court Struggles to Right Some Wrongs without Trampling Some Rights." *Rocky Mountain News,* May 24, 1995.

de Jasay, Anthony. "After Socialism, What? Socialism Dominated Europe for Half a Century, Defining Its Opponents As Well As Its Adherents. Now It Is Dead, and in Its Place May Come a Resurgent Right, with a Surprising Power Base." *National Review* 43, no. 9 (May 27, 1991): 25 ff.

de la Torre, Adela. "Getting a Piece of the Mexican Rock; NAFTA Could Open the Vast, Underinsured Markets of Mexico and Latin America to U.S. Insurance Companies." *Los Angeles Times,* August 11, 1993.

———. "Perspective on Ethnic Studies: Activism Isn't Enough Any More; Scholarship and Intellectual Rigor Are Required If Programs Are to Move into the Academic Mainstream." *Los Angeles Times,* December 12, 1996.

Delgado, Richard. "The Imperial Scholar: Reflections on a Review of Civil Rights Literature." *University of Pennsylvania Law Review* 132, no. 561 (1984).

———. *The Rodrigo Chronicles: Conversations about America and Race.* New York: New York University Press, 1995.

Desimore, Laura M. "Racial Discourse in a Community: Language and the Social Construction of Race." *Journal of Negro Education* 62, no. 4 (Fall 1993).

Dezell, Maureen. "Boston's Celeb Complex: Many Stars, Little Glitter." *Boston Globe,* November 29, 1996.

DiBacco, Thomas V. "Social Work's Slow Rise; Profession Faced Opposition for Decades." *Washington Post,* November 15, 1994.

"Don't Fear Multicultural Education." *Advocate,* March 15, 1994.

D'Souza, Dinesh. "We the Slaveowners; In Jefferson's America, Were Some Men Not Created Equal?" *Policy Review* 74 (Fall 1995): 30 ff.

Du Bois, W. E. B. *The Autobiography of W. E. B. Du Bois.* New York: International Publishers, 1991.

———. *Black Reconstruction in America, 1860–1880,* ed. David L. Lewis. New York: Macmillan, 1991.

———. *The Souls of Black Folk.* New York: Bantam Books, 1989.

Edgerton, Russel. "The Re-examination of Faculty Priorities." *Change* 25, no. 4 (July 1993): 10 ff.

Elshtain, Jean Bethke. "Battered Reason: The New Feminist Jurisprudence." *New Republic* 207, no. 15 (October 5, 1992): 25 ff.

Endicott, William. "Don't Need PC to Know a Slur." *Sacramento Bee,* July 18, 1993.

Estrada, Leo F. "Latinos in California's Future." *California Journal Weekly,* January 1, 1995.

"Europe's Unfolding Dilemmas: What's Good for Markets Isn't Always Good for Democracy." *Guardian,* June 4, 1996.

Fein, Bruce. "By Every Other Name Racism Smells As Foul." *New Jersey Law Journal* (May 2, 1991): 14 ff.

———. "The Economics of Professional Racism." *Texas Lawyer,* May 6, 1991.

Ferber, Marianne A., and Julie A. Nelson. "Humanizing the 'dismal science.'" *Chicago Tribune,* August 4, 1993.

Ferguson, Tim W. "Dear Stan." *Forbes* (September 9, 1996): 47 ff.

Fields, Suzanne. "Afrocentrism Can Be a Trap for Black Children" *Atlanta Journal and Constitution,* September 9, 1993.

———. "The Double-Edged Sword of 'Reverse' Racism." *Atlanta Journal and Constitution,* July 29, 1993.

Fink, Carole F. *Marc Bloch: A Life in History.* New York: Cambridge University Press, 1989.

Folkart, Burt A. "French Historian Fernand Braudel Dies; He Ignored Elite, Recorded How the People Spent Their Lives." *Los Angeles Times,* November 30, 1985.

Foner, Eric. "Reconstructing Reconstruction." *Newsday,* February 16, 1992.

Forman, Paul. Review of *Telling the Truth About History,* by Joyce Oldham Appleby. *Science* 269, no. 5223 (July 28, 1995): 565 ff.

Forrest, Anne. "Women and Industrial Relations Theory: No Room in the Discourse." *Industrial Relations* (Canadian) 48, no. 3 (June 22, 1993): 409 ff.

Fox-Genovese, Elizabeth. "Political Correctness Stifles Thought and Speech." *News & Record* (Greensboro, N.C.), May 1, 1994.

Fuller, Steve. "Being There with Thomas Kuhn: A Parable for Postmodern Times." *History and Theory* 31, no. 3 (October 1992): 241–275.

Garcia, Phil. "Firebrand Rep. Dornan Apparently Loses in Orange." *Sacramento Bee,* November 13, 1996.

Garza, Melita Marie. "Culture Wars: Across the Nation, Universities Find Themselves on the Front Line of the Ethnic Studies Debate." *Chicago Tribune,* July 18, 1995.

Genovese, Eugene D. "Voices Must Unite for Victory in the Cultural War." *Chicago Tribune,* December 22, 1993.

Gewirtz, Paul. "On 'I know it when I see it.'" *Yale Law Journal* 105, no. 4 (January 1996): 1023–1047.

Giddens, Anthony. "In Defence of Sociology." *New Statesman & Society* 8, no. 347 (April 7, 1995): 18 ff.

Gillmore, Robert. "Buchanan: Not Just Another Wordsmith." *Chicago Tribune,* January 29, 1987.

———. "For Liberals, 'Compassion' Is Not Enough." *Chicago Tribune,*. April 26, 1987.

Glidden, David G. "Why Not Reward a Political Scientist Who Helps a Neighborhood? UC: Research Should Be More Than Specialized Investigation. It Should Include Applying Scholarship to the Classroom and to the World." *Los Angeles Times,* November 17, 1991.

Goetz, Thomas. "Oh, the Humanities!" *Village Voice,* April 18, 1995.

Goldberger, Paul. "Historical Shows on Trial: Who Judges?" *New York Times,* February 11, 1996.

Goldsborough, James O. "Pete Won, His Party Lost." *San Diego Union-Tribune,* November 18, 1996.

Goleman, Daniel. "Researcher Is Criticized for Test of Journal Bias." *New York Times,* September 27, 1988.

Goode, Stephen. "When the Truth Yields to Political Pressure." *Washington Times,* December 20, 1995.

Goodman, Neville W. "Paradigm, Parameter, Paralysis of Mind: Use of Language and Statistics in Biomedical Research." *British Medical Journal* 307, no. 6919 (December 18, 1993): 1627 ff.

Gordon, Larry. "UC Adopts Policy to Place More Emphasis on Teaching; Education: New Promotion Guidelines Are Aimed at Rewarding Excellence in Instruction As Well As Research." *Los Angeles Times,* July 17, 1992.

———. "UC Panel Urges Less Emphasis on Research; Education: Report Calls for Professors to Focus More on Teaching, Public Service and Attempts to Solve Real-Life Problems." *Los Angeles Times,* November 5, 1991.

Gottschalk, Louis Reichenthal. *Understanding History.* 2nd ed. New York: Knopf, 1969.

Gough, Barry. "Goodbye Columbus? Canada's Chains of History: Christopher Columbus Quincentenary Uncelebrated in Canada." *History Today* 43 (March 1993): 8 ff.

Gould, Stephen Jay. *The Mismeasure of Man.* New York: W. W. Norton, 1981.

Gramsci, Antonio. *Selections from Political Writings 1910–1920.* New York: International Publishers, 1977.

———. *Selections from Political Writings 1921–1926.* New York: International Publishers, 1978.

Gray, Katti. "Black Group Rallying for Curriculum." *Newsday,* July 22, 1990.

Greeley, Andrew M. "The Last Fellow Travelers Dig Their Heels." *Plain Dealer,* September 19, 1994.

Green, Joelette. "History, Ourstory." *Essence,* June 1992.

Gross, Netty C. "Studying for Their Own Sake." *Jerusalem Post,* February 5, 1993.

Gross, Susanna. "Defiant Champion of the Workers." *Daily Mail,* September 2, 1993.

Gunson, Phil. "Poll Puts Mexican Opposition Ahead; The Ruling PRI's Fiesta May Soon Be Over." *Guardian,* August 1, 1994.

Guzda, Henry P. Review of *Workplace Industrial Relations and the Global Challenge,* ed. Jacques Belanger, P. K. Edwards, and Larry Haiven. *Monthly Labor Review* 118, no. 7 (July 1995): 80 ff.

Handlin, Oscar. *Truth in History.* Cambridge, Mass.: Harvard University Press, 1979.

Harding, Sandra. *The Science Question in Feminism.* Ithaca, N.Y.: Cornell University Press, 1986.

Harper, Timothy. "Memories of a Polish Democracy." *Newsday,* September 18, 1989.

Hay, Colin. "Narrating Crisis: The Discursive Construction of the 'Winter of Discontent.'" *Sociology: The Journal of the British Sociological Association* 30, no. 2 (May 1996): 253–277.

Hayden, Tom, and Connie Rice. "California Cracks Its Mortarboards; Abolishing Affirmative Action at the University of California, July 1995." *Nation* 261, no. 8 (September 18, 1995): 264 ff.

Hayward, Brad. "UCD Creates Department for American Indian Studies." *Sacramento Bee,* October 23, 1993.

Helfand, David. "I Turned Down Tenure; Why Other Professors Should, Too." *Washington Monthly* 18 (June 1986): 13 ff.

Hendricks, Jon. "The Social Power of Professional Knowledge in Aging: What It Means to Be a Professional in the Field of Aging." *Generations* 19, no. 2 (June 22, 1995): 51 ff.

Hernandez, Peggy. "Afro-American Studies Show Strength." *Boston Globe,* November 16, 1990.

Heron, G. A., "Running from Racism 'Is No Solution.'" *Guardian,* October 13, 1993.

Herubel, Jean-Pierre V. M. "The 'Annales Movement' And Its Historiography: A Selective Bibliography." *French Historical Studies* 18, no. 1 (Spring 1993): 346–355.

Himmelfarb, Gertrude. "The Group: Bourgeois Britain and Its Marxist Historians." *New Republic* 194 (February 10, 1986): 28.

———. "What to Do about Education: The Universities." *Commentary* 98, no. 4 (October 1994): 21.

Hoagland, Jim. "A Witches' Brew in Europe." *Washington Post,* May 8, 1990.

Hobsbawm, Eric, and Terence Ranger, eds. *The Invention of Tradition.* Cambridge: Cambridge University Press, 1983.

Hockenos, Paul. "Making Hate Safe Again in Europe; Right Cultural Revolutionaries." *Nation* 259, no. 8 (September 19, 1994): 271 ff.

Hoftstader, R., and C. D. Hardy. *The Development and Scope of Higher Education in the United States.* New York: Columbia University Press, 1952.

Holding, Reynolds. "UC Barred from Using Prop. 209: 2nd Setback for Newly Passed Law." *San Francisco Chronicle,* December 7, 1996.

Hollinger, David A. "Truth by Consensus." *New York Times,* March 27, 1994.

Hondagneu-Sotelo, Pierrette. *Gendered Transitions: Mexican Experiences of Immigration.* Berkeley: University of California Press, 1994.

"Hooked; Divisions over Diversity." Interviews by Robert MacNeil and Judy Woodruff, with Sen. Joseph Biden, [D] Delaware; William Bennett, National Drug Policy Director; Patricia Williams, Law Professor; John Bunzel, former University President; Roderic Park, University Administrator; Ronald Takaki, Ethnic Studies Professor. Also includes an interview of Derrick Bell, Law Professor, by correspondent Charlayne Hunter-Gault. *MacNeil/Lehrer NewsHour*, May 10, 1990, transcript no. 3729.

"How the GOP Lost So Many Latino Voters." *Sacramento Bee*, November 24, 1996.

Howard, Philip. "Trouble with Fraggles." *Times*, August 5, 1993.

Howkins, Alun. "A Past for the People. History Workshop Journal." *New Statesman & Society* 8, no. 337 (January 27, 1995): 36 ff.

Hu-DeHart, Evelyn. "The History, Development, and Future of Ethnic Studies; Multicultural Education." *Phi Delta Kappan* 75, no. 1 (September 1993): 50 ff.

Huggins, Nathan I. "The Deforming Mirror of Truth: Slavery and the Master Narrative of American History." *Radical History Review* 49 (Winter 1991): 25–47.

Hunt, Shelby D. "Positivism and Paradigm Dominance in Consumer Research: Toward a Critical Pluralism and Rapprochement." *Journal of Consumer Research* 18, no. 1 (June 1991): 32 ff.

Innerst, Carol. "Most Faculty Say No to Special Treatment: Administrators Look Out of Step." *Washington Times*, December 2, 1996.

———. "Putting Africa on the Map: 'Racist' History Assailed." *Washington Times*, November 13, 1990.

Jackson, Derrick. "Less Government Hurts Working Blacks." *Dallas Morning News*, November 30, 1994.

———. "White Women Passed Prop. 209." *Austin American-Statesman*, November 13, 1996.

———. "Who's to Blame for Prop. 209?" *Boston Globe*, November 8, 1996.

Jimenez, Manuel. "Scholar Challenges Latino Stereotypes." *Nuestro Tiempo*, March 18, 1993.

Jones, Brian W. "Two Views on Questions of Morality in Racial Issues." *Washington Times*, December 8, 1996.

Jones, Maldwyn A. "Putting a Lid on the Melting Pot." *New York Times*, January 15, 1989.

Jones, Marc T. "Missing the Forest for the Trees: A Critique of the Social Responsibility Concept and Discourse." *Business and Society* 35, no. 1 (March 1996): 7 ff.

Kahlenberg, Richard D. "D'Souza Falls Prey to Conservative Excess." *Connecticut Law Tribune*, March 4, 1996.

Kealy, Gregory S. "Herbert G. Gutman, 1928–1985, and the Writing of Working-Class History." *Monthly Review* 38 (May 1986): 22 ff.

Kelly, Dennis. "Afrocentric Studies: A Concept Rooted in Controversy." *USA Today*, January 28, 1992.

Kettle, Martin. "Economic Spasmodics." *Guardian*, October 28, 1995.

Kiernan, Victor. Review of *Protest and Survival: Essays for E. P. Thompson*, ed. John Rule and Robert Malcolmson. *History Today* 45, no. 2 (February 1995): 53 ff.

Kimball, Roger. "Attacking but Not Offending: Why Won't Robert Hughes Admit He's a Conservative?" *Daily Telegraph*, June 7, 1993.

Klausner, Samuel Z. "The Religious 'Other' in Black-Jewish Relations; African American–Jewish Relations." *Society* 31, no. 6 (September 1994): 51 ff.

Klein, Jeffrey S., and Nicholas J. Pappas. "Discrimination in Tenure Decisions." *New York Law Journal* (October 2, 1995): 3 ff.

Koury, Renee. "UC Spent Millions to Settle Sex Bias Cases: Incidents May Still Occur, Say Officials." *San Diego Union-Tribune*, July 8, 1996.

Kramer, Rita. "Politically Correct Is Scientifically Fatal: Was Newton Really A Rapist?" *Newsday*, July 9, 1995.

Krikorian, Greg. "Study Questions Justice System's Racial Fairness." *Los Angeles Times*, February 13, 1996.

Kuhn, Thomas S. *The Structure of Scientific Revolutions*. 2nd ed. Chicago: University of Chicago Press, 1970.

Kull, Andrew. *The Color-blind Constitution*. Cambridge, Mass.: Harvard University Press, 1992.

Kuttner, Robert. Review of *Rival Views of Market Society and Other Recent Essays*, by Albert O. Hirschman. *New Republic* 197, no. 21 (November 23, 1987): 46.

Lam v. The University of Hawaii, Ninth Circuit, U.S. Court of Appeals, No. 91-16537, 95 *Daily Journal*, D.A.R, October 12, 1994.

"The Landscape: Internet and Colleges." *Change* 28, no. 1 (January 1996): 41 ff.

"Latinos in California: the Next Italians." *Economist*, December 14, 1996.

Leff, Lisa. "A Major Choice for Midshipmen; Academy Pushes Engineering over Humanities." *Washington Post*, March 26, 1989.

"The Left, the Right and the Third World: Review of *States or Markets? Neo-Liberalism and the Development-Policy Debate*, ed. Christopher Colclough and James Manor. *Economist* (March 14, 1992): 103 ff.

Lempinen, Edward W. "Debate over CCRI Effect on Women: Legal Meaning of Clause in Dispute." *San Francisco Chronicle*, September 10, 1996.

Leo, John. "Affirmative Action Has Always Lacked Popular Support." *Tampa Tribune*, March 7, 1995.

———. "The Espresso Uprising." *U.S. News & World Report* 120, no. 18 (May 6, 1996): 23.

Leonard, John. "Culture Shock." *Newsday*, July 5, 1990.

———. Review of *Culture and Imperialism*, by Edward W. Said. *Nation* 256, no. 11 (March 22, 1993): 383 ff.

Lepiscopo, Peter. "Proposition 209 Should Be Upheld." *San Diego Union-Tribune*, December 22, 1996.

Lester, Julius. "Race: A Conversation Peace." *Washington Post*, May 25, 1995.

"Let's Face It, We're on Automatic Fast Forward." *Record*, December 1, 1994.

Levine, David O. *The American College and the Culture of Aspiration, 1915–1940.* Ithaca, N.Y.: Cornell University Press, 1986.

Levine, Lawrence W. *The Opening of the American Mind: Canons, Culture, and History.* Boston: Beacon Press, 1996.

Lewy, Guenter. "Academic Ethics and the Radical Left." *Policy Review* no. 19 (Winter 1982): 29 ff.

Lively, Donald E., and Stephen Plass. "Equal Protection: The Jurisprudence of Denial and Evasion." *American University Law Review* 40 (Summer 1991): 1307.

Locke, Robert R. *The End of the Practical Man: Entrepreneurship and Higher Education in Germany, France and Great Britain, 1880–1940.* Greenwich, Conn.: JAI Press, 1984.

Lopez, Julie Amparano. "How Your Job Jargon So You Don't Disconnect." *Arizona Republic*, May 5, 1996.

Loury, Glenn. "Absolute California." *New Republic*, November 18, 1996.

Maloney, Linda M. Review of *Who Killed Jesus? Exposing the Roots of Anti-Semitism in the Gospel Story of the Death of Jesus*, by John Dominic Crossan. *America* 173, no. 6 (September 9, 1995): 24.

"Many Cultures, Many Claims: Yes, Revise History Books, but Not Just to Bolster Ethnic Pride." *Newsday*, December 30, 1990.

Marable, Manning. "History and Black Consciousness: The Political Culture of Black America." *Monthly Review* 47, no. 3 (July 1995): 71 ff.

Marley, Sara. "Educators Receive Credit: Wharton Rated Top Program for Risk, Insurance Studies." *Business Insurance*, March 29, 1993.

Marquand, David. "A Stake through the Heart of Old Simplicities; Neither Old Left nor New Right Understands Tony Blair's Stakeholder Economics, but They Know It Spells Death to the Old Form of Politics in This Country." *Independent*, January 15, 1996.

Marquez, Myriam. "Insensitive Words but Fair Actions? Lay That on the Jurors, Judge." *Orlando Sentinel*, December 12, 1994.

Marriot, Michael. "Educators See Need for Diversity on Campus, but Debate How to Achieve It." *New York Times,* December 19, 1990.

Marrus, Michael R. "Good Scholar, Good Frenchman." *New York Times,* October 1, 1989.

Martin, Ralph Drury. "Cracking Crimes through Language: In Fascinating Detail, Roger W. Shuy Chronicles How the Scientist Can Bring Understanding to Something We All Think We Know So Well—Everyday Conversation." *Legal Times,* July 11, 1994.

———. "Cracking Crimes through Language Analysis." *Recorder,* August 4, 1994.

Martinez, Draeger. "Parents Learn How to Help Youths at Mendota Conference." *Fresno Bee,* April 20, 1996.

Martinez, Gebe. "O.C. Precinct Typifies Latino Voter Apathy." *Los Angeles Times,* November 28, 1994.

Marty, Myron A. "Creating an American Past: How We Have Reshaped Our Memories to Shape Our Culture." *St. Louis Post-Dispatch,* March 8, 1992.

Massy, William F., Andrea K. Wilger, and Carol Colbeck. "Overcoming 'Hollowed' Collegiality: How Departmental Cultures Affect Teaching." *Change* 26, no. 4 (July 1994): 11 ff.

Mathews, Jay. "Politics in Academia Questioned at Stanford: Conservative Wasn't Targeted, Probe Finds." *Washington Post,* May 25, 1986.

McCaughan, Michael. "Current Neoliberal Wisdom in Latin America Challenged." *Irish Times,* May 18, 1996.

McDougall, Walter A. Review of *The Age of Extremes: A History of the World, 1914–1991,* by Eric J. Hobsbawm. *Commentary* 100, no. 2 (August 1995): 56.

McGinn, Colin. Review of *The Construction of Social Reality,* by John R. Searle. *New Republic* 212, no. 21 (May 22, 1995): 37 ff.

McPhee, Mike M. "CSU Faculty OKs Plan for Tough Tenure Review." *Denver Post,* December 10, 1996.

Megill, Alan. "Introduction: Four Senses of Objectivity." In *Rethinking Objectivity,* ed. Megill. Durham, N.C.: Duke University Press, 1994.

Menand, Louis. "The Thrashing of Professionalism." *New York Times,* March 5, 1995.

Mendel, Ed. "Prop. 209 Is Declared a Winner." *San Diego Union-Tribune,* November 6, 1996.

Miller, Marjorie. "Salinas Accused of Doctoring the Books on Mexico's History: New School Texts Cast Villains and Heroes in a Different Light. Critics Say the President Is Distorting the Past for Political Gain." *Los Angeles Times,* September 22, 1992.

Mills, David. "Half-Truths and History: The Debate over Jews and Slavery." *Washington Post*, October 17, 1993.

"Missing the Point About 'Afrocentrism.'" *Washington Post*, September 29, 1990.

Mitchell, Don. *The Lie of the Land: Migrant Workers and the California Landscape*. Minneapolis: University of Minnesota Press, 1996.

Moreno, Sylvia. "UT's Minority Recruiting Shows Court Ruling's Effects; Officials Tread New Path without Affirmative Action." *Dallas Morning News*, October 11, 1996.

Morgan, Glenda, and E. J. Levy. "Debunker of 'Feminist Fictions' Is Soft on Truth Herself." *Star Tribune*, September 3, 1994.

Morrow, Carlotta. "This Afrocentrism Is Reverse Racism." *San Diego Union-Tribune*, November 12, 1995.

Morse, Rob. "Fighting Bullets with Hope." *San Francisco Examiner*, April 25, 1996.

Mundy, Liza. "What They Talk About When They Talk About Talk; To Deborah Tannen and Her Fellow Georgetown Sociolinguists, Conversation Is More Than Just a Field of Study. It's the Way Human Beings Define Themselves." *Washington Post*, February 4, 1996.

Munson, Lynne A. "Art by Committee." *New York Times*, September 21, 1995.

Muwakkil, Salim. "The Ugly Revival of Genetic Determinism." *San Francisco Examiner*, December 6, 1994.

Myrdal, Gunnar. *An American Dilemma: The Negro Problem and Modern Democracy*. Vols. 1–2. New York: Harper & Row, 1944.

Navarette, Ruben, Jr. "New Victims? Weighing the Charges of Reverse Discrimination." *Change* 25, no. 2 (March 1993): 8 ff.

"The Neo-Liberals Push Their Own Brand of Reform." *Business Week* (January 31, 1983): 96 ff.

Nichols, John. "Recalling a Guide through the Mists of History." *Capital Times*, April 1, 1994.

———. "'We Need to Change the Political Culture.'" *Capital Times*, November 3, 1995.

Nichols, Rodney W. "Federal Science Policy and Universities: Consequences of Success; The Impact of Federal Sponsorship on American University Research." *Daedalus* 122, no. 4 (September 22, 1993): 197.

Nicholson, David. "The Mind of a Prophet." *Washington Post*, February 22, 1987.

———. "Whose American Dilemma?" *Washington Post*, October 1, 1995.

Njeri, Itabari. "Academic Acrimony: Minority Professors Claim Racism Plays Role in Obtaining Tenure." *Los Angeles Times*, September 20, 1989.

Norman, Tony. "Space Is the Place." *Pittsburgh Post-Gazette*, October 24, 1993.

Notturno, M. A. "Thomas Kuhn and the Legacy of Logical Positivism." *History of The Human Sciences* 10, no. 1 (February 1997): 131–133.

Novick, Peter. *That Noble Dream: The 'Objectivity Question' and the American Historical Profession*. Cambridge: Cambridge University Press, 1988.

Odom, Maida. "Prophetic Pioneer: Biographer Says Civil-Rights Leader W.E.B. Du Bois Called Today's Crisis." *Chicago Tribune*, February 14, 1994.

Oliande, Sylvia L. "Latinos Map Out Activism in Wake of 209; Conference: At a Statewide Meeting of 1,200 At CSUN, Chicano Leaders Say They See the Initiative's Passage as a Catalyst For Political Mobilization." *Los Angeles Times*, November 10, 1996.

Omi, Michael, and Howard Winant. *Racial Formation in the United States: From the 1960s to the 1990s*. 2nd ed. New York: Routledge, 1994.

Owens, Madeleine. "Blameless Nation: Has Bob Dole Forgotten Slavery? Vietnam? The Indians? McCarthyism? Watergate?" *Columbian*, September 10, 1995.

Page, Clarence. "Bush, Quayle, Media All Ignore 'R' Word." *St. Louis Post-Dispatch*, May 31, 1992.

Parr, Joy. "Gender History and Historical Practice." *Canadian Historical Review* 76, no. 3 (September 1995): 354 ff.

Pemberton, J. Michael. "The Importance of Theory and Research to Records and Information Management." *Records Management Quarterly* 26, no. 2 (April 1992): 46 ff.

Pertman, Adam. "Affirmative Action's Loss in Calif. Expected to Spur Similar Battles." *Boston Globe*, November 7, 1996.

Pfeffer, Jeffrey. "Barriers to the Advance of Organizational Science: Paradigm Development As a Dependent Variable." *Academy of Management Review* 18, no. 4 (October 1993): 599 ff.

Phillips, Jim. "Are Research Universities Selling Out?" *Austin American-Statesman*, January 14, 1996.

Pierard, Richard V. "Denying the Holocaust: The Growing Assault on Truth and Memory." *Christianity Today* 38, no. 4 (April 4, 1994): 97.

Pinkerton, James P. "General Schwarzkopf's New Paradigm: Domestic Lessons of Desert Storm." *Policy Review* 57 (Summer 1991): 22.

Pinsker, Sanford. "Lost on Campus: Civility, Rational Debate." *Christian Science Monitor*, November 30, 1995.

———. "Why Faculty Preference Is for No Preference." *Christian Science Monitor,* December 2, 1996.

Pisik, Betsy. "The Semantics of Hate: Are Racist Code Words Masquerading As Political Straight Talk?" *Washington Times,* November 14, 1991.

Popper, Karl R. *The Logic of Scientific Discovery.* New York: Harper & Row, 1968.

Portch, Stephen R., Nancy J. Kaufman, and Jaqueline R. Ross. "From Frog to Prince: From Post-Tenure Review to Faculty Roles, Development, and Rewards." *Change* 25, no. 4 (July 1993): 17 ff.

Porter, Horace. "Reflections of a Black Son; First Printed in February, 1977." *Change* 26, no. 3 (May 1994): 22.

Pressley, Darrell S. "'Virtual University' Proposal Being Developed by Educators: Students Could Earn Credits, Degrees on Internet, Interactive TV." *Cincinnati Enquirer,* August 29, 1996.

Prewitt, Kenneth. "America's Research Universities under Public Scrutiny." *Daedalus* 122, no. 4 (September 22, 1993): 85 ff.

Purvin, George. "A Little Ethnic Cheerleading Would Do History No Harm." *Washington Times,* August 1, 1990.

Rasch, Sara B. Review of *Rethinking Labor History: Essays on Discourse and Class Analysis,* ed. Leonard Berlanstein. *Labor Studies Journal* 20, no. 2 (June 22, 1995): 58.

Raspberry, William. "Combining Ideas on Racial Justice Could Be Useful." *Fresno Bee,* November 22, 1996.

———. "Culture, Schooling and Eurocentrism." *Chicago Tribune,* September 7, 1990.

———. "End Racial Preferences but Also Stop Excluding." *Cincinnati Enquirer,* November 24, 1996.

———."Picking Racial Justice Apart." *Chicago Tribune,* November 26, 1996.

Ravitch, Diane, and Arthur Schlesinger Jr. "Should Teach History, Not Ethnic Cheerleading." *Newsday,* June 29, 1990.

Regents of the University of California v. Bakke, Supreme Court of the United States, 438 U.S. 265; 98 S. Ct. 2733; 1978 U.S. LEXIS 5; 57 L. Ed. 2d 750; 17 Fair Empl. Prac. Cas. (BNA) 1000; 17 Empl. Prac., June 28, 1978.

Reid, S. A. "The Du Bois Chronicles: Eight-Year Odyssey to Define a Man and His Genius Pays Off in High Praise for Historian David Levering Lewis." *Atlanta Journal and Constitution,* December 5, 1993.

Reilly, Joseph. "Under the White Gaze: Jim Crow, the Nobel, and the Assault on Toni Morrison." *Monthly Review* 45, no. 11 (April 1994): 41 ff.

Reinhold, Robert. "The Past Examined." *New York Times*, January 8, 1989.

Rejwan, Nissim. "Frenchman and Jew." *Jerusalem Post*, September 7, 1990.

Reske, Henry. "Peer Pressure." *ABA Journal* 75 (November 1989): 48.

"Return of the revisionists." *Jerusalem Post*, January 6, 1993.

Reveler, Norma. "Understanding Words in Context." *Daily Yomiuri*, August 1, 1994.

Roark, Anne C. "UCLA Accused Of 'Apartheid-Like' Hiring Policy." *Los Angeles Times*, June 26, 1987.

Robertson, Alonza. "Black Students' Protest at SF State: Budget Cuts, New Class, Called Threat to Ethnic Studies Program." *San Francisco Chronicle*, September 14, 1990.

Robinson, Paul H. "Moral Credibility and Crime: Why People Obey Law." *Current* 373 (June 1995): 10 ff.

Rocco, Raymond. "The Theoretical Construction of the 'Other' in Postmodernist Thought: Latinos in the New Urban Political Economy." *Cultural Studies* 4, no. 3 (October 1990): 321–330.

Rodríguez, Roberto, and Patrisia González. "Ethnic Minorities Continue to Battle School Segregation." *Fresno Bee*, May 11, 1994.

———. "Proposition 209 is part of trend, 'politics of hate.'" *Fresno Bee*, November 11, 1996.

Roediger, David R. *The Wages of Whiteness: Race and the Making of the American Working Class.* London: Verso, 1991.

Rosaldo, Renato. *Culture and Truth: The Remaking of Social Analysis.* Boston: Beacon Press, 1993.

Rosenblatt, Robert A. "A Shortage of Skills? Analysts Fear Minorities' Education Won't Keep Pace." *Los Angeles Times*, June 1, 1993.

Roser, Mary Ann. "Tenure Not in Peril at UT; While President Says Reviews Should Be Seen Positively, Some Faculty Remain Concerned. UT Faculty Told Reviews Won't Jeopardize Tenure." *Austin American-Statesman*, September 17, 1996.

Ross, John. "Mexican Bishops Opt More for the Poor; Speaking Out on the State of the Mexican Economy." *National Catholic Reporter*, October 11, 1996.

Rothenberg, Randall. Letter to Editor, "Neo-Liberals Have a Message for the Democrats." *New York Times*, March 17, 1985.

Ruggles, Clifton, and Olivia Ruggles. "Clashing Colors." *Gazette* (Montreal), December 6, 1992.

Ruggles, Rick. "Speaker Decries Trends in Higher Education." *Omaha World Herald*, December 16, 1995.

Saltzman, Amy. "Life after the Lawsuit." *U.S. News & World Report* (August 19, 1996): 57 ff.

Salvatore, Nick. Review of *Perspectives on American Labor History: The Problems of Synthesis*, ed. J. Carroll Moody and Alice Kessler-Harris. *Business History Review* 64, no. 1 (March 22, 1990): 166 ff.

Salzer, James. "Tenured Faculty Reviews Sought." *Florida Times-Union* (Jacksonville), April 11, 1996.

Sama, Dominic. "New U.S. Issue Honors W. E. B. Du Bois." *Chicago Tribune*, February 2, 1992.

Sanchez, Felix. "Hispanic, Indian Applicants Dip at UC, but the Riverside Campus Notes a Rise in Number of Chicano and Latino Hopefuls." *Press-Enterprise* (Riverside, Calif.), February 14, 1996.

Sanchez, Rosaura. "Ethnicity, Ideology, and Academia." *Cultural Studies* 4, no. 3 (October 1990): 294–302.

Sanoff, Alvin P., and Nancy Linnon. "Harvard's Helmsman Quits the Rat Race." *U.S. News & World Report* 108, no. 23 (June 11, 1990): 54.

Schlesinger, Arthur M., Jr. *The Disuniting of America: Reflections on a Multicultural Society.* New York: W. W. Norton & Co., 1992.

Schneider, William. "The Ups and Downs of the Economy: Is the Recession the President's Biggest Enemy? Or the Democrats? The Opposition: Bush Picks His Shots." *Los Angeles Times,* February 2, 1992.

Schrag, Peter. "Backing off Bakke: The New Assault on Affirmative Action. *Regents of the University of California v. Bakke.*" *Nation* 262, no. 16 (April 22, 1996): 11 ff.

Schwartz, Stephen. "Challenge to Campus Policies: New Group Seeks to Maintain Quality of State Education System." *San Francisco Chronicle,* January 5, 1991.

Schwartzkopff, Fran. "They'll Tell Us Firsthand about the Jim Crow South." *San Diego Union-Tribune,* April 18, 1993.

"Scientists File Suit to Open Peer Panel." *National Law Journal* (March 28, 1994): A5.

Scott, David Clark. "Mexican Opposition Denounces Politics of New School Texts." *Christian Science Monitor,* September 21, 1992.

Searle, John R. *The Construction of Social Reality.* New York: Free Press, 1995.

———. "Rationality and Realism, What Is at Stake? Ongoing 'Debate' over the Objectives of Higher Education Curriculum, Academic Requirements and Enhancement of Western Culture." *Daedalus* 122, no. 4 (September 22, 1993): 55 ff.

"The Secret's Out: Affirmative Action Lacked Support." *Times-Picayune,* March 7, 1995.

Senior, Peter A., and Raj Bjopal. "Ethnicity As a Variable in Epistiological Research." *British Medical Journal* 309, no. 6950 (July 30, 1994): 327 ff.

Shah, Reena. "When the Melting Pot Breaks Down." *St. Petersburg Times,* April 5, 1992.

Shivakumar, Dhananjai. "The Pure Theory as Ideal Type: Defending Kelsen on the Basis of Weberian Methodology." *Yale Law Journal* 105, no. 5 (March 1996): 1383–1414.

Shore, Marlene. "'Remember the Future': The Canadian Historical Review and the Discipline of History, 1920–95." *Canadian Historical Review* 76, no. 3 (September 1995): 410.

Shuy, Roger W. *Language Crimes.* Oxford: Blackwell Publishers, 1993.

Silberberg, Michael C. "Work Product Privilege of Internal Investigations." *New York Law Journal* (August 16, 1996): 3 ff.

Simmons, Judy, Jill Nelson, Gordon Chambers, and Cherella Cox. "A House Divided." *Essence* (January 1992): 58 ff.

Simpson, Ann. Review of *Ethics and Environmental Policy: Theory Meets Practice,* ed. Frederick Ferre and Peter Hartel. *Alternatives* 21, no. 3 (July 1995): 39.

Singer, Alan. "Reflections on Multiculturalism." *Phi Delta Kappan* 76, no. 4 (December 1994): 284 ff.

Sivanandan, A. "The New Racism." *The New Statesman & Society* 1, no. 22 (November 4, 1988): 8–9.

Sneider, Daniel. "Judges Raise Conservative Hackles." *Christian Science Monitor,* December 6, 1996.

———. "Legal Test for California's Affirmative Action Ban." *Christian Science Monitor,* December 18, 1996.

Soley, Lawrence. *The Leasing of the Ivory Tower.* Boston: South End Press, 1995.

Solomon, Martin B. "What's Wrong with Multimedia in Higher Education?" *THE (Technological Horizons In Education) Journal* 21, no. 7 (February 1994): 81 ff.

Sommer, Robert. "Serving Two Masters: Center for Consumer Research at the University of California, Davis, 1976–1992." *Journal of Consumer Affairs* 28, no. 1 (June 22, 1994): 170 ff.

Sowell, Thomas. "Multicultural Propagandists Disregard Facts." *Ethnic NewsWatch* 6, no. 5 (May 31, 1994): 7.

Spivak, Gayatri Chakravorty. "Can the Subaltern Speak?" In Nelson, Cary and Lawrence Grossberg, *Marxism and the Interpretation of Culture,* ed. Cary Nelson and Lawrence Grossberg, 217–313. Urbana: University of Illinois Press, 1987.

Stall, Bill, and Dan Morain. "Prop. 209 Wins, Bars Affirmative Action Initiatives: Wilson Says It Will Undo a 'Terrible Unfairness.' Limits on Campaign Donations, Hiking Minimum Wage Are Among Nine Measures That Win or Lead." *Los Angeles Times,* November 6, 1996.

Stanfield, Rochelle L. "The New Faces of Hate." *National Journal* 26, no. 25 (June 18, 1994): 1460 ff.

"Stanford Upheld in Rejecting Historian." *Los Angeles Times,* September 6, 1991.

Steele, Shelby. *The Content of Our Character: A New Vision in America.* New York: St. Martin's Press, 1990.

Steelman, Ben. "Middle-Class Blacks' Disillusionment: N.C. Native Knows It Well; White America Missing Its Chance, Fullwood Warns." *Sunday Star-News* (Wilmington, N.C.), June 23, 1996.

Stefancic, Jean, and Richard Delgado. *No Mercy: How Conservative Think Tanks and Foundations Changed America's Social Agenda.* Philadephia: Temple University Press, 1996.

Steigerwald, Bill. "The Right Honorable Intellectual: William F. Buckley Jr., High Priest of Conservatism, Throws around Impressive Words in Plugging His New Book." *Pittsburgh Post-Gazette,* September 19, 1995.

Stewart, C. Evan. "Self-Critical Analysis: An Emerging Privilege?" *New York Law Journal* (December 17, 1992): 5 ff.

Stoianovich, Traian. "Past Imperfect: French Intellectuals, 1944–1956." *Society* 31, no. 3 (March 1994): 93.

Suggs, Ernie. "Chambers: Program Cuts Will Help NCCU UNC System Streamline Offerings across Board." *Herald-Sun* (Durham, N.C.), February 6, 1995.

Swanson, K. C. "A Redefined Target?" *National Journal* 28, no. 20 (May 18, 1996): 1125 ff.

Tannen, Deborah. *Gender and Discourse.* Cambridge: Oxford University Press, 1994.

Tapia, Andres. "L.A. after the Ashes: Churches Help Post-Riot Rebuilding Effort in Los Angeles, California." *Christianity Today* 37, no. 5 (April 26, 1993): 42 ff.

Taylor, Peter. "Left Laments Lost Heroes of Deep Thought." *Sunday Telegraph,* September 5, 1993.

Taylor, Stuart, Jr. "Affirmative Action and Doublespeak." *American Lawyer* (July/August 1996): 31.

Teixeira, Diogo. "Executive View: Client Server Is Brightest Spot on the Technological Horizon." *American Banker,* July 6, 1993.

Thomas, Irene Middleman. "The Big Chill: Ivy League Colleges and Hispanic Professors." *Hispanic* 7, no. 11 (December 1994): 18.

Thompson, E. P. (Edward Palmer). *Folklore, Anthropology and Social History.* Brighton: Noyce, 1979.

———. *The Making of the English Working Class.* London: Penguin, 1991.

————, ed. *Visions of History: Interviews with E. P. Thompson [et al.]*. Manchester: Manchester University Press, 1983.

Tobar, Hector. "Rigoberta Menchu's Mayan Vision: Revered for the Symbolic Power of Her Nobel Prize but Attacked for Her Continuing Life in Exile, the Guatemalan Leader Focuses on Bringing a 'New Dawn' to the World's Indigenous Peoples." *Los Angeles Times Magazine* (January 23, 1994): 16.

Tofel, Richard. "The Case for a National Reporter's Shield Law." *New Jersey Law Journal* (March 21, 1991): 9 ff.

Tompkins, Philip. "Quality in Community College Libraries; Perspectives on Quality in Libraries." *Library Trends* 44, no. 3 (January 1996): 506 ff.

Turner, Jenny. "Left In and Out of History." *Guardian*, June 30, 1995.

Turner, Sarah E., and William G. Bowen. "The Flight from the Arts and Sciences: Trends in Degrees Conferred." *Science* 250, no. 4980 (October 26, 1990): 517 ff.

"Univ. Of California Regents End System's Affirmative Action." *Jet*, August 7, 1995.

"University of Pennsylvania v. EEOC 58 U.S.L.W." *National Law Journal* (August 13, 1990): 27.

"University of Pennsylvania v. EEOC 88-493." *National Law Journal* (December 26, 1988–January 2, 1989): 26.

University of Pennsylvania v. Equal Employment Opportunity Commission No. 88-493, Supreme Court of the United States. 493 U.S. 182.

U.S. Senate. "Hearing of the Senate Judiciary Committee Subject: California Affirmative Action Chaired By: Senator Orrin Hatch (R-UT)." Witnesses: Pete Wilson, Governor of California; Ward Connerly, University of California Regent, and Chairman, California Civil Rights Initiative; Lee Cheng, Law Student, UC Berkeley; Audrey Rice Oliver, CEO, Integrated Business Solutions, San Ramon, CA; Erwin Chemerinsky, Professor, USC Law School; Linda Chavez, President, Center for Equal Opportunity. *Federal News Service*, April 30, 1996.

Valenzuela, Abel, Jr. "California's Melting Pot Boils Over: The Origins of A Cruel Proposition." *Dollars & Sense* 198 (March 1995): 28–41.

Valverde, Mariana. "The Dialectic of the Familiar and the Unfamiliar: 'The Jungle' in Early Slum Travel Writing." *Sociology: The Journal of the British Sociological Association* 30, no. 3 (August 1996): 493–509.

van Dijk, Teun. *Communicating Racism: Ethnic Prejudice in Thought and Talk*. Newbury Park, Calif.: Sage, 1986.

————. *Elite Discourse and Racism*. Newbury Park, Calif.: Sage, 1993.

van Dusen Wishard, William. "The New Era of Human Affairs: Security and the Information Environment." World Trends Research Pres. Wm. van Dusen Wishard speech, transcript. *Vital Speeches* 62, no. 8 (February 1, 1996): 236.

Vélez-Ibañez, Carlos. *Border Visions: Mexican Cultures of the Southwest United States.* Tucson: University of Arizona Press, 1996.

———. "The Challenge of Funds of Knowledge in Urban Areas: Another Way of Understanding Resources of Poor Mexicano Households in the U.S. Southwest and Their Implications for National Contexts." *Annals of The New York Academy of Sciences* 749 (1995): 253–280.

Vélez-Ibañez, Carlos, and James B. Grenberg. "Formation and Transformation of Knowledge Among U.S.-Mexican Households." *Anthropology and Education Quarterly* 23, no. 4 (December 1992): 313–335.

Vellinga, Mary Lynne. "Guards Hit Jackpot with Overtime Pay." *Sacramento Bee,* April 23, 1995.

Wadley, Denis. "An American Century: Has It Been One? Should It Be Our Goal?" *Star Tribune,* September 27, 1992.

Walker, Ruth. "Fresh Air from Hyde Court." *Christian Science Monitor,* November 17, 1993.

Wallach, Eric J., and Jane H. Farkas. "Businesses Fear Case May Bring Courts into Partnership Matters." *National Law Journal* (September 24, 1990): 18 ff.

Walsh, Sharon. "Tape Analysis Disproves Racial Slurs, Texaco Says: Company Calls 'Tone, Context' Unacceptable." *Washington Post,* November 12, 1996.

Ware, Leland. "*Hopwood* Disregarded U.S. Black Experience." *National Law Journal* (April 22, 1996): A23.

Warner, Gary A. "The Development of Public Relations Offices at American Colleges and Universities." *Public Relations Quarterly* 41, no. 2 (June 1996): 36 ff.

"W. E. B. Du Bois; The Bold Advocate of Black History and Identity." *Life,* Fall 1990, special issue.

Weber, Eugen. "History Is What Historians Do." *New York Times,* July 22, 1984.

Weil, Eric. "Philosophical and Political Thought in Europe Today; Assessment of the Impact of Change in Traditional Social Beliefs and Cultural Ideology." *Daedalus* 123, no. 3 (June 22, 1994): 185 ff.

Weil, Martin, and Lisa Leff. "Naval Academy Relieves Head of Department: Chairman Was Asked to Raise Grades." *Washington Post,* February 25, 1990.

West, Martha S. "The Case against Reinstatement in Wrongful Discharge." *University of Illinois Law Review* 1988, no. 1.

Westcott, John. "A Forgotten Battle against Segregation: Fifty Years Ago, a Westminster Case Became One of the First Steps in the March toward Civil Rights." *Orange County Register,* February 18, 1996.

"What Are Lessons of Our Time?" *Independent,* March 17, 1991.

Wiener, Jon. "When Historians Judge Their Own: British Historian Norman Davies Denied Tenured Professorship at Stanford University." *Nation* 245, no. 17 (November 21, 1987): 584.

Williams, Patricia J. *The Alchemy of Race and Rights.* Cambridge, Mass.: Harvard University Press, 1991.

Willmott, Hugh. "What Has Been Happening in Organization Theory and Does It Matter?" *Personnel Review* 24, no. 8 (1995): 33–54.

Wilson, Danton. "Deciphering Racial Code Words 101." *Michigan Chronicle,* November 23, 1994.

Wilson, Mike. "Racism Standard: Deeds or Words?" *St. Petersburg Times,* February 9, 1995.

Wilson, William Julius. *When Work Disappears: The World of the New Urban Poor.* New York: Knopf, 1996.

Wilson, Yumi. "Where Have All the Marchers Gone?" *San Francisco Chronicle,* December 5, 1996.

Witham, Larry. "Professor Decries Academia's Religious Bias." *Washington Times,* November 22, 1993.

Woodward, C. Vann. Review of *That Noble Dream: The "Objectivity Question" and the American Historical Profession,* by Peter Novick. *New Republic* 200, no. 8 (February 20, 1989): 40 ff.

Worden, Blair. "Englishman or Briton? Blair Worden on a Study of How Britain Became a Nation Rather Than a Grouping of Countries." *Sunday Telegraph,* September 13, 1992.

"World War II History Exhibit Causes Controversy." Interviews by Dean Olsher, with Simon Shama, Historian, Columbia University; Michael Heymann, Smithsonian Institute; Peter Novick, University of Chicago; John Coatsworth, Historian, Harvard University. *All Things Considered,* National Public Radio, March 28, 1995, transcript no. 1800-3.

Wynn, Graeme. "Maps and Dreams of Nationhood: A Review of the *Historical Atlas of Canada." Canadian Historical Review* 76, no. 3 (September 1995): 482 ff.

Yoder, Edwin M., Jr. "They Took Their Stand." *Washington Post,* June 11, 1995.

Young, Eric. "Connerly Raises Stakes on Affirmative Action." *Sacramento Bee,* December 5, 1996.

Zacharias, Fred C. "Rethinking Confidentiality II: Is Confidentiality Constitutional?" *Iowa Law Review* 75 (March 1990): 601.

Zak, Michele. "The Deep Structure of the Field." *Journal of Business Communication* 33, no. 4 (October 1996): 503–511.

Index

academe: and American paradigm, 53–55; conformity in, 145–47; culture of, 83, 205; and justice system, 167; and media, 184; political infighting, 183; resistance to change, 91–94; secrecy of, 183, 210, 250 n. 1

Academic Freedom Defense Fund, 75

academic presses, 168, 174, 178, 251 n. 4

Academic Questions, 75

academic specialization, 87, 92–93, 215

Accuracy in Academia (Bloom), 63

activism, 110, 114

Acuña, Frank, 127

Acuña, Rodolfo: academic review of, 159–63, 163–65, 187; background of, 143–45; IRS audits of, 240 n. 7; support of, 243 n. 20; testimony about, 175–77, 179–81, 190–99

Acuña v. The Regents of the University of California: background, 123–27; in conclusion, 151–53; defense counsel, 127–30; depositions, 168–69, 188–89, 237–38 n. 7; discovery process, 128, 135, 167–68, 205, 240 n. 4, 240 n. 10; documentation, 153–65; exclusion of evidence, 138; in federal court, 133–42; importance of, 211; judges, 134–42 (*see also* Collins, Audrey); jurors, 138; jury, 140–41; plaintiff's counsel (*see* Corbett & Kane); psychiatric

examinations, 128, 240 n. 5; strategies, 142–44; testimony, 131–33, 139–40, 143–44, 170–81, 188–89, 190–99; venues, 127; verdict, 140–42; witnesses, 139–40, 143–44

Adler, Polly, 224

Adolph Coors Foundation, 236 n. 10

advocacy, 221–22

affirmative action: attacks on, 11–18; conspiracy against, 77–81; effects of, 1–10; impact of Proposition 209, 3–6; legal cases affecting, 232 n. 23; meaning of, 208; original intent of, 18–22; and remedies, 220; support of, 6–8

African Americans: and affirmative action, 18–20; as faculty, 219; as historians, 118, 121; and Jews, 72; law school admission declines, 218, 229 n. 4, 234 n. 10; and Proposition 209, 9–10, 220; scholarly networks of, 146; unemployment rates of, 225; in work force, 227

African American studies, 80, 97, 112, 216

Afrocentrism, 66

age discrimination, 244 n. 27, 247 n. 45

The Alchemy of Race and Rights (Williams), 51

Alcoa, 73

Allegheny Foundation, 236 n. 10

alternative institutions, 216

amendments to Constitution. *See*
Constitution of the United States
American Association of University
Professors, 3
American Civil Liberties Union
(ACLU), 6, 128
*The American College and the Culture
of Aspiration, 1915–1940* (D. O.
Levine), 85
American Council of Learned
Societies, 3
An American Dilemma (Myrdal),
94–95
American Enterprise Institute, 65, 73,
236 n. 10
American Historical Association, 71,
117, 118
American Indian Studies Association,
99
American Sociological Association,
115
And We Are Not Saved (Bell), 51
anti-affirmative action organizations,
3–4
Anti-Discrimination and Employment
Act, 21–22
anti-Semitism, 62, 72, 116–17, 118
Anything But Mexican (Acuña), 129,
138–39, 168, 251 n. 8
applied research, 171
Arizona State University, 106
Asian Americans, Proposition 209
vote of, 9–10, 220
Asian American Studies Association,
99
Association of American Colleges, 87
Association of Puerto Rican Studies,
99

Bakke, Allan, 21–22, 228
Bancroft Library, 190
Banks, James, 97
Beard, Charles, 116, 117, 119, 234 n. 11
Becker, Carl, 117, 119, 234 n. 11
Bell, Derrick, 16–17, 51
The Bell Curve (Herrnstein and
Murray), 73, 77, 209

Bender, Thomas, 66
Bennett, William, 63, 65, 74
Birnbaum, David, 134
Black, Hugo, 48
Blackmun, Harry, 22–23
Bloom, Allan, 52, 63, 74
Blum, John Morton, 66
Boorstin, Daniel, 118
Bork, Robert, 48
Boyer, Ernest, 92
Brookings Institution, 236 n. 10
Brown, Donald, 93
Brown v. Board of Education, 18, 28–30,
48
Broyles-González, Yolanda: in
Acuña's review, 244 n. 26,
247 n. 44, 248 n. 48; appointment
of, 246 n. 37, 250 n. 2; CAP report
on, 160; initiatives of, 104,
239–40 n. 1; promotion of,
246 n. 39; against University of
California, 153
Bruner, Jerome, 66
Buchanan, Pat, 64
Bunzel, John, 4, 11, 73
Burger, Warren, 21
Burns, James MacGregor, 66
Bush, George, 20
Bustamante, Andrés, 198–99
Bustamante, Cruz, 9

Caballero, Miguel, 132–33
Calder v. Bull, 48
California: Chicana/o studies in,
104–6; curriculum in, 71, 238 n. 9;
equal protection clause of, 81;
Fair Housing and Employment
Act, 21; Supreme Court of, 80–81
California Association of Scholars, 12,
77
California Civil Rights Initiative
(CCRI). *See* Proposition 209
California Public Information Act, 212
California State University, 1–2, 90,
105–6, 237 n. 2, 238 nn. 9, 13
Campa, Arthur, 198
capitalism, against socialism, 39

Carnoy, Martin, 227
Caro, Robert, 66
Carr, Edward Hallett, 115–16
Carter, Stephen, 14–15
Carthage Foundation, 75, 236 n. 10
Casa Blanca Colonia, 239 n. 3
Castañeda, Carlos, 198
Castells, Manuel, 226
Cato Institute, 73
Celler (House Judiciary chairman), 24
Center for Constitutional Rights, 127,
    135, 240 n. 3
Center for Equal Opportunity, 73
Center for Individual Rights, 73, 75
Center for Strategic and International
    Studies, 236 n. 10
Center for the Study of Popular
    Culture, 76
Central America, holocausts in, 70–71
Central American studies, 106, 111,
    239 n. 2
César Chávez Center, 104
Chafe, Wallace, 132–33, 160, 213,
    247 n. 47
Chávez, Linda, 12, 17
Chavis, Patrick, 228
Cheney, Lynne, 64–65
Chicana/o scholars: accusations
    against *Occupied America*,
    241–42 n. 15; assimilation of,
    119–22, 215–16; direction of,
    221–24; political choices of,
    146–47; in review process, 150–51
Chicana/o studies: and American
    paradigm, 103; in California,
    104–6; controversy over *Occupied
    America*, 175–78; criticism of,
    58–59; expertise in, 108–9,
    239 n. 3; identity politics in,
    114–15; institutional resistance
    to, 223; justification for, 144–45;
    linked with multiculturalism, 97;
    literary analysis of, 109–14;
    methodologies of, 170–71; and
    paradigm shifts, 37; and
    Proposition 209, 80; status of,
    103–7; suspicion of, 121; think

tanks against, 76; well-known
    programs, 106–7
Christy, Alberta, 230 n. 8
citizenship, 145–47
City of Richmond v. J. A. Croson, 22
Civil Rights Act, 19, 21, 23–27, 77, 80,
    186, 224–25
civil rights law, in Warren Court, 47
Claremont College, 105
Clinton, Bill, 65, 225, 231 n. 19
The Closing of the American Mind
    (Bloom), 74
Cody-Váldez, Martha, 124–25,
    240 n. 2
cold war paradigm, 119
colleges. *See* universities
Collegiate Network (CN), 74
Collier, Peter, 76
Collins, Audrey, 134–42, 151, 169,
    240 n. 9, 241 n. 12, 242 n. 16,
    251 n. 8
colonialism, 203–4, 246 n. 42
The Color-blind Constitution (Kull), 28
color-blind society, 22–29, 207–8,
    210
Commager, Henry Steele, 66
Committee of Scholars in Defense of
    History, 66–73
Committee on Academic Personnel
    (CAP), 89–90, 131–32, 159–63,
    163–65, 185, 213, 248–49 n. 55
The Common Law (Holmes), 49
communication, distortion of, 214
communism, demise of, 39
A Community Under Siege (Acuña),
    155, 161, 194, 248 n. 49,
    251–52 n. 10
Comte, Auguste, 42–43
conformity, 145–47
El Congreso, 126
Connerly, Ward, 12, 78–80
conservatism, 2–3. *See also* New Right
Constitution of the United States, 44,
    233–34 n. 7; Fifteenth
    Amendment, 30; First
    Amendment, 47, 185–86;
    Fourteenth Amendment, 6, 21,

Constitution of the United States (*cont.*)
    23, 28–29, 30, 31, 80, 232 n. 24;
    Thirteenth Amendment, 30
The Content of Our Character (Steele),
    12–13
The Contours of American History
    (Williams), 119
Coors Foundation, 75
Corbett & Kane, 127, 128–30, 133–34,
    137, 139–40, 142, 168–69, 240 n. 6
corporations, relationships with
    universities, 61–62, 85, 235 n. 3
courts, 167, 203, 204, 232 n. 24
Critical Legal Studies (CLS), 50–53
critical race theory, 50–51, 52–53
critical social science, 234–35 n. 13
Cruz, Jesús, 137
Cuban Americans, voting of, 230 n. 9
cultural nationalism, 99–100
culture: of academe, 83, 205; of courts,
    203; of faculty, 86–89, 91, 216–17;
    of graduate schools, 87; meanings
    of, 83; of universities, 119–22, 203
culture war, 4–5, 57, 60–63, 63–66,
    73–76, 209
Cunliffe, Marcus, 66
curriculum: in California, 71, 238 n. 9;
    control of, 57–60, 66–69; creation
    of core, 194–95; historical
    perspective of, 84–86; influences
    on, 84–86; relevance to societal
    problems, 223
Custred, Glynn, 77

Dartmouth Review, 74
degrees, in ethnic studies, 104
de la Torre, Adela, 17–18, 109, 111–13,
    115
DeLeon, Arnoldo, 196
Delgado, Richard, 51–52, 53, 76
Deukmejian, George, 80–81
Díaz, Porfiro, 40–41
dissertations, publishing as books,
    245–46 n. 32
The Disuniting of America (Schlesinger,
    Jr.), 97
Diversity and Diversion, 74
Dole, Bob, 8, 58

dominative racism, 53
Dornan, Bob, 8, 230 n. 8
Dred Scott v. Sanford, 233–34 n. 7
D'Souza, Dinesh, 52, 63, 73–74
Du Bois, W. E. B., 121, 221
Duke, David, 123
Durón, Armando, 128

Earhart Foundation, 64
educational traditions, 84–85
elitism, in universities, 215
employment, of Latinos, 3
employment discrimination lawsuits,
    128, 131, 184–87, 200–201, 205,
    211–12, 252 n. 2
England, educational tradition of,
    84–85
English Language Education for
    Immigrant Children, 220–21
English Only movement, 209
equal educational opportunities,
    232 n. 24
Equal Employment Opportunity
    Commission (EEOC), 128, 131,
    184–87, 205
equality, 19, 23–29
esoteric scholarship, 92, 93
Espinoza, Tony, 230 n. 8
Estrada, Leo, 240 n. 9
ethnic studies: and American
    paradigm, 103; arguments
    against, 80, 95–98; associations
    for, 99; degrees in, 104; de la Torre
    on, 111–13; importance of, 65;
    linked with Afrocentrism, 66; and
    Myrdal, 94–95; objectivity in,
    172–73; parity struggle of,
    99–101; programs at University
    of California, 104–5
evaluation process. *See* review
    process
experts, 215. *See also* academic
    specialization
extramural letters, 191–99

faculty: code of silence, 184;
    conservatism of, 2–3; culture of,
    86–89, 94, 216–17; established

interests of, 214; minorities in,
16–17, 219; remuneration, 90–91,
93; review process at University
of California, 89–91
faculty governance, 85, 149, 151, 215,
237 n. 1, 243–44 n. 22
Farrakhan, Louis, 72
Favela, Rámon, 126
Federal Housing Act (1968), 19
Federation of American Immigration
Reform (FAIR), 77–78, 131,
233 n. 2
Fellerman, Ian, 138, 169, 190
feminism, 65, 110, 114
Ferguson, Thomas, 236 n. 10
La Feria de Libros, 251 n. 5
FitzGerald, Frances, 66
Flores, Yvonne, 241 n. 12
F. M. Kirby Foundation, 73
Ford Foundation, 155
F. O. R. (Friends of Rudy) Acuña
Committee, 152–53, 240 n. 4
foundations, 73–76, 74 table 1,
75 table 2, 209
Fox-Genovese, Elizabeth, 64
Foxx, Redd, 21
France, educational tradition of, 85
free market politics, 43
Fregoso, Rosalinda, 139
funding: against affirmative action,
77; of foundations, 73–76; for
research, 65; of University of
California, 245 n. 29

Galarza, Ernesto, 198
García, Ignacio M., 109–11, 113–15,
239 n. 6
García, Jorge, 163, 197
Garcia, Margaret, 230 n. 8
García, Mario, 164, 198, 245 n. 30,
245–46 n. 32, 246 nn. 37, 39,
247 n. 46, 248 n. 48
Gardner, David, 93, 217
Garrow, David, 66
Gates, Henry Louis, 111, 112
gender, within Chicana/o studies,
106
Genovese, Eugene, 63–64

Germany, educational tradition of,
84–85
gerrymandering, 46
ghettos, 15
Ginsberg, Ruth Bader, 45–46
Glidden, David, 93–94
globalization, 38
Golding, William, 183–84
Gomez, Luis J., 230 n. 8
Gómez-Quiñones, Juan, 163, 176, 195,
246 n. 33
González, Deena, 162, 196
graduate schools, culture of, 87
Graff, Henry, 66
Graham, Otis, Jr., 77–78, 131, 252 n. 3
Gramsci, Antonio, 34
Great Britain, educational tradition of,
84–85
Grodin, Joe, 127
Grossman, Eliot, 169–81, 189–98
Guinier, Lani, 234 n. 9
Gunn, Giles, 132, 141, 160, 213,
247 n. 47
Gutiérrez, José Angel, 107
Gutierrez, Juana, 243 n. 20

Hammes, Gordon, 124, 164, 187
Hammond, Phillip, 131, 159
Hand, Learned, 233–34 n. 7
Handlin, Oscar, 116, 118, 119
Harris, Teresa, 45
Harrison, Jenny, 211–12
Harris v. Forklift Systems, Inc., 45
Hart, Gary, 130
Harvard University, 5–6, 14–15,
16–17, 112
Hayden, Tom, 130
Hayes-Bautista, David E., 191–93
Heartland Institute, 73
Helms, Jesse, 22
Henderson, Thelton, 209–10
Henry Salvatori Foundation, 73
Heritage Foundation, 59, 65, 73,
236 n. 10
Heterodoxy, 76
higher education. See universities
historical interpretation, 68, 70,
115–19, 175–76, 179–81

historical reality, 176–77
Hobbes, Thomas, 42
Holmes, Oliver Wendell, Jr., 49
holocausts, 70–71
Holst, James, 130
Holtby, David, 169–81, 189, 213
Honig, Lisa, 127
Hoover Institution, 73
Hopwood, Cheryl, 232 n. 23
Hopwood v. University of Texas, 75, 218,
    220, 232 n. 23, 234 n. 10
Horowitz, David, 76
Horton, Willie, 20
House Committee on Un-American
    Activities, 119
Hu-DeHart, Evelyn, 100
Hudson Institute, 73
Huerta, Ray, 141, 241 n. 12, 244 n. 25
Hull, Charles, 118
Humphrey, Hubert, 23–24, 25
Hunger of Memory (Rodríguez), 17
Hupp (Federal Justice), 134

identity politics, 95–96, 114–15
Illiberal Education (D'Souza), 73–74
immigrant groups, 72, 144–45,
    242–43 n. 19
immigrants, curricular change driven
    by, 85–86
income gaps, 224–25, 226–27
Individual Rights Foundation, 76
Institute for Justice, 73
Integrity in the Curriculum
    (Association of American
    Colleges), 87
intellectual property, legal status of,
    129
interdisciplinary rivalry, 107–8
intergroup education movement, 96
Internal Revenue Service audits,
    240 n. 7
Invisible Victims (Lynch), 73
Iriye, Akira, 66
The Iron Heel (London), 206

Jackson, Andrew, 71, 186
Jay, John, 48

Jewish Community Foundation, 64
Jews: and African Americans, 72;
    exclusion from higher
    education, 86; as historians,
    116–17, 118; and Mexicans,
    251–52 n. 10; Proposition 209
    voting of, 220; vilification by
    Gospels, 62
John M. Olin Foundation, 64, 73, 74,
    75, 236 n. 10
Johnson, Lyndon B., 10, 19, 47
John William Pope Foundation, 64
Jones, Bill, 230 n. 8
"Juncture in the Road" (García),
    109
justice system. *See* courts

Kammen, Michael, 66
Kaplow, Louis, 17
Katz, Stanley N., 66
Kelley, Robert: on ad hoc committee,
    153–59, 160, 246 n. 37, 247 n. 47,
    248 nn. 48, 49; background of,
    131–32; testimony of, 179, 213,
    244 n. 28; written works of, 138,
    241 n. 11
Kennedy, Anthony M., 31
Kennedy, John F., 19
Keyes, Judith Droz, 127, 141
King, Martin Luther, Jr., 4, 18–19, 79,
    209, 229 n. 4
King, Rodney, 78, 131, 208
Kirby, Robion, 212
Kristol, Irving, 74
Kuhn, Thomas, 34–37, 38, 169, 173–75,
    178, 181, 205, 233 n. 3
Kull, Andrew, 28

Labyrinth of Solitude (Paz), 108
laissez-faire doctrine, 42–43
Lam, Maivan Clech, 200–201
Lamm, Richard, 64
Lam v. University of Hawaii, 200–201,
    244 n. 27
Landmark Legal Foundation,
    236 n. 10
language, 205, 206, 207

Latin American studies, 103,
238–39 n. 1
Latinos: affected by Proposition 209, 7;
and affirmative action, 20;
earnings statistics, 219;
enrollment statistics, 1–3, 13–14;
faculty statistics, 219; against
glass ceiling, 218–19; income
gaps of, 225, 226–27; law school
admission declines, 218;
population statistics, 8, 58;
unemployment rates of, 225;
voting of, 8–10, 220, 230 n. 9;
in work force, 227
law: and employment bias, 184–87,
200–201; legal formalism, 45;
legal instrumentalism, 52; legal
positivism, 47; legal realism,
49–50, 234 n. 11; and morality, 49,
234 n. 10; mythicization of,
44–47; parallels to social sciences,
234–35 n. 13; positivist theory of,
19; rule of, 54–55
laws of reason, 47
Leadership Institute, 75
Lee, Marilyn, 136–37
legal education, 44–45
Léon, Arnoldo de, 162
Leuchtenburg, William, 66
Levine, David O., 85
Levine, Lawrence W., 84, 86
Lincoln Institute, 73
Link, Arthur S., 66
Lomeli, Francisco, 139, 141, 241 n. 13,
246 n. 39, 250 n. 2
London, Jack, 206
Lord of the Flies (Golding), 183–84
Los Angeles Times, 136, 155
Loury, Glenn, 14
Lungren, Daniel, 78–79
Lynch, Frederick R., 73
Lynde and Harry Bradley Foundation,
64, 73, 75, 236 n. 10

McNeill, William H., 67
McWilliams, Cary, 108
Madison, James, 233–34 n. 7

Madison Center for Educational
Affairs (MCEA), 74–75
Maivan Lam v. University of Hawaii,
200–201, 244 n. 27
Manchester, William, 66–67
Manhattan Institute for Policy
Research, 73
manufacturing jobs, disappearance
of, 15
Marable, Manning, 210
Marbury v. Madison, 54, 233–34 n. 7
marginalization, 206
Marshall, John, 186, 233–34 n. 7
Marshall, Thurgood, 27–28, 47, 48, 54
Marx, Karl, 42
Marxism, 64, 242 n. 18
Mazón, Mauricio, 162, 193–94,
249 n. 65, 251 n. 9
Medicare, 39
Méndez, Gonzalo, 31
meritocracy, 89–91, 148–51
Merriman, Roger, 118
methodology, 222
Mexican Americans, 175–76, 219,
229 n. 1
Mexican Revolution, 40
Mexicans, and Jews, 251–52 n. 10
Mexico: holocausts in, 70–71;
neoliberal policies in, 40–41;
support of University of
California, 245 n. 29; Treaty of
Guadalupe Hidalgo, 23
Mexus-Nexus, 245 n. 29
microcomputers, 216, 226
Mills, C. Wright, 172
minorities. See also under specific
minorities: in faculty, 16–17, 219;
against glass ceiling, 220; law
school admission declines, 218;
preferential treatment, 33–34; in
review process, 149, 244 n. 23
Minsky, Beth, 127, 128, 134, 240 n. 8
Minsky, Leonard, 61–62, 126–27
Mitchell, John, 20
Montejano, David, 168, 178
Moore, Calvin, 211–12
morality, and law, 49, 234 n. 10

moral relativism, 43
Morrison, Samuel Eliot, 117
Morrissey, Jim, 230 n. 8
Mothers of East Los Angeles, 177, 243 n. 20, 250 n. 2
Mountain States Legal Foundation, 73
Moviemiento Chicanos de Aztlán (MECHA), 109–10
Muhammed, Khalid Abdul, 72
multiculturalism, 65, 66, 96–98, 238 n. 13
multimedia computing, 216
Mumford, Lewis, 117
Murray, Charles, 52
Myrdal, Gunnar, 94–95

Nader, Ralph, 236 n. 10
narrative storytelling, 51–52, 53
National Association for Chicana/o Studies (NACCS), 99, 106, 108, 109–11, 114–15, 195, 251 n. 5
National Association of Ethnic Studies, 99
National Association of Scholars (NAS), 60–63, 64, 74, 75
National Coalition of Universities in the Public Interest, 62, 126–28
National Council of Black Studies, 99
National Endowment of the Humanities, 65
National Humanities Alliance, 65
Native Americans, faculty statistics, 219
Native American studies, 216
Nativist scholars, 223
natural law, 47–49, 234 n. 8
neoliberalism, 38–41, 41–44, 64, 111–13, 142–43, 222
neo-Marxism, 110, 114
Neu, John, 212
Nevins, Allan, 117
New Deal era, 38–39, 49
New Left Review, 119
The New Republic, 74
New Right: critique of education, 84; culture war of, 60–63; curriculum control by, 57–60; foundations of,

209; hegemony of, 203; ideologies of, 34; and Proposition 209, 77–81, 209
New York, curriculum control in, 66–69
No Mercy (Stefancic and Delgado), 76
North American Free Trade Agreement (NAFTA), 40, 245 n. 29
North from Mexico (McWilliams), 108
Notestein, Wallace, 118
Novick, Peter, 50, 54, 116–18, 251 n. 6
"NY Should Teach History, Not Ethnic Cheerleading" (Ravitch and Schlesinger, Jr.), 66–69

objectivity: in culture war, 60–63; definitions of, 204–5; in ethnic studies, 172–73; in historical context, 115–19; meaning of, 222–23; and scholarship, 169–81; in women's studies, 172–73
Occupied America (Acuña): accusations against, 241–42 n. 15; in CAP review, 161–62; on Chicana/o communities, 251–52 n. 10; dismissal of, 248 n. 49; as evidence, 138; reviews of, 249–50 n. 1; Ruiz on, 145; testimony on, 125, 155–56, 158, 169, 170, 175–77, 179–80, 189, 191–92, 194, 197
Ochoa, Ralph, 123, 126
O'Connell, Jack, 130
O'Connor, Sandra Day, 31, 45–46
The Opening of the American Mind (L. W. Levine), 84
Out of the Barrio (Chávez), 17

Pacheco, Nick, 230–31 n. 10
Pacific Research Institute, 73
Padilla, Raymond, 143–44
palanca, 33, 217
Palerm, Juan, 245 n. 29
paradigms, concept of, 35–37, 233 n. 3
paradigm shifts, 35–36, 173–74, 178, 181

Paredes, Raymond, 100–101
Paz, Octavio, 108
peer pressure, 147
peer review, 148–51, 151–52, 184–87
Peltason, Jack, 130
People v. Lemmon, 49
Personal Responsibility and Work
    Opportunity Act (1996), 16
"Perspective on Ethnic Studies" (de la
    Torre), 109
Pioneer Fund, 75, 77
Pister, Karl, 91–94, 237–38 n. 7
Planned Parenthood v. Casey, 54
Plan of Santa Bárbara, 109, 110, 114
Plessy v. Fergusson, 32
pluralism, 68, 70
Polanco, Richard, 130
polemics, 174
political correctness, 64, 98
politics: and Chicana/o scholars,
    146–47; in education, 62; of free
    market, 43; and history, 57–60; of
    identity, 95–96, 114–15; and
    review process, 192–93, 243–44 n.
    22; and scholarship, 120–21
Polk, James K., 10
porfiriato, 40–41
positivism, 35, 38, 41–44, 45, 47–49, 97,
    206–7
positivist theory of law, 19
postmodernism, 64, 65, 97
Prall, Stuart, 67
preferential treatment, 79–80
presentism, 241–42 n. 15
Price, Glenn, 10
professionalization, 88–89
professors. *See* faculty
Proposition 187, 7–8, 209, 230 n. 8
Proposition 209: and *Bakke* case, 29–30;
    and Chicana/o studies, 80; effects
    of, 1–10; future ramifications of,
    218; impact on affirmative action,
    3–6; language of, 79; and
    minority groups, 9–10, 220;
    passage of, 77–81, 229 n. 3;
    reflections on, 208–10; and
    religion, 79, 236 n. 11; voting
    statistics, 220

publication, of scholarly works, 87,
    174–75, 178
Pythagoras, 60

quotas, 11, 21–22

race theory, 50–51, 52–53
racial equality, 19, 23–29
racial gerrymandering, 46
racial quotas, 11, 21–22
Racine, Robert, 134
racism, 20–21, 33, 112–13, 241–42 n. 15
Ramirez, Manuel A., 230 n. 8
Ramparts, 76
Rand Corporation, 73, 227
Ranke, Leopold von, 116
Ravitch, Diane, 66, 71, 72–73
La Raza Studies, 105
Reagan, Ronald, 20, 39
realism, 49–50, 234 n. 11
reason, 41–42, 47
Reflections of an Affirmative Action Baby
    (Carter), 14–15
"Reflections on Multiculturalism"
    (Singer), 71–72
Regents of the University of California v.
    Bakke: about, 21–30; and anti-civil
    rights movement, 34; citations of,
    231–32 n. 22; language of, 207–8;
    Marshall on, 47; as neoliberalism,
    203; as precedent, 232 n. 23
Rehnquist, William, 21, 48
religion, 79, 236 n. 11
remediation, 32, 232 n. 25
research institutions, 119–20, 149,
    152
review process: cliques in, 237 n. 2;
    and Committee on Academic
    Personnel (CAP), 131–32, 159–63,
    163–65; and minority scholars,
    149, 244 n. 23; politics of, 192–93,
    243–44 n. 22; positivism of, 206;
    as reward, 120; secrecy of, 183,
    184–87, 205; sloppiness in,
    199–201; at University of
    California, 89–91, 237 n. 6
Richardson, Robert L., 230 n. 8
rivalry, among disciplines, 107–8

Rockefeller Humanities Fellowship, 155
Rodney King uprisings, 78, 131
The Rodrigo Chronicles (Delgado), 51–52
Rodríguez, Richard, 17
Roe v. Wade, 234 n. 8
Roll, Jordan, Roll (Genovese), 63–64
Romano, Octavio, 221
Romero, Noemi C., 230 n. 8
Rosaldo, Renato, 111
Ross, Ian, 133
Ruiz, Ramón, 140, 143, 145, 162, 196–97, 247 n. 46
Russell, Jeffrey, 60, 131, 135, 164, 177, 213–14, 237 n. 4, 242 n. 18

Salinas de Gortari, Carlos, 40–41, 245 n. 29
San Antonio Independent School District v. Rodriguez, 232 n. 24
Sánchez, George I., 198
Sánchez, Loretta, 8
Sarah Scaife Foundation, 73, 74, 75, 236 n. 10
Scaife, Richard Mellon, 236 n. 10
Scalia, Antonin, 30–31
Schlesinger, Arthur, Jr., 64, 66, 71, 72–73, 97, 118
Schlesinger, Arthur, Sr., 118, 119
scholarship, 120–21, 155, 169–81, 194–99, 211, 245 n. 30
Schwartz, Murray, 134
scientific method, 170–72, 178
scientific positivism, 42–43
scientists, in culture war, 61
segregation, 31, 52
Segura, Denise, 139, 241 n. 12, 241–42 n. 15
self-sufficiency, 16
Sennett, Richard, 67
separate-but-equal doctrine, 28–29
set-aside programs, 22
sex bias lawsuits, 185, 210–12
sexism, 239–40 n. 1, 241–42 n. 15
sexual harassment, 45–46
Shaw v. Reno, 46

Sheinbaum, Stanley, 243 n. 21
Simon, William, 34, 74, 209
Singer, Alan, 71–72
Slater, James, 136
slavery, and natural law, 48–49
Smith, Adam, 43
Smith, James P., 227
Smith, Page, 120
Smith Richardson Foundation, 64, 73, 74, 75, 77
socialism, 39
social sciences, 36, 61, 234–35 n. 13
Social Security, 39
societal problems, and curriculum, 223
Solis, Hilda, 130
Sonoran Strongman (Acuña), 155, 190–91, 194, 197, 248 n. 49
Souter, David H., 31
The Southern Tradition (Genovese), 64
Southwest Labor Studies Council, 195, 251 n. 5
Sowell, Thomas, 12, 52
Spencer, Glenn, 12, 78, 80
Sprecher, David, 133, 164, 179, 187–89, 189–99, 250 n. 2, 251 nn. 6, 7
Steele, Shelby, 12–13, 52
Stefancic, Jean, 76
Stevens, Ronald, 128, 136
storytelling, 51–52, 53
The Structure of Scientific Revolutions (Kuhn), 34–37, 173–75
Student Army Training Corps program, 85
Supreme Court: civil rights under Warren, 47; on color-blindness, 22–29; image of, 204; on peer review confidentiality, 185–86; on racial gerrymandering, 46; on racial quotas, 21–22; on rule of law, 54–55; on sexual harassment, 45–46
surname voting, 8, 230 n. 8, 230–31 n. 10
Suzuki, Bob, 163, 246 n. 34
Sweet, David, 162

Takaki, Ronald, 111
Tanton, John, 233 n. 2
television, racism issues on, 20–21
Telling the Truth (Cheney), 64–65
tenure, lure of, 114, 120
That Noble Dream (Novick), 116–18
think tanks, 73–76
Thomas, Clarence, 30–31, 48,
    234 nn. 8, 9
Thompson, Sid, 229 n. 2
Time for Truth (Simon), 34
Title VI. *See* Civil Rights Act
Title VII. *See* Civil Rights Act
Tofosky, David, 230–31 n. 10
Tomas Rivera Center, 105
The Tragedy of American Diplomacy
    (Williams), 119
Treaty of Guadalupe Hidalgo, 23
Trefousse, Hans, 67
Tribe, Laurence H., 48, 234 n. 8
truth, 60–63, 204, 222–23
Truth in History (Handlin), 116, 118
tuition costs, 231 n. 17
Tung, Rosalie, 185

Uehling, Barbara, 126, 164, 213
unemployment, 15, 225
universities: admissions policies, 5–6,
    14–15, 75, 218, 229 n. 4, 234 n. 10;
    confidentiality in, 184;
    conservatism of faculty, 2–3;
    corporation relationships of,
    61–62, 85, 235 n. 3; culture of,
    119–22; curriculum influences,
    84–86; departmental autonomy,
    100–101, 149; elitism in, 215;
    image concerns, 86; Latino
    enrollment statistics, 1–3, 13–14;
    power agendas of, 205, 212;
    private vs. public, 230 n. 6;
    research at, 85, 217–18, 237 n. 1;
    resistance to change, 91–94, 101;
    scandals at, 217; statistics on,
    86–87
University of Arizona, 111
University of California. *See also*
    Committee on Academic

Personnel (CAP): against
    affirmative action, 230 n. 7; and
    Bakke case, 21–22; Chicana/o
    studies at, 104–5, 187–88, 191–93,
    251 n. 4; faculty credentials, 142;
    in discrimination cases, 212;
    disparity at, 219; ethnic studies
    department, 99–101; faculty
    remuneration, 90–91; judicial
    system network of, 215; Latino
    enrollment statistics, 2; minority
    faculty at, 244 nn. 24, 25; Pister
    Report, 91–94; politicization of,
    62; racial preferences elimination,
    218–19; review process of,
    237 n. 6; sex bias lawsuits against,
    210; support system of, 136–37,
    245 n. 29
University of New Mexico, 90
University of Notre Dame, 13–14
University of Pennsylvania v. EEOC,
    128, 131, 184–87, 205
University of Texas, 75, 107, 218,
    229 n. 4, 234 n. 10
university presses, 168, 174, 178,
    251 n. 4
Unruh, Jesse, 209

Vargas, Zaragosa, 164
Vasquez, Ana Y., 230 n. 8
Vázquez, Moisés, 128, 134, 136, 137,
    139–40, 153
Vélez-Ibáñez, Carlos, 143, 162, 197–98,
    247 n. 46
Vietnam War, 117, 120, 144
Villaraigosa, Antonio, 130
virtual universities, 216
Voice of Citizens Together, 12, 78
voting, 8–10, 220, 230 nn. 8, 9,
    230–31 n. 10
Voting Rights Act, 1, 19, 27, 46

Wade, Richard, 67
WAGE (We Advocate Gender Equity),
    212, 240 n. 7
Wall Street Journal, 74
Wang, Marcy, 211, 252 n. 2

Warren, Earl, 21, 47, 50
Warren, Edward "Bull," 44
wars of position, 34
Washington Legal Foundation, 73
Weber, David, 66
Welfare Reform Act, 16
Westminster School District of Orange County et al. v. Méndez et al., 31
What Is History? (Carr), 115
When Work Disappears (Wilson), 15
white backlash, 20
Whitman, Walt, 68
Wiegrand Foundation, 73
William H. Donner Foundation, 64
Williams, Patricia J., 51
Williams, William Appleman, 119
Wilson, Brenda, 237 n. 2

Wilson, Pete, 8, 20, 22, 62, 78, 80–81, 219, 230 n. 8
Wilson, William Julius, 15–16, 231 n. 19
women, income gaps of, 225
women's studies, 172–73, 216
Wood, Thomas, 77, 80
Woodward, C. Vann, 67
Wright, Cathie, 230 n. 8

Young, Charles, 100–101

Zacarias, Rubén, 229 n. 2
Zamora, Juan, 198
Zelmanowitz, Julius, 124, 140, 142, 146, 164, 214, 248–49 n. 55
Zurcher, Rita, 61

19

1

DATE DUE